ART AND ARTISANS OF MERIDEN

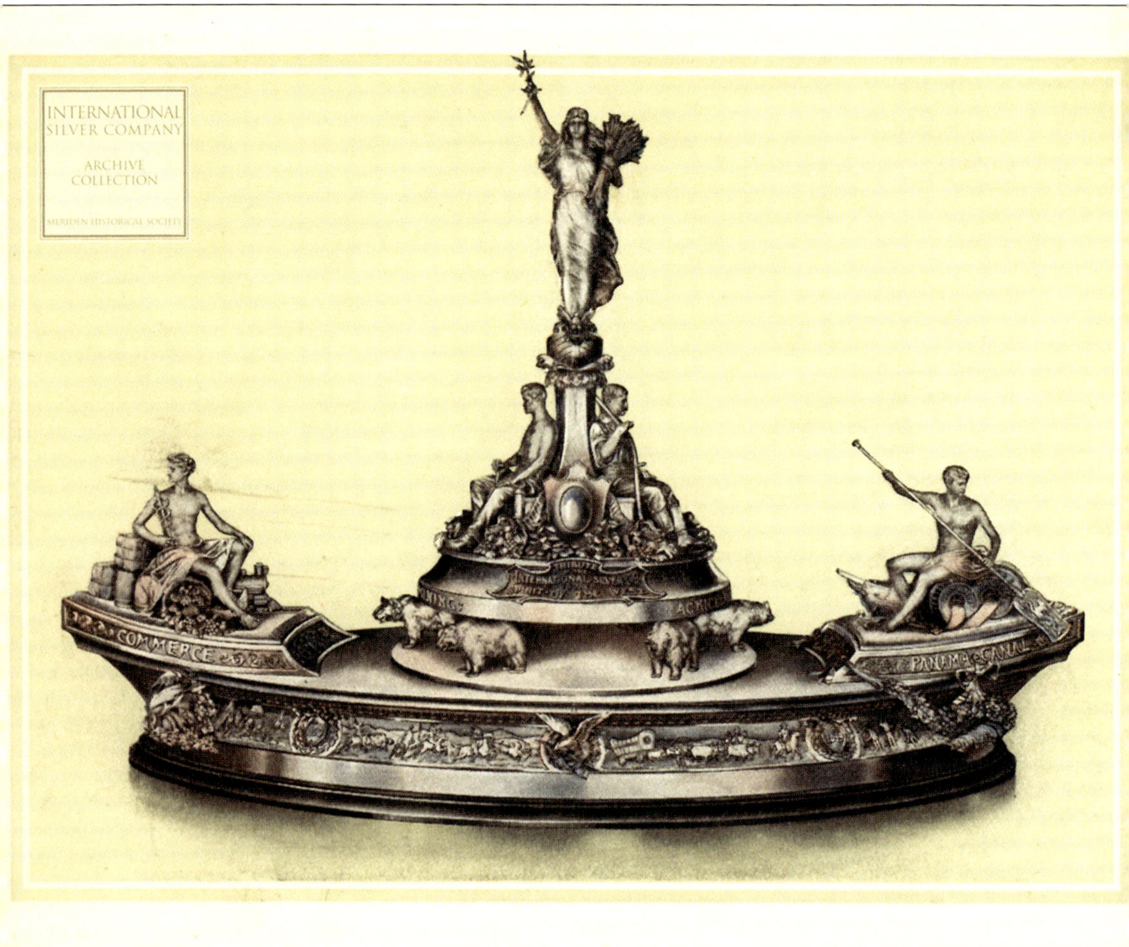

The Spirit of the West. The International Silver Company produced this exquisite masterpiece, *The Spirit of the West*, for the 1915 Panama-Pacific International Exposition, which celebrated the completion of the Panama Canal. Described in a San Francisco newspaper as "the largest piece of sculpted silver in the world," the sculpture was created by Meriden artist Louis Gudebrod with the collaboration of Samuel Stohr and Louis Hiller of the International Silver Company design staff. (Courtesy of the Meriden Historical Society.)

Front Cover (top): *Meriden Landmarks* by John Neff (Courtesy of the Meriden Historical Society.)

Front Cover (bottom, from left to right): Jean Tamburine Bertolli (Courtesy of the Meriden Public Library.), Burton Hubbell (Courtesy of the Connecticut Historical Society.), *Member of the Band* by Sara Cambria (Courtesy of Sherwin Borsuk.), *John Yale* by A. Patrick (Courtesy of Meriden Historical Society.), Philip Julius Handel (Courtesy of the Meriden Historical Society.)

Back Cover (top): *Undine Rising from the Waters* by Chauncey B. Ives (Courtesy of the Yale University Art Gallery.)

Back Cover (bottom): *Meriden, Connecticut Railroad Station, Circa. 1940* by Steven Cryan (Courtesy of Steven Cryan.)

ART AND ARTISANS OF MERIDEN

JUSTIN PICCIRILLO

ARCADIA
PUBLISHING

ISBN 978-1-4671-0933-8

Published by Arcadia Publishing
Charleston, South Carolina

Printed in the United States of America

Library of Congress Control Number: 2022944004

For all general information, please contact Arcadia Publishing:
Telephone 843-853-2070
Fax 843-853-0044
E-mail sales@arcadiapublishing.com
For customer service and orders:
Toll-Free 1-888-313-2665

Visit us on the Internet at www.arcadiapublishing.com

Dedicated to Gloria Ghezzi, Linda Ransom, and Julie Meucci, the best teachers one could have. Thank you for all that you have done for the Meriden art community.

Contents

Acknowledgments

This book would not have been possible without the support and assistance of Brian Cofrancesco. Thank you for your friendship and unparalleled wisdom. Thank you to Allen and Neda Weathers, both of whom have graciously shared their memories, their love for Meriden, and their *Silver City* memorabilia; Sandy Goodyear, Chris Webster, Rose Devlin, Alison Green, and the entire staff at Gallery 53 for your concern and support while entrusting me with your prestigious collection; and to Sherwin and Ruth Borsuk for welcoming me into your home and sharing with me your amazing Meriden collection. Your generosity is greatly appreciated.

A very special thank-you to David Emmett Cooley; Kathy Matula; Angela Long and family; Diantha Morse; Mike Zaffino, Chris Ruel, Lesley Solkoske, Paul Butkus, and the entire staff and volunteers of the Meriden Historical Society; the late "Butch" Kiss and his wife, Charlene; Thomas Rockwell, Jane Rockwell Braithwaite, and the Rockwell family; Pete Wilson; Robert Charles Gruppe; Keith Murphey, Cliff Monges and Seth Eddy; Jeffrey Nelson of the Eisenhower Presidential Library and Museum; Ric and Len Suzio; the family of Bruce Raven; Ray and Janet Gawlak; Christopher Aguirre of Penguin Random House LLC; Peter Wnek; Lynn Keeler Fisher; Wendy Ronitz-Baker; Erik Allison, Liz White Notarangelo, and the *Record-Journal*; Kevin Cook; Ryan Brechlin and the staff at Nest Egg Auctions; George Kirschmann Jr.; Becky Starr, Prescott Hazeltine, Lauren Thompson, and Wanda Guzman at the Meriden Public Library; Marcus Hamilton; Diane Calabro of the Cheshire Historical Society; Donna Hunter and the Hunter family; Jon Dunford at Miller and Miller Auctions; Sharon Cioffi; Nadeau's Auction Gallery Inc.; Igor Karpov and family; Regina Muni and family; Ellie Bender; Susan Reale; Bill Hyatt and Alice Meigs; Cindy Upham Hall; Warren Sattler; the Lamphier family; Jeff Griffin; Henrietta and Roseann Scalise; Sarah Bogdanski-Bourdon; Mike Glynn at Prentis Printing Solutions Inc.; and Josh Cohn, Faith Twining, and the staff of Edison Middle School.

My sincerest appreciation to my editor, Caroline Anderson Vickerson.

Thank you to my parents, Duane and Diana Piccirillo, for instilling a great sense of art, family, and history in me.

Lastly, words cannot express my gratitude for my wife, Jennifer, and my sons, Clayton, Adam, and Anders, and their families.

Unless otherwise noted, all images appear courtesy of the author.

Introduction

Although the history of Meriden as a township does not begin until its incorporation in 1806, the story of its settlement starts many, many years before that date. Predating the first colonial settlements, Native Americans traveled and hunted on this land; the Quinnipiacs traversed the area known as South Meriden, and the Mettabessets hunted in today's eastern Meriden, adjacent to Middletown. These indigenous groups provided the first artworks made on these premises. Whether hand-built clayware, decorative quilts, or functional utensils marked with ornamentation, these peoples were our first artisans.

Fast forward to the quarter century that followed the Revolutionary War. Meriden, then a part of neighboring Wallingford and several other New England towns, experienced a rapid increase in the demand for artwork and paintings, specifically portraiture. Breaking away from traditional styles practiced in larger cities, many relatively unknown artists found eager patrons in the small but developing communities. Although little is known about how these early artisans were trained, it is likely that many were self-taught.

While some artists preferred to create their works at home, others, like portrait painter A. Patrick, found it more lucrative to travel. In the first quarter of the 19th century, countless artisans took to the road, for at least part of the year, selling their works door-to-door like the peddlers of that era who sold household goods. The artists sold portraits, landscapes, historical scenes, and subject pieces to residents for both home decoration and personal satisfaction.

Meriden was a budding town by the early 1800s, and its residents were industrious. Farmers were at their plows, carpenters were at their benches, and artists were at their easels working hard to make a living. This emerging community soon attracted new manufacturing industries that produced products such as pewterware, guns, buttons, ivory combs, organs, coffee grinders, silverware, and a plethora of other items. The fabrication of these varied items required innovative design and creative mechanics. For over a century, artistic workers flocked to Meriden to work in these industries.

Artists, designers, decorators, and sculptors were soon called artisans. By the mid-19th century, this catchall term encompassed engravers, photographers, printers, and silversmiths, and by 1900, it also included crafters.

Of Meriden's highly distinguished artists, few achieved greater notoriety than former resident Chauncey Bradley Ives. Born in 1810, Ives became synonymous with high-quality sculpture. He is best known for his statues of Connecticut's colonial leaders Gov. Jonathan Trumbull and Roger Sherman installed in the US Capitol in Washington, DC, as part of the National Statuary Hall Collection. His artwork can also be seen in many major museums around the world.

Miniature paintings also became fashionable during this period. Talented artists like Meriden-born Samuel Holt were commissioned to create miniatures as a less expensive alternative to full-sized portraits.

Photography was introduced to the world in 1839, and when the new medium arrived in the United States that same year, it first became popular in major eastern cities. Local directories and newspapers show advertisements for Meriden's first photography studios by the 1860s. Early local photographers like E.B. Everitt, David French, and some years later Burton Hubbell saw photography as an art form as well as a profitable business.

Meriden also became an important place for innovations in graphic arts. As literature became increasingly popular throughout the 19th century, so did the art of printmaking. Copper and steel engravings and woodcuts were used for advertisements and other custom business graphics. Skilled printmakers such as Horton Printing, Kelsey Printing, and the Meriden Gravure Company employed engravers, photographers, and other artisans to create their products. Initially driven by the needs of Meriden's booming silver manufacturing industry, each company established expertise in high-quality image reproduction.

The tradition of plein air painting—painting outdoors—grew in popularity in the mid-19th century. For the first time, painters could purchase portable easels and oil paints in tubes in order to create their paintings while outdoors. This led to the Hudson River School and French Impressionism movements, which inspired local artists like Daniel Wentworth and Robert Durrie.

In the late 19th century, it became more acceptable for women to have professional talents like painting. The Yale School of Art and other schools admitted female students, which made these talents more accessible to women. Charlotte Lilla Yale, an educated and technically proficient painter, perhaps best represents this generation of female artists in Meriden. Yale was formally trained at the Art Students League of New York and studied with famed artist William Merritt Chase. She returned to Meriden where she taught private art lessons, with several of her pupils becoming noteworthy in their own right.

Art education, in its most primitive form, was introduced into the nation's public schools in 1826, mostly in the eastern states. Seventy years later in 1896, art education was mandated in Meriden. Incorporating art in the schools had a profound impact on the city's youth, especially as they entered the workforce. Rosemary Brady, a former student of Charlotte Lilla Yale, became one of Meriden's first art teachers during this time. As teachers like Brady made drawing a generally accepted skill, there was a rapid increase in the number of students who pursued vocational paths in art. For the first time, a child growing up in Meriden may have heard that becoming an artist could benefit a city *and* assure their employment.

The late 19th century was a period of opulence and wealth in America. Known as the "Gilded Age," it brought about enormous industrial expansion. Manufacturing was a stronghold in Meriden as the city became a silver capital, a lamp-making mecca, and home to several national manufacturing institutions. These companies thrived, in part, because they employed artists to unify the practical and the ornamental in their products. An ever-increasing number of skilled artisans continued to flock to Meriden in search of steady employment, with some particularly talented metal workers coming from as far away as Europe. These immigrants helped shape the economic and cultural complexion of the city for many years, and art was a common denominator.

Meriden had become a thriving artistic community by its 1906 centennial celebration. That same year, a group of local artists led by Indianna Thomas and Julia Lansing Hull arranged an art exhibit. The exhibit proved such a success that Thomas was asked to hold another the following year. Helen Roby, a Meriden artist who had recently returned from Paris with a portfolio of her watercolors, asked Thomas to sponsor an exhibit of her work at the building later known as the 1711 Inn and Solomon Goffe House Museum. The successful display paved a path for other exhibits and a series of meetings of local artists starting on December 7, 1907. A mere three months later, on March 11, 1908, this new group convened at the Curtis Memorial Library and named itself the Arts and Crafts Association of Meriden. From this beginning, the small but active group of members provided Meriden with talks and annual exhibits like those coordinated by Thomas. Edward Bradstreet succeeded Indianna Thomas as president, and the group expanded its focus to include donating reproduction artwork to the public schools and establishing an Indianna Thomas Memorial Book Fund to supply books about art to the Curtis Memorial Library. The association remained active until 1917 when, due to World War I, it discontinued its annual event and donated the contents of its treasury to a local day-care center.

Although the association was inactive for nearly 16 years, Meriden's art scene blossomed in the early 20th century. Businesses such as John F. Butler Painting Supplies and the Horton Printing Company catered to artists, and companies that employed local artisans saw their wares hit record sales. The Meriden Britannia Company, which merged into the International Silver Company in 1898, earned worldwide acclaim for its beautiful items crafted by skilled artisans. C.F. Monroe Opal and Crystal Decorating Works and Kelsey Printing also employed trained artists, and their products were in high demand.

In the first two decades of the 20th century, the Handel Lamp Company was a haven of sorts for artists. Known for having some of the top artists in Meriden, at one time Handel employed 20 highly skilled decorators, a high percentage of its workforce in comparison with other businesses. The company was known for its glass lampshades decorated from the inside with different motifs, often from the mind of chief designer Albert Parlow. Decorators copied his designs freehand, embellishing them so that no two lampshades were painted exactly the same.

Many of these Handel artists had side businesses of their own, creating deep roots in Meriden's art history and adding considerable value to their Handel pieces. Handel lamps often feature the signatures of their artists, including Henry Bedigie, Frank Gubisch, Joseph Palme, and the aforementioned Parlow. The combination of these artistic talents, clever marketing, and fine quality materials led the Handel Lamp Company to great success.

Political strife in Europe following World War I forced many artists to immigrate to the United States in the 1920s. They brought along their traditions and ideas as well as a willingness to work to communities like Meriden. However, the stock market crash of 1929 and the ensuing Great Depression catapulted Meriden's once booming industries into inconsistency. Many businesses reduced their workforces, and some, like the once-flourishing Handel Lamp Company, closed their doors permanently. By 1932, one in every four American workers was unemployed, and leading artists like Walter Wilson and Frederick Matzow found themselves bouncing from company to company looking for a paycheck. Work was scarce, and some artists attempted to supplement their income with freelance work. It was a 10-year-long economic struggle that ended only with the onset of World War II.

Americans hoped the federal government would intervene to ease their sufferings. In time, the Works Progress Administration, or WPA, was created to provide jobs for some two million workers. People were put to work performing useful services for a nominal paycheck rather than accepting welfare payments. The WPA focused on public works projects. including more than 5,000 public murals, paintings, and sculptures produced by statewide artists. The WPA employed at least three notable Meriden artists: John Backstrom, Isabella Ruth Doerfler, and Ernst Lohrmann.

In the spring of 1933, through the efforts of a Meriden native, Louise Connaway, the Macbeth Gallery offered to loan some of its paintings for an exhibition in Meriden. The Meriden Women's Club agreed to sponsor the exhibit, and Indianna Thomas was appointed as chairman of the project. This Depression-era revival of the arts in Meriden led to the reactivation of the Arts and Crafts Association of Meriden in April 1933, which sustained until 1946.

By the late 1930s, the city's attention shifted from the Depression to menacing moves overseas and the start of World War II. Meriden answered the call for support of the war through industrial and patriotic contributions, and in March 1944, the city was honored with the moniker "The Nation's Ideal War Community." Whether serving in military or civilian positions, some Meriden artists helped create a pictorial record of World War II, but they also aided local and national campaigns to boost morale, promote conservation, sell war bonds, and encourage national unity among all Americans.

In 1956, after World War II and the Korean War, the Arts and Crafts Association of Meriden returned as a reinvigorated organization. The association capitalized on its rebirth with a special 32nd annual exhibit, a retrospective showcasing works by former members and famous artists in honor of Meriden's sesquicentennial celebration. The exhibit was held at the Horace C. Wilcox Technical School and attracted more than 1,500 attendees.

In the decade following the retrospective, the Arts and Crafts Association of Meriden cultivated relationships between its local members and out-of-town artists. One such bond was established with the Rockport Art Association in the seaside community of Rockport, Massachusetts, where legendary artists like Emile Gruppe conducted plein air seaside painting classes. The association coordinated several bus trips from Meriden to Rockport for its members to learn from Gruppe, which subsequently altered several members understanding of the principles of making art. Meriden artists Earl Bushnell and Irma Morse saw transformations in the composition and subject matter of their own art.

In subsequent years, the Arts and Crafts Association of Meriden struggled with its identity and securing a permanent home. This was remedied in June 1981 when the association purchased the building at 53 Colony Street to create a dedicated space to foster the visual arts in Meriden. Spearheaded by then president and local artist Irma Peckham Morse, the building was a prominent location in downtown Meriden adjacent to the century-old Butler Paint. The association soon changed its name to Gallery 53, a name to define its new focus and work downtown. Gallery 53 remains active today and over the years has attracted the finest of American artisans as members and exhibitors, most notably Winslow Homer, John Taylor Arms, Eric Sloane, and Harry Ballinger.

The creation of Gallery 53 on Colony Street ignited a downtown renaissance with Meriden artists eager to create subcultures within the arts. The Meriden Arts Council emerged in response, fueled by artisans of all media types as a collaboration between artists, musicians, actors and actresses, and dancers. For years, the council was known for its annual Main ARTery event that combined local artists exhibiting their works with a wine-tasting event.

Today, Meriden continues to strive for a full arts renaissance. The talent, the opportunity, and the downtown arts spaces are alive, but stigmas of today's downtown have kept the concept of an arts colony from coming to fruition. With new artwork and unique mediums being discovered each day in Meriden, there is optimism that a rebirth is forthcoming.

The artwork that graces this city is remarkable. Some works have stood the test of centuries, others are preserved in museums and independent collections, and others reflect new ideas about art and design. While change and advancements have altered Meriden's landscape over the centuries, the varied artworks that remain reflect our city's rich history, telling the stories of innovative art and accomplished artisans who have left their indelible marks on Meriden.

One

Early Art and Artisans of Meriden

As a hub for innovation and advancements in art and art making in the 19th century, Meriden shaped countless artisans across a variety of mediums. When Meriden was being incorporated as an independent town in 1806, miniature painting was becoming fashionable in America. Although originally conceived for ornamental purposes, miniature paintings evolved into small portraiture. Meriden's Samuel Holt became one of the town's first bona fide painters to adopt working with this fine-painting technique.

In addition to the fine artists of the day, sculptors and photographers also made Meriden their home in the early decades of the 19th century. As American sculpture grew in popularity, Connecticut boasted one of the greatest artists of this medium, Chauncey Bradley Ives, who briefly resided in Meriden. By the mid-century mark, photography had arrived in the United States, and Meriden's first photographic portrait studios opened shortly after. The *Meriden Daily Republican* newspaper featured advertisements for local artisan photographers like E.B. Everitt; his successor, David French; and Jeremiah F. Green as early as the 1860s, offering an inexpensive alternative to painted portraits.

By the 1880s, the United States was experiencing a shift in artistic styles and taste. Young painters were now pursuing an artistic style that embraced visible brushstrokes and emphasized light and shadow. Known as American Impressionism, this style was the hallmark of Meriden's pioneer painter, Charlotte Lilla Yale. Educated and well-connected in social circles, Yale was a fixture among the Connecticut artists of the period as well as a respected art educator. Many of Yale's students advanced the trajectory of Meriden art.

By the later decades of the 19th century, Meriden was defined by its manufacturing economy. The artisans and designers employed by major Meriden companies made art their profession but also pursued recreational art as a pastime in order to counterbalance their work in the factories. This inevitably brought together artists from all over Meriden.

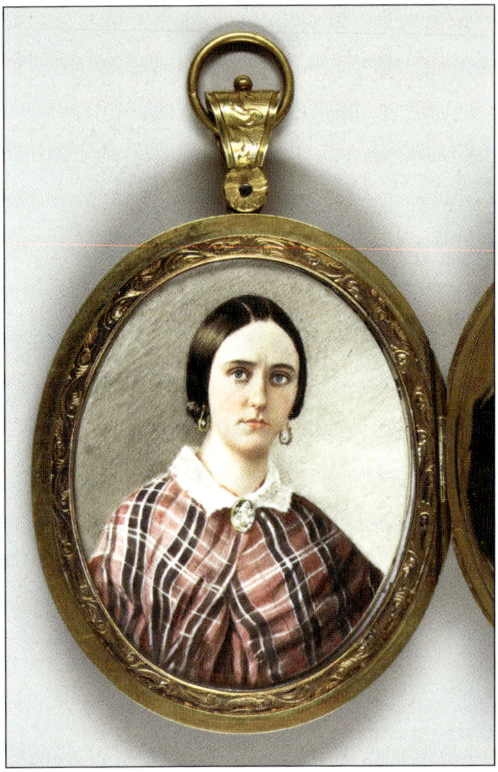

Samuel Holt. Portrait painter Samuel Holt was born in Meriden in 1801. Holt was not trained as an artist until he was 30 years old and thereafter painted fine miniature portraits for years. His failing eyesight eventually forced him to undertake the coarser work of car decorating. Holt's artwork is scarce today and is often unattributed. This miniature portrait was not painted by Holt but is reminiscent of his work. (Courtesy of Yale University Art Gallery.)

George Henry Durrie. Best known as a painter of New England landscapes, George Henry Durrie was born in New Haven, Connecticut, in 1820. From about 1839 to 1841, Durrie and his brother studied with Nathaniel Jocelyn, a famed painter and banknote engraver. Durrie then worked as an itinerant artist with early stops in Meriden, Hartford, Naugatuck, and Bethany. Durrie died in 1863. (Courtesy of the National Gallery of Art, Collection of Mr. and Mrs. Paul Mellon.)

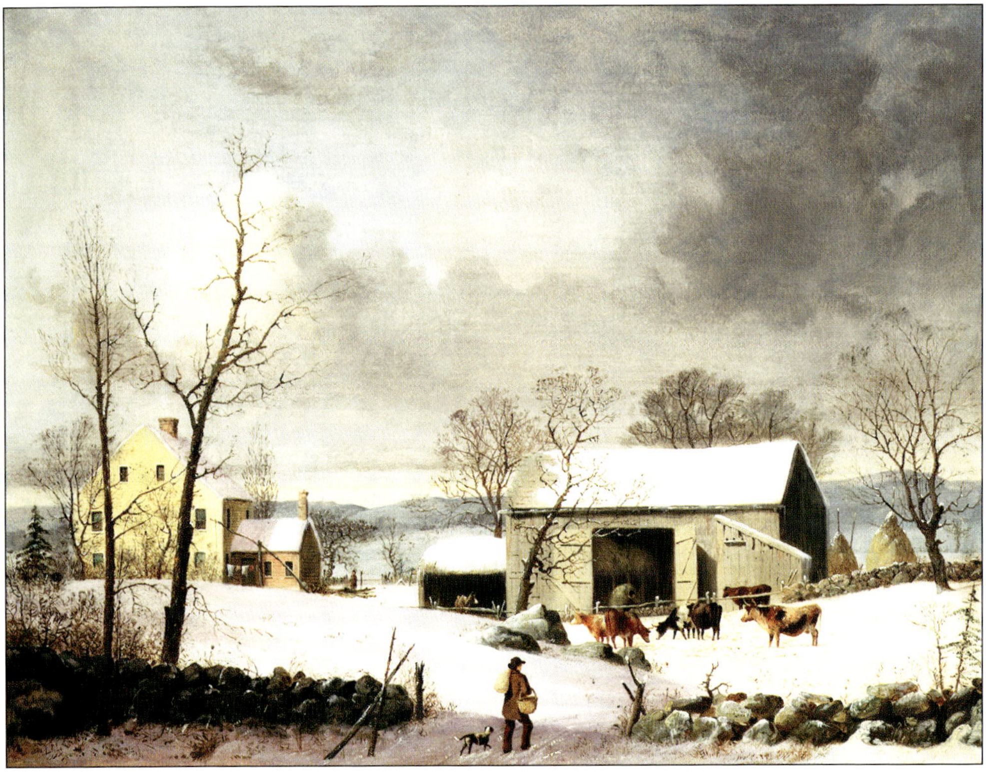

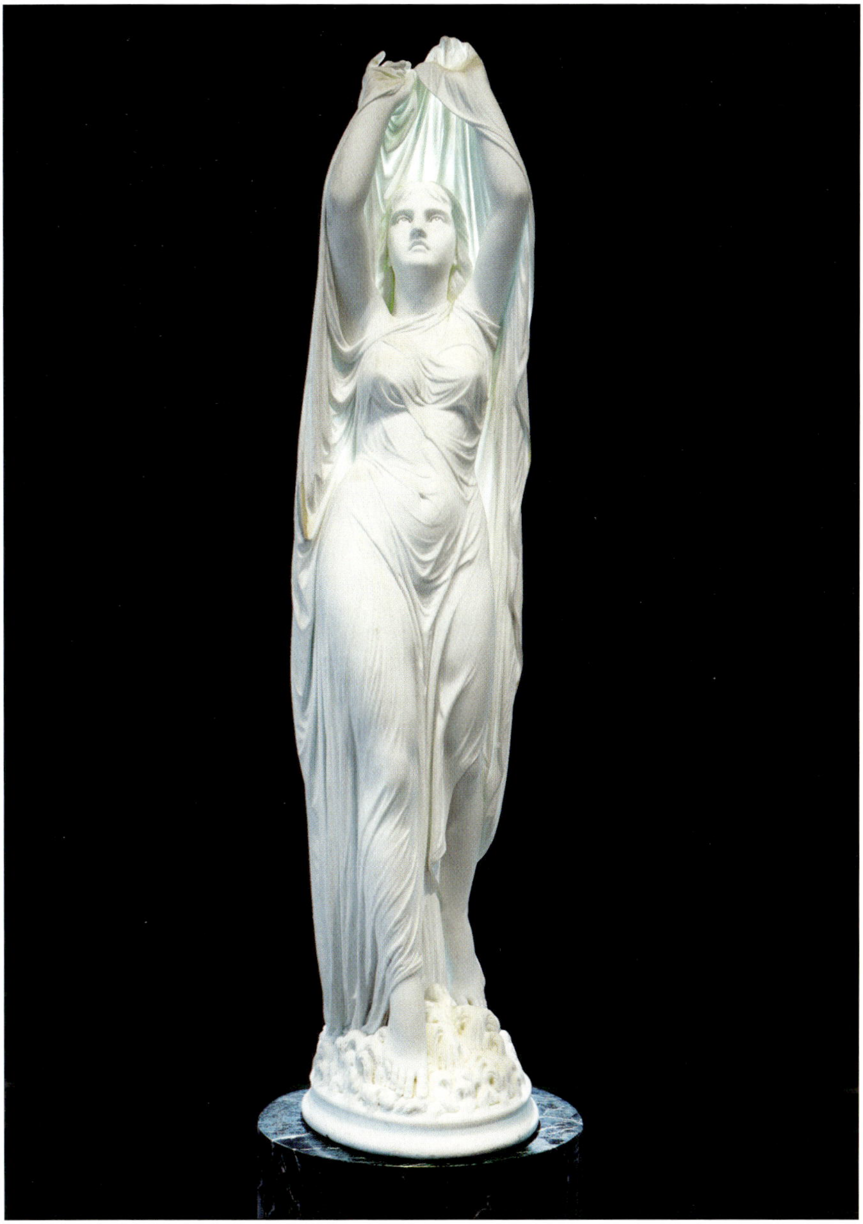

CHAUNCEY BRADLEY IVES. Born in Hamden, Connecticut, in 1810, Chauncey Bradley Ives received his early training in wood carving. At the age of 27, he began studying sculpture. In 1841, while Ives was making plaster casts in Meriden, a doctor commented on his declining health and advised him to go to Europe. Three years later, Ives moved to Italy where he worked in Florence before permanently settling in Rome. Ives made frequent trips to the United States to sell his work and acquired many patrons. His native state gave him commissions for the statues of Jonathan Trumbull and Roger Sherman, which are displayed in the Connecticut State Capitol and the US Capitol. His work can also be found in many major museums around the world, most notably the Smithsonian Museum of Art and the Metropolitan Museum of Art. Though Ives was remembered with lively affection, toward the end of his life he was known among American sculptors and students in Rome as "Old Bear Ives." Ives died in 1894 in Rome, Italy. (Courtesy of the Yale University Art Gallery.)

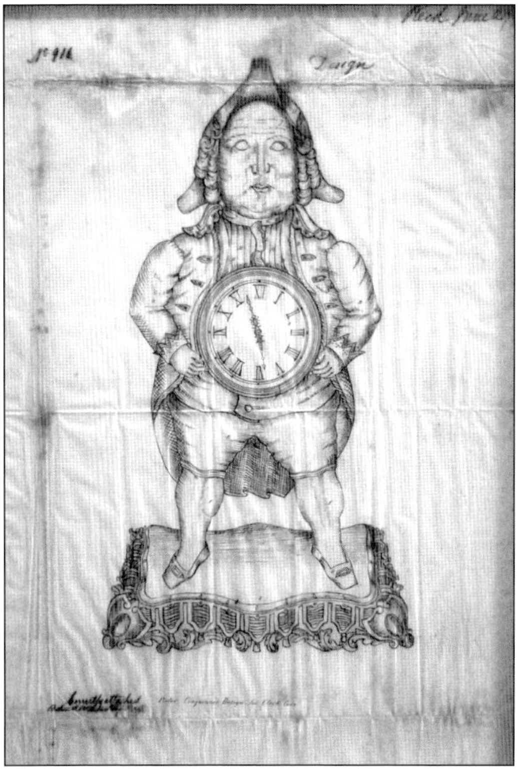

BRADLEY & HUBBARD "BLINKING EYE" CLOCK CASE. This pen-and-ink drawing by Meriden engraver Pierre Cinquinne was a design for Bradley & Hubbard Manufacturing Company's "blinking eye" clock case. Cinquinne, a talented artist and a fine educator, had an ambition of opening an art school in Meriden. This drawing, which accompanied Bradley & Hubbard's 1857 patent application, and the clock case are in the collection of the Meriden Historical Society. (Courtesy of the Meriden Historical Society.)

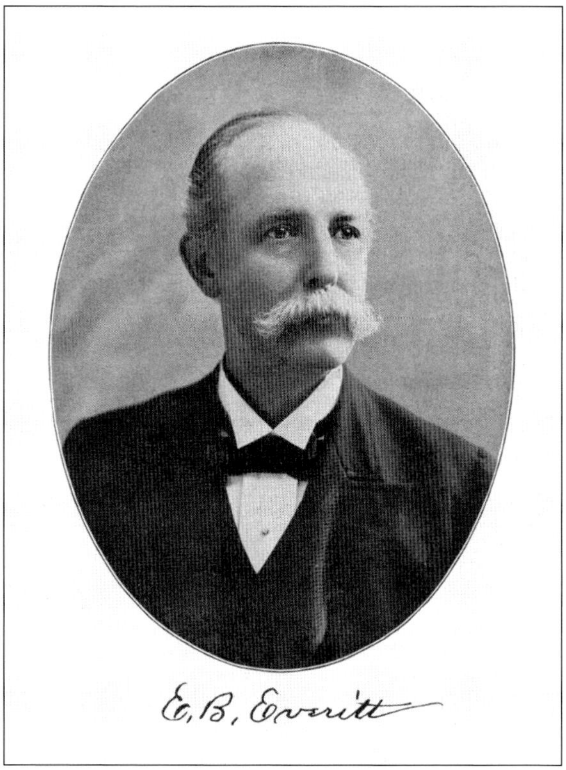

EDWIN BROWNSON EVERITT. Edwin Brownson Everitt was born in Waterbury, Connecticut, in 1835. He came to Meriden in the early 1860s and opened a successful photographic gallery. Years later, Everitt's ill health forced him to sell his business to fellow Meriden photographer David French. Everitt then worked in insurance and later, around 1890, was employed in the office of the Meriden Britannia Company. Everitt died in Meriden on March 22, 1907.

John Jameson. A talented young man in both art and music, John Jameson was born in Hartford, Connecticut, in 1842 to two accomplished musicians. Jameson often traveled to Meriden to accompany his parent or to perform in the local churches. Later, his family moved to New York where famed artist Frederic Edwin Church took him in as a student. Jameson died tragically in Andersonville Prison during the Civil War.

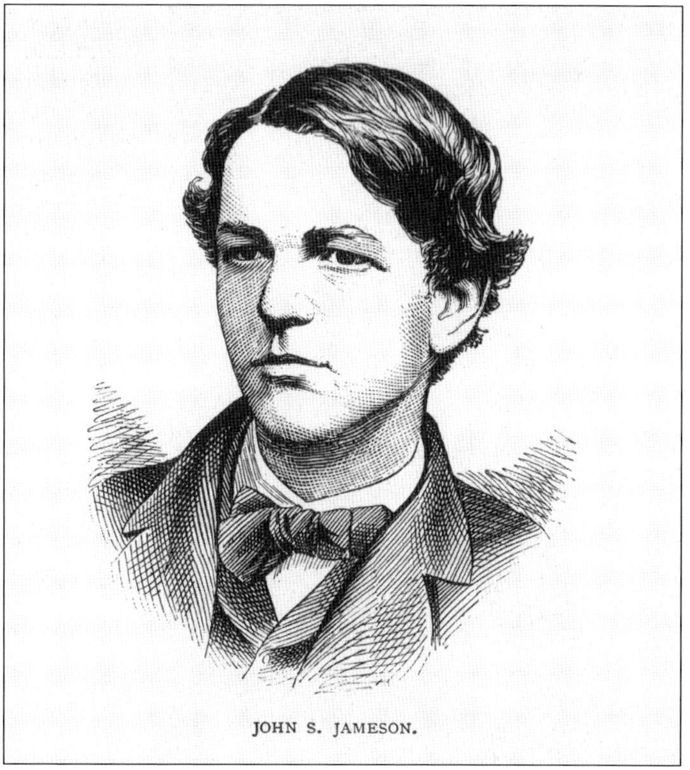

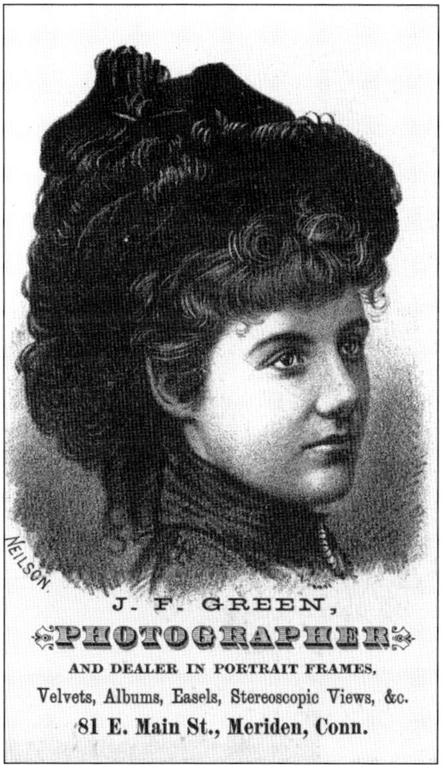

Jeremiah F. Green. Jeremiah F. Green, one of Meriden's earliest and most successful photographers, was born in New York in 1842. A lover of flowers, Green was prominent in church and society, the Meriden community, and all political matters. He died on September 12, 1887, at the age of 45. After Green's death, his widow and J.F. Green Photographic Studio supervisor Alfred Pritchard reopened the shop and ran the business together.

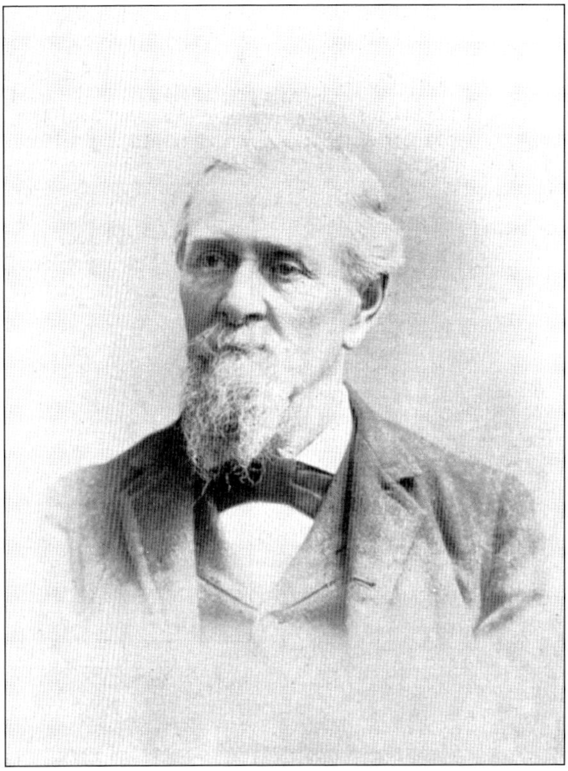

Bela Carter. Bela Carter was born February 6, 1828, in Hardwick, Massachusetts. A child of natural artistic ability, Carter focused his talents on painting and interior painting. In 1850, he relocated to Meriden and two years later went into business for himself, operating a business that became Meriden's first painting firm. Carter also had interests in real estate and politics and died in 1893 at the age of 65.

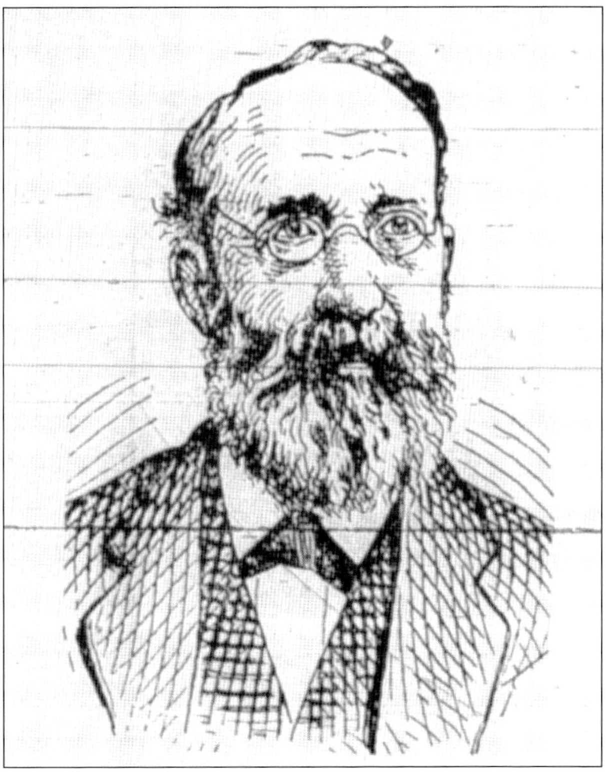

Augustine Busch. One of the Silver City's most revered artisans was Wilcox Silver Plate Company engraver Augustine Busch. Born in Baden, Germany, around 1838, Busch attended the best schools and graduated from the esteemed Heidelberg University. Fluent in six languages, Busch came to America and settled in Meriden, making a name for himself as "Meriden's Oldest Engraver," according to an 1895 *Meriden Daily Journal* newspaper article. Busch died in Meriden in 1905.

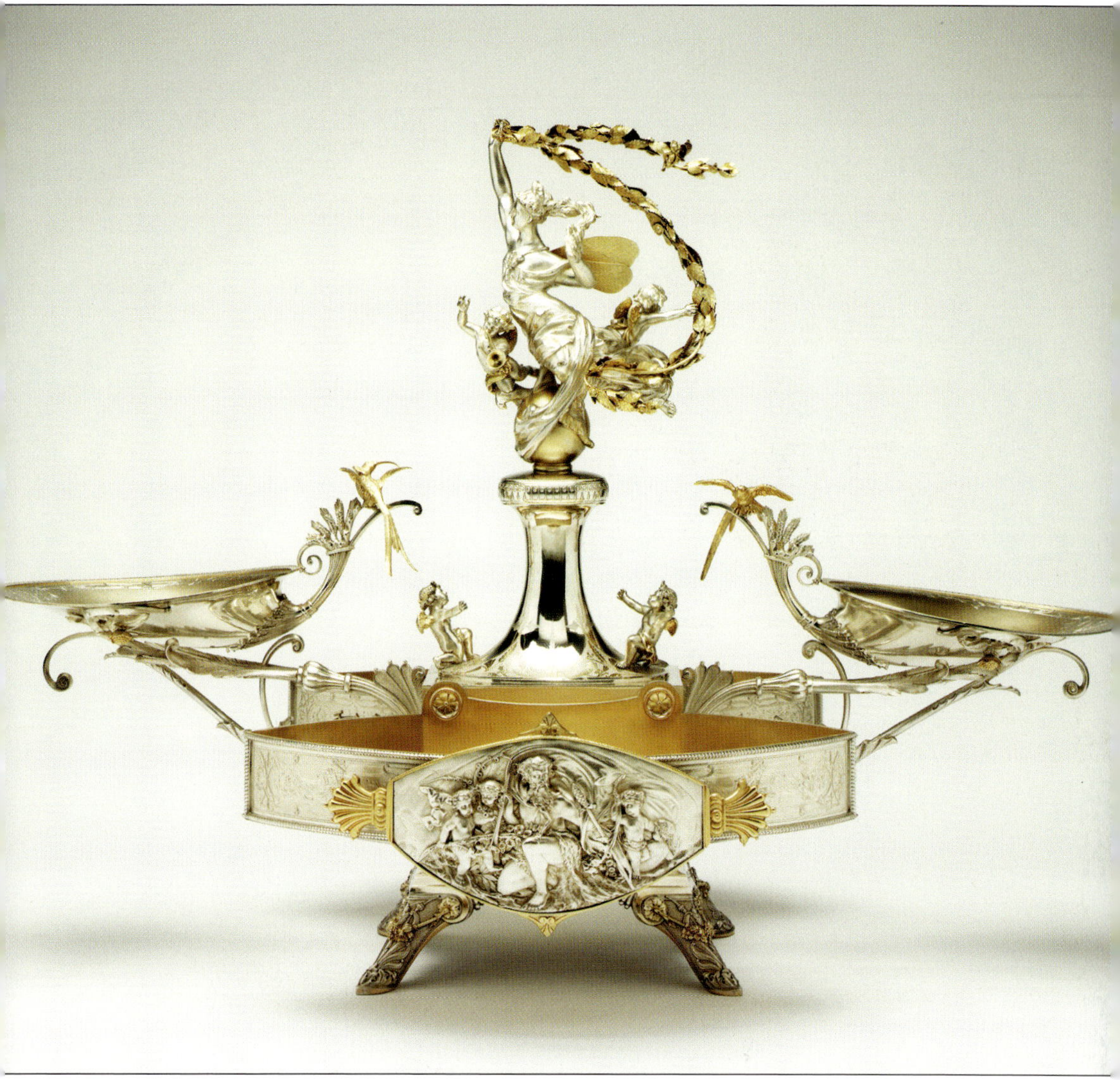

THOMAS PAIRPOINT. Thomas Pairpoint created this design prior to his coming to Meriden in 1877 to become a designer at the Meriden Britannia Company. After years of studying art abroad, his work exemplified the meticulous and intricate design skills of Meriden artists. While abroad, Pairpoint prepared a series of articles titled *Art Work & Silver* about silver as an art medium. This notoriety led to Pairpoint being regarded as "one of the most skillful and artistic designers of the present day, having a reputation which is worldwide." Soon after receiving this commendation, Pairpoint and 50 other workers suddenly left Meriden for New Bedford, Massachusetts, for new positions at Pairpoint Manufacturing Company, aptly renamed after Pairpoint, who was named the company's superintendent. While at the helm of Pairpoint Manufacturing Company, Pairpoint was considered to be the foremost silver designer in the country. The company prospered and received favorable attention for its designs, with its success attributed to the abilities of Thomas Pairpoint. (Courtesy of the RISD Museum, Providence, Rhode Island.)

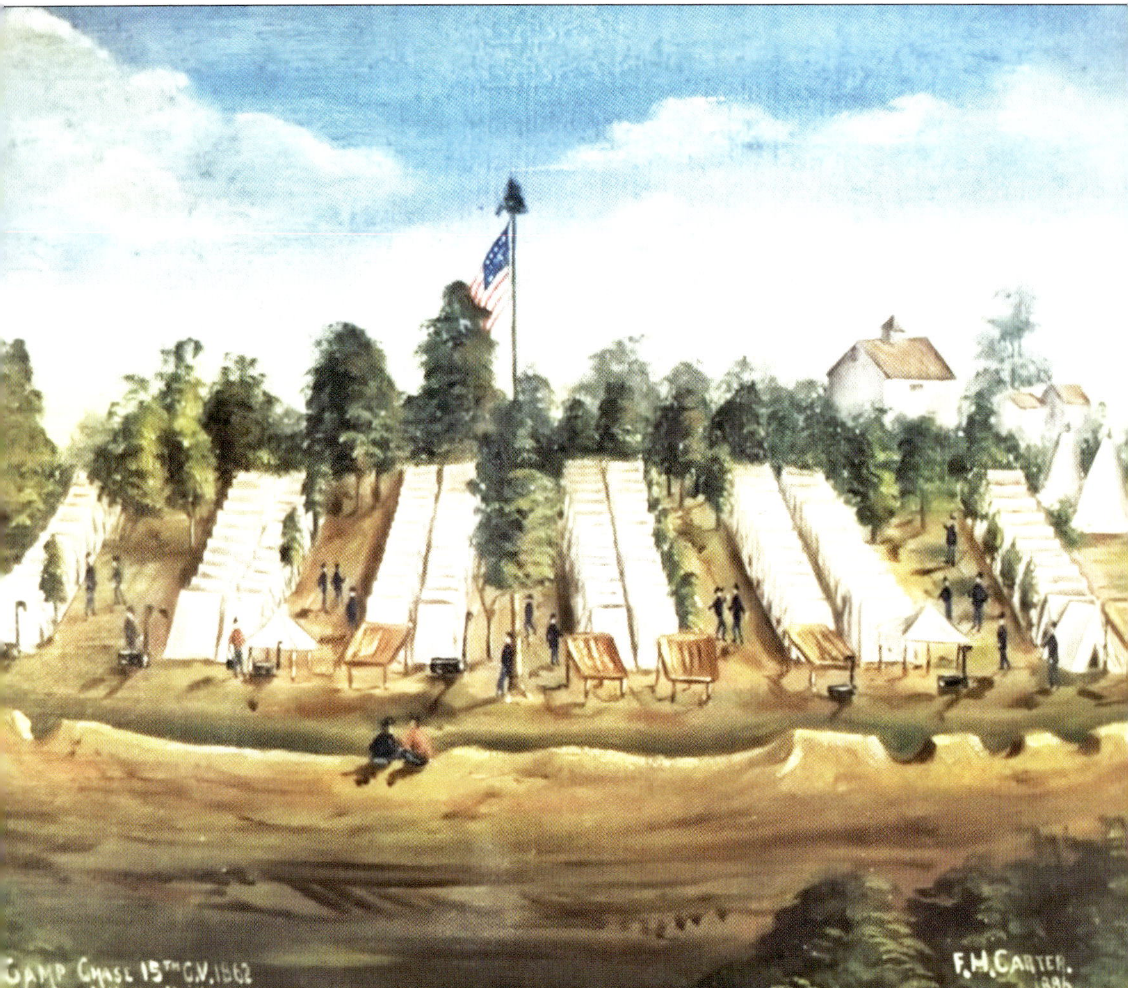

Comdr. Frederick Howard Carter. Frederick Howard Carter was born in Providence, Rhode Island, in May 1847 but moved to Meriden at an early age. After enlisting in the military, Carter served in the Civil War and advanced to the rank of corporal, a title he proudly held for the remainder of the war. Upon his return to Meriden, Carter was employed by Little, Somers & Hyatt as an artist-painter and paper hanger before opening his own shop on South Colony Street. In 1893, Carter was chosen as commander of the local Merriam Post of the Grand Army of the Republic, a fraternal organization for Union army veterans. He died in 1904 at the age of 56 following the injuries sustained in a fall at a local paint shop. Carter painted this depiction of Camp Chase, a military staging and training camp in Columbus, Ohio, in 1886. (Courtesy of the Meriden Historical Society.)

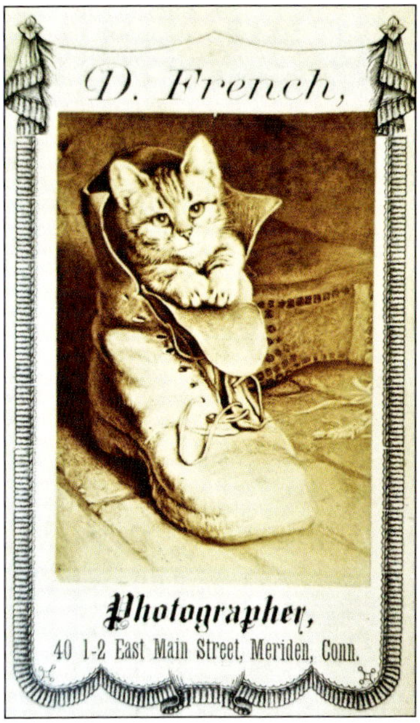

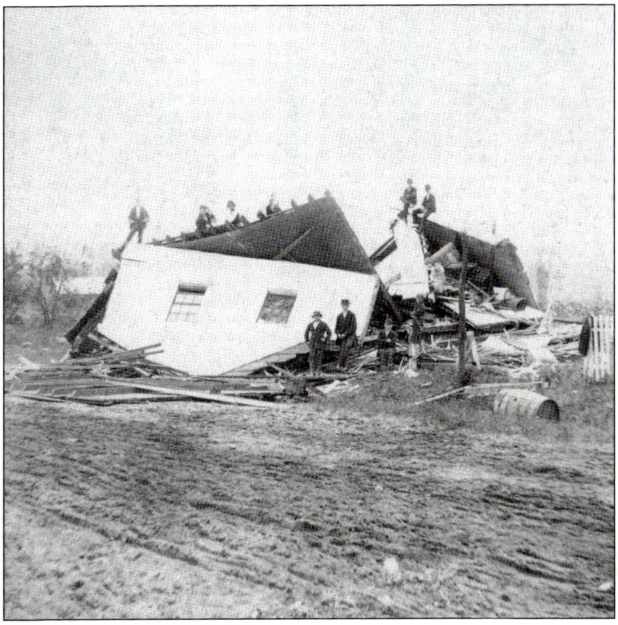

DAVID FRENCH. David French was born in 1840 and came to Meriden in 1870. When E.B. Everitt's ill health forced him to sell his photographic studio, French purchased the business and became a highly successful studio portrait photographer. French was also an avid recreational photographer, noted for his captivating images like this photograph of the aftermath of the August 9, 1878, tornado that devastated neighboring Wallingford. French lived in Meriden until 1910 and died in 1919.

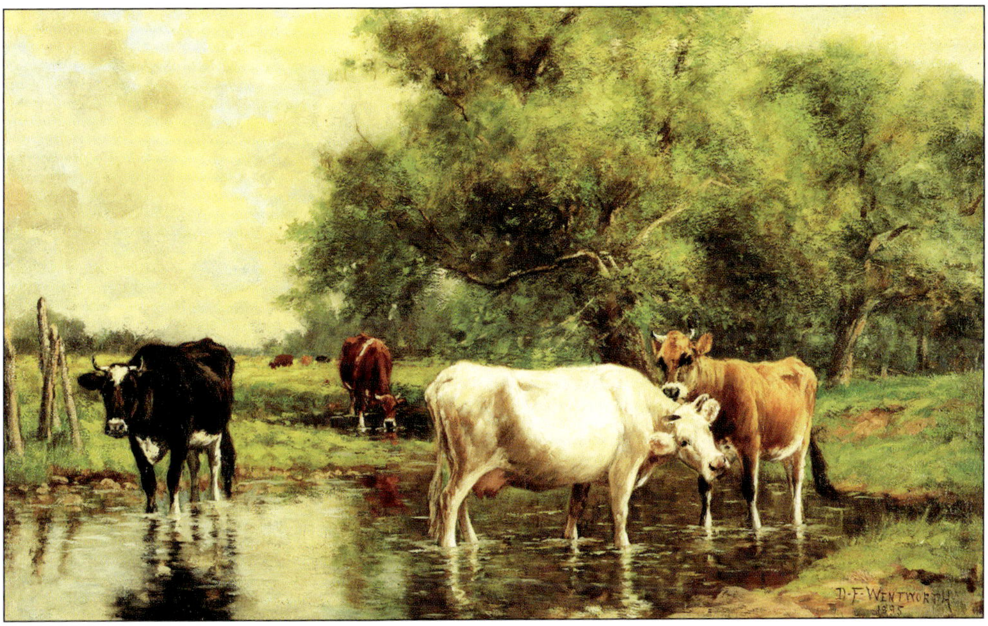

DANIEL F. WENTWORTH. Daniel F. Wentworth was born in Maine in 1850 but lived and worked in Connecticut for most of his adult life. Associated with the second generation of Hudson River School painters, he lived in Meriden from 1884 to 1887 where he painted realistic landscapes rich with marshes, streams, and cattle. Wentworth died in New Milford, Connecticut, on May 31, 1934. (Courtesy of the Connecticut Historical Society.)

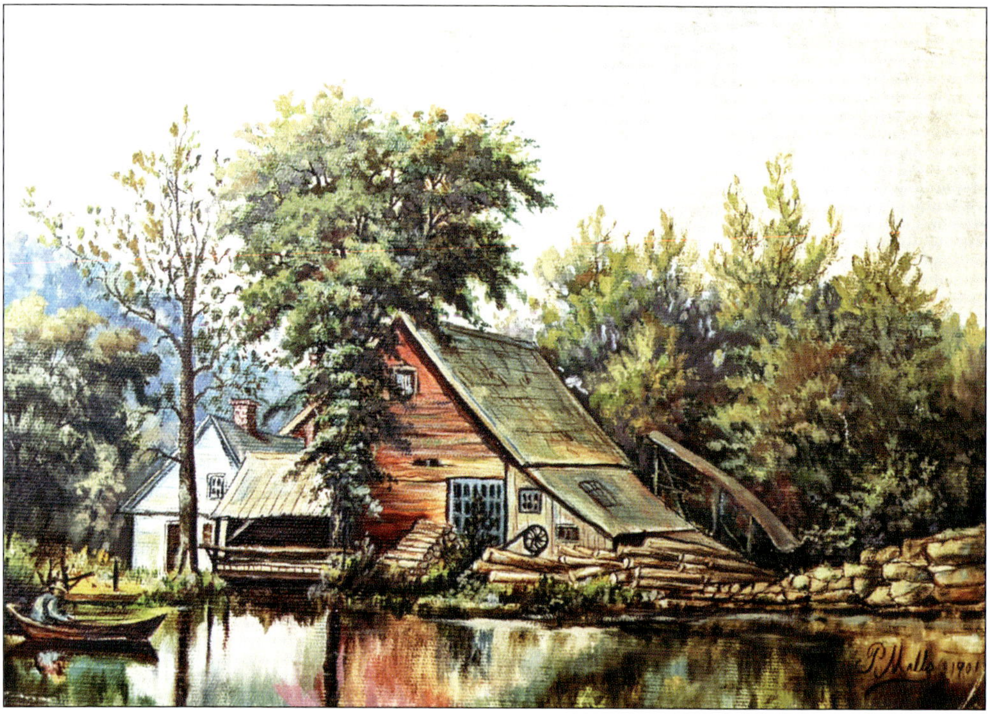

PHILIP MILLS. Philip Mills was born around 1860. A very religious man, he joined the church in 1880 but later left to work as an insurance agent. Mills was also a skillful and energetic artist, as demonstrated in this painting of Hough Mill near Red Bridge and the South Meriden sawmill. Mills died in February 1897. (Courtesy of the Cheshire Historical Society.)

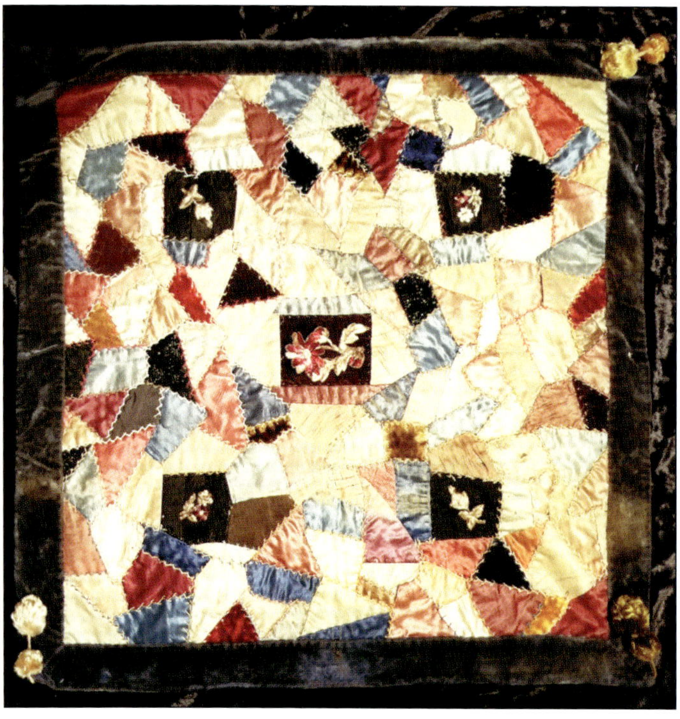

CRAZY QUILT. The textile art of crazy patchwork, known as "crazy quilts," was popular in the late 1800s. This art style rapidly became a national fashion among urban, upper-class women, who used the wide variety of fabrics available from the booming textile industry to piece together single quilts from hundreds of different fabrics. This Meriden-made crazy quilt was created sometime around 1880. (Courtesy of the Meriden Historical Society.)

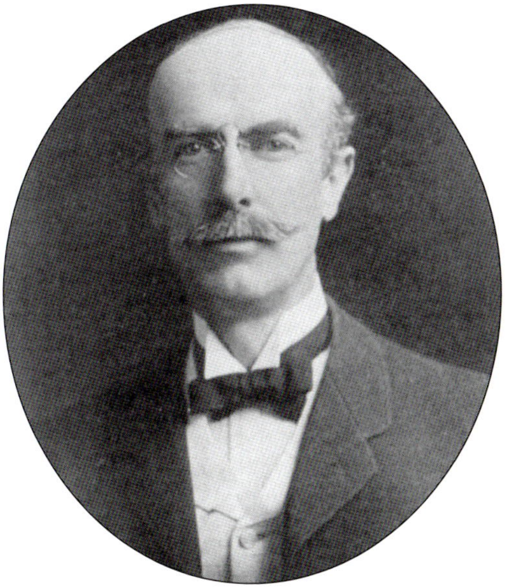

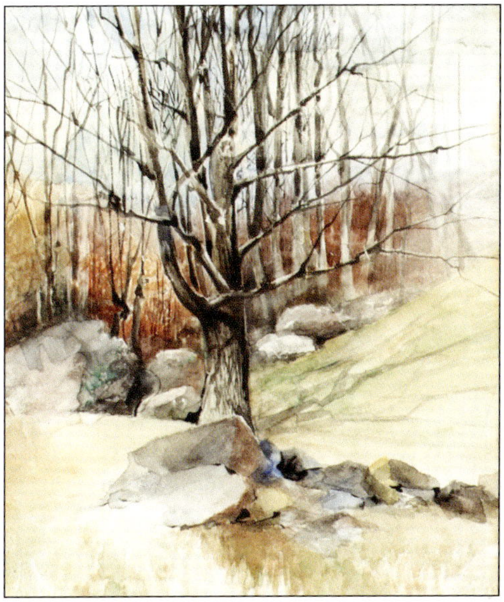

CHARLES FABYAN MONROE. Charles Fabyan Monroe was born in Providence, Rhode Island, on April 16, 1855. As a young man, he lived and worked in New Bedford, Massachusetts. Upon moving to Meriden a few years later, he was hired by leading industrialist Horace C. Wilcox as a designer at the Meriden Flint Glass Company, one of Wilcox's many business enterprises. After a few years, Monroe left the Meriden Flint Glass Company and spent the next year in Europe. When he returned to Meriden, Monroe began decorating glass and marketing art goods of his own design, opening a retail store, C.F. Monroe Opal and Crystal Decorating Works, on State Street. In 1886, Wilcox urged Monroe to move his business to the intersection of West Main Street and Capital Avenue, where it flourished. The company prospered for decades but the economic challenges caused by World War I and a change in public taste caused the company to close its doors in 1916. Monroe was also an enthusiastic sportsman. His yacht, the *Sylph*, was considered one of the finest of its class on the Atlantic coast. Monroe died in Meriden on November 19, 1919.

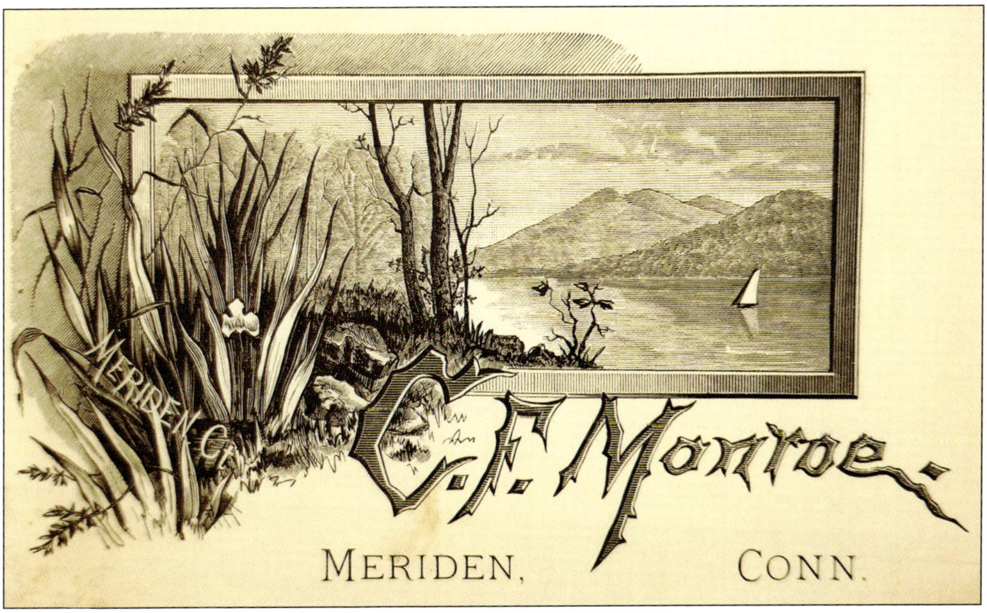

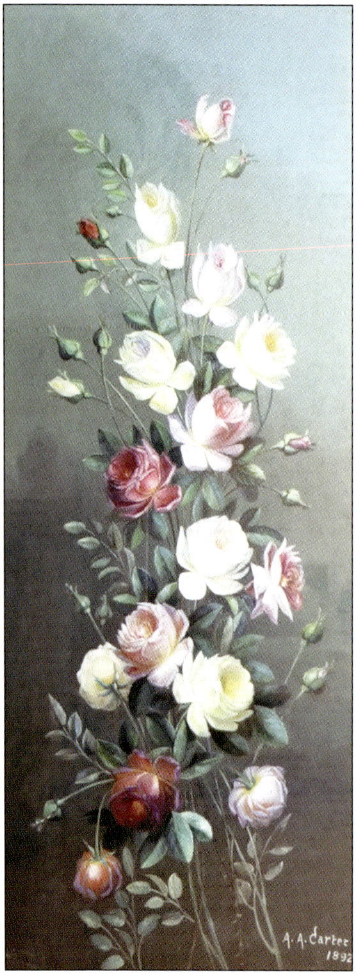

Albert A. Carter. Albert A. Carter was born about 1848 and served in the Civil War. After the war, he and his brother Frederick Howard Carter opened an art dealership on Center Street in Meriden. His paintings of floral arrangements were highly acclaimed throughout the city. Carter died in St. Louis, Missouri, in 1899. (Courtesy of Gallery 53.)

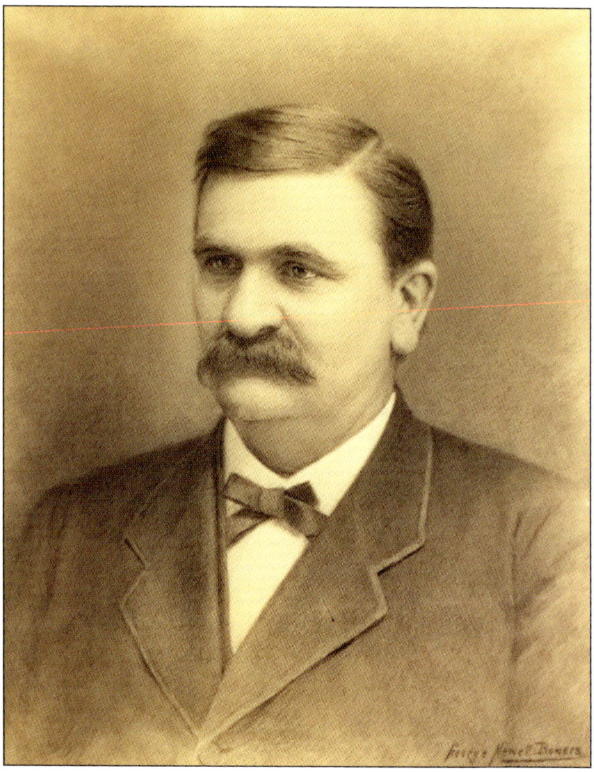

George Newell Bowers. This charcoal on half-tone paper of Meriden industrialist Horace C. Wilcox was drawn by well-known artist George Newell Bowers. Bowers was born in Berlin, Connecticut, but traveled to Springfield, Massachusetts, at an early age. He studied art in New York and spent five years in Paris before moving to Meriden where he set up a studio at Meriden City Hall. Bowers died in 1909 at the age of 59. (Courtesy of Sherwin Borsuk.)

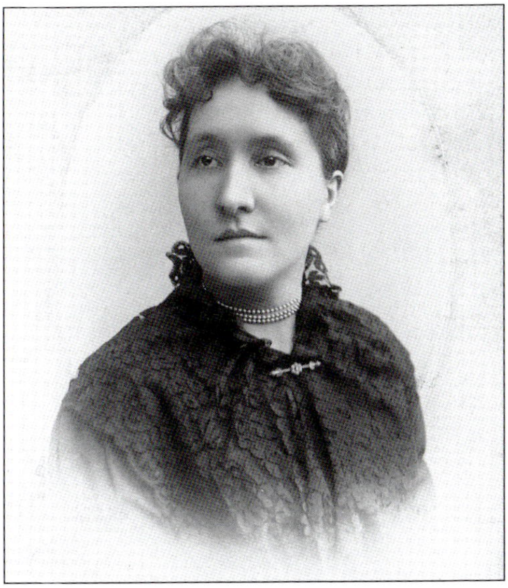

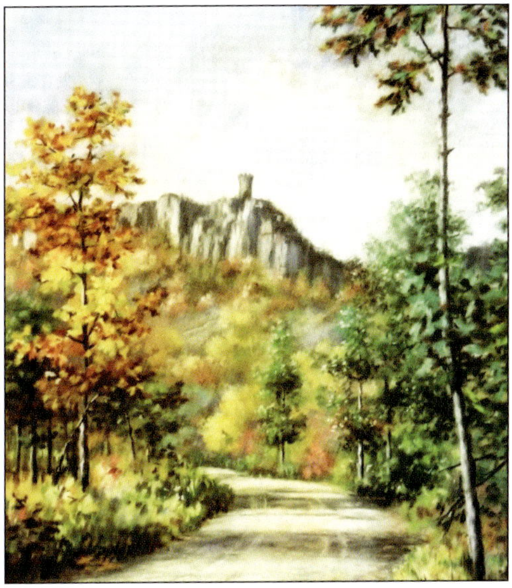

CHARLOTTE LILLA YALE. One of Meriden's pioneering artists was Charlotte Lilla Yale. A member of one of Meriden's oldest families, Yale was born in 1855 and educated in local schools. She continued her schooling at the Art Students League in New York City under famed American Impressionism painter William Merritt Chase. Years later, Yale opened a painting studio at 208 West Main Street in Meriden, opposite All Saints Church. She worked primarily in oil paints, and her work was collected by many in the city. She drew inspiration from the scenes around Meriden and along the lower Connecticut River Valley and was especially well-known for her renditions of flowers and her portraits. Never married, she devoted her entire life to painting and teaching. Among her many students were Julia Manley, Ethel Easton Paxson Du Clos, Nellie Nagel, and Frederick Rettenmeyer. Yale died of pneumonia in Meriden on March 7, 1929. (All, courtesy of the Meriden Historical Society.)

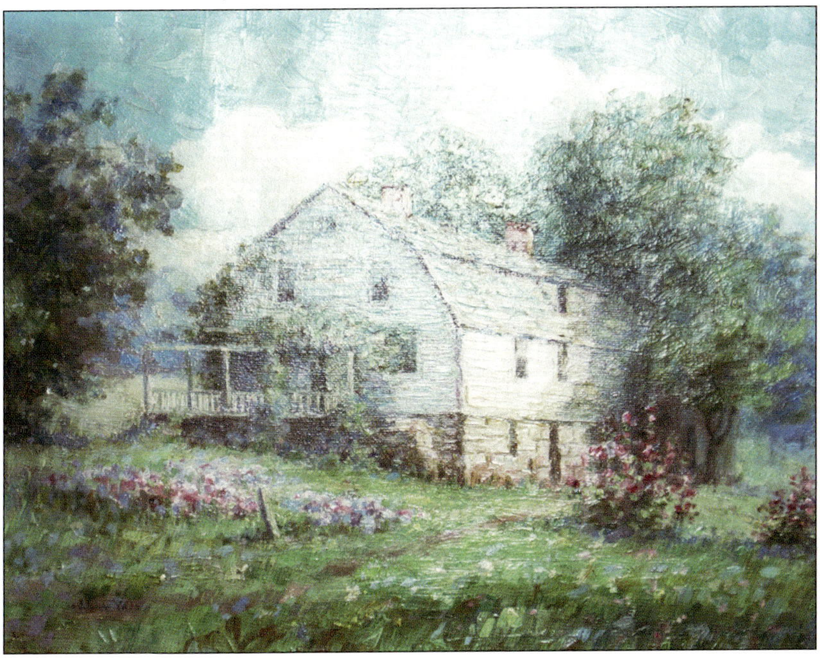

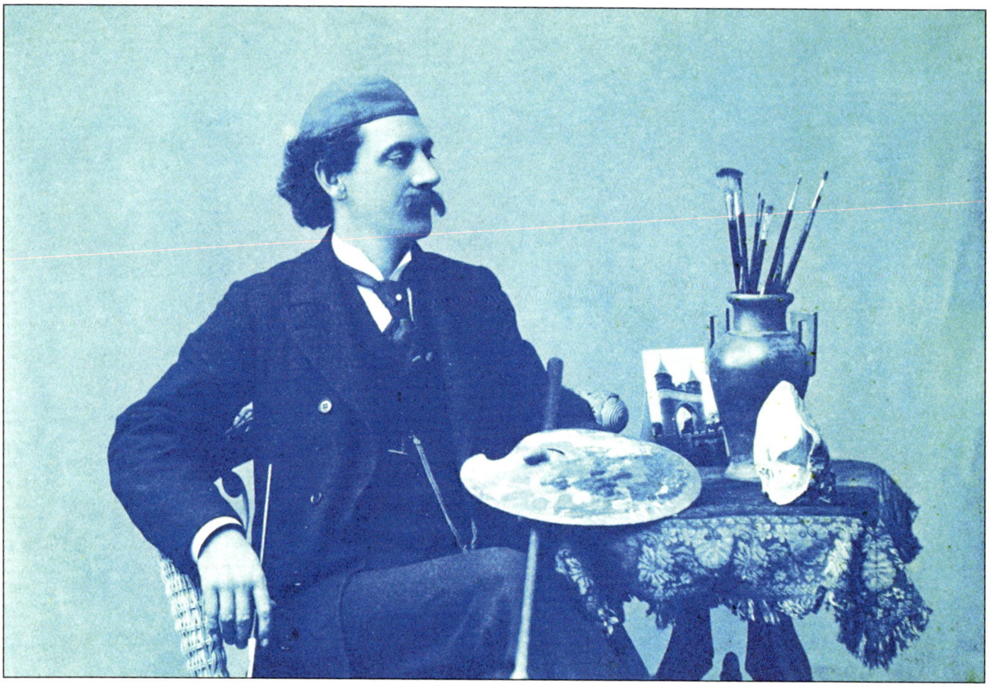

Burton H. Hubbell. Burton H. Hubbell was born in Hamden, Connecticut, on March 20, 1863. He was a painter by trade and had worked alongside his father in a contracting business. After his father's death, he continued the family business while exploring his talents as an artist. He was skilled in both painting and photography, sometimes combining the two to create hand-tinted photographs. Years later, Hubbell was employed by Edward Miller & Company and worked there until his death at his home in Meriden on October 23, 1912, at the age of 49. Hubbell's photography is still regarded as iconic and timeless. (Top, courtesy of the Connecticut Historical Society; bottom, courtesy of Allen Weathers.)

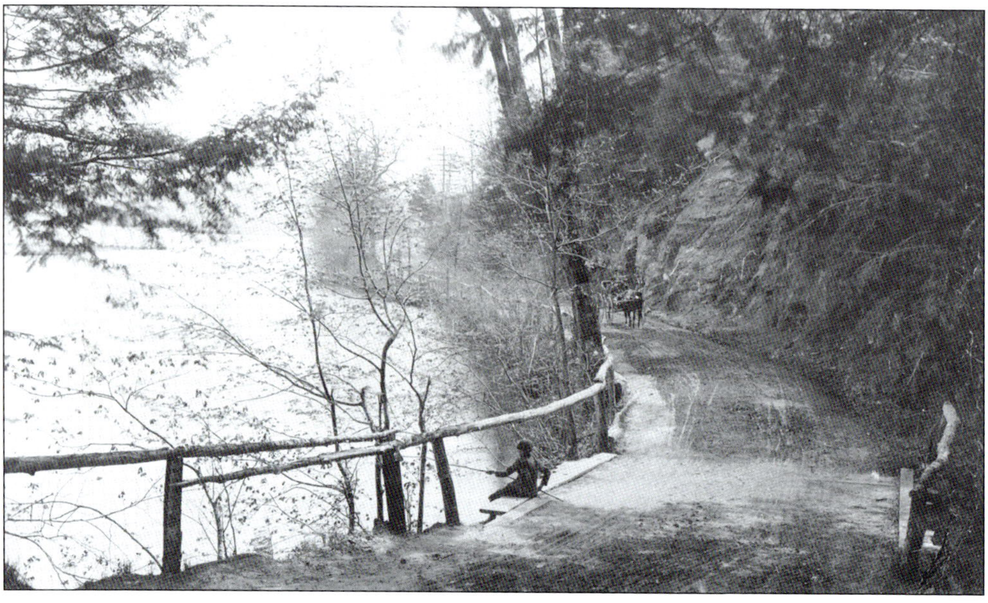

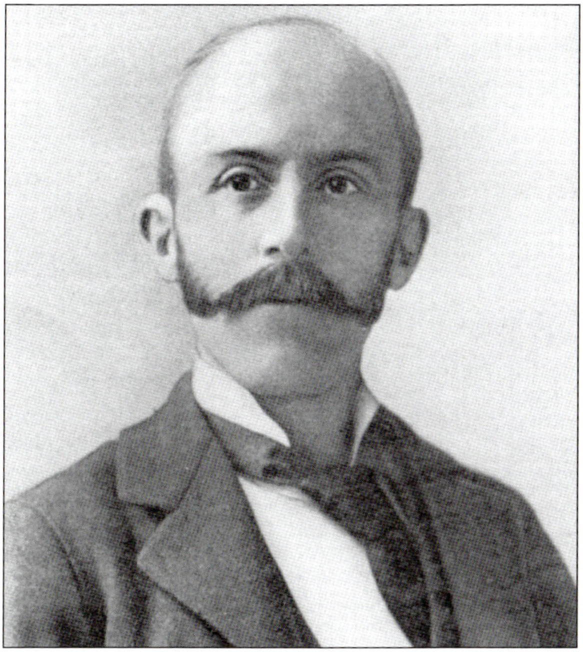

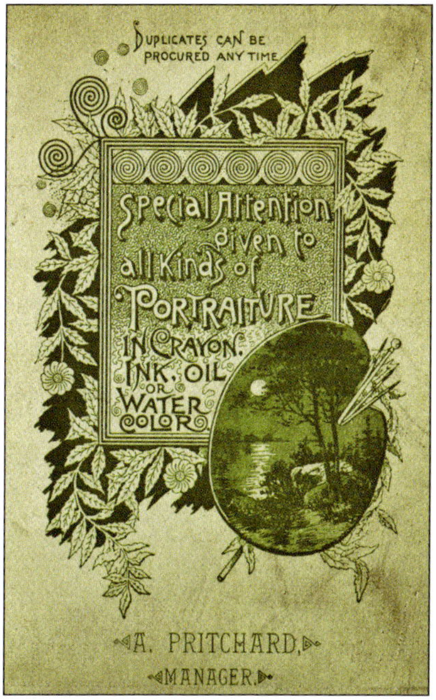

ALFRED PRITCHARD. For years, Alfred Pritchard was Meriden's leading photographer. He made his debut as a photographer in 1879 as manager of the J.F. Green Studio, a job he held for 12 years. In 1890, he opened his own short-lived studio on East Main Street, soon accepting an offer to work with famed photographer Colonel Marceau in his photography business on Fifth Avenue in New York City. Pritchard soon returned to Meriden and died in 1938.

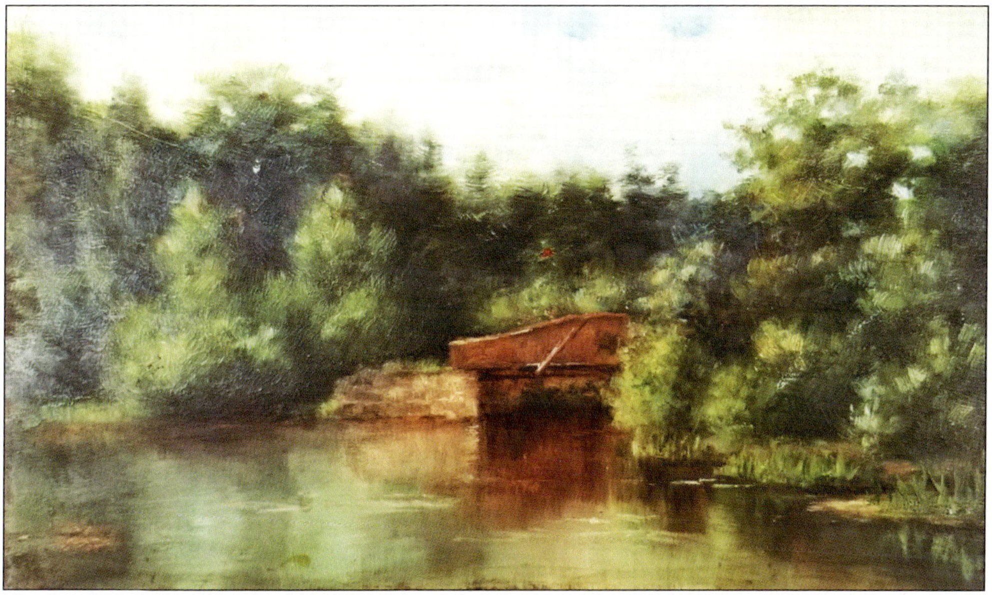

RED BRIDGE. This late-19th-century oil painting of Red Bridge by an unidentified artist features the techniques and style of American Impressionism. These Impressionists adopted bright palettes and loose brushstrokes to capture the intimate beauty of American everyday life. Once a popular recreation spot for swimming, boating, fishing, and gathering, Red Bridge sits at the southwestern edge of Hanover Lake in South Meriden. (Courtesy of Chris Ruel.)

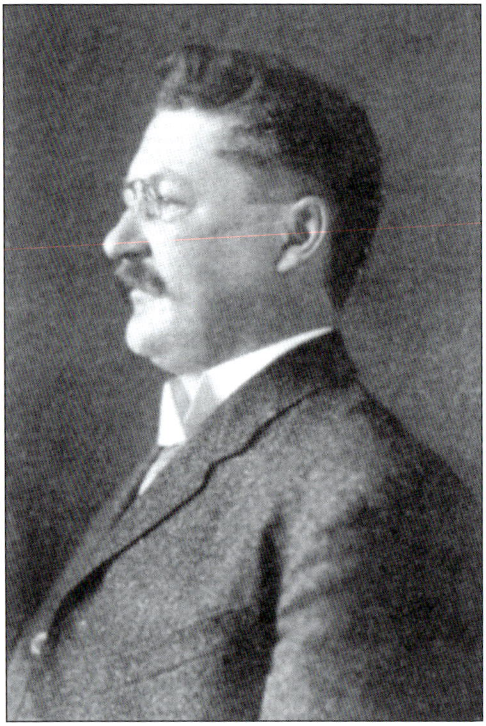

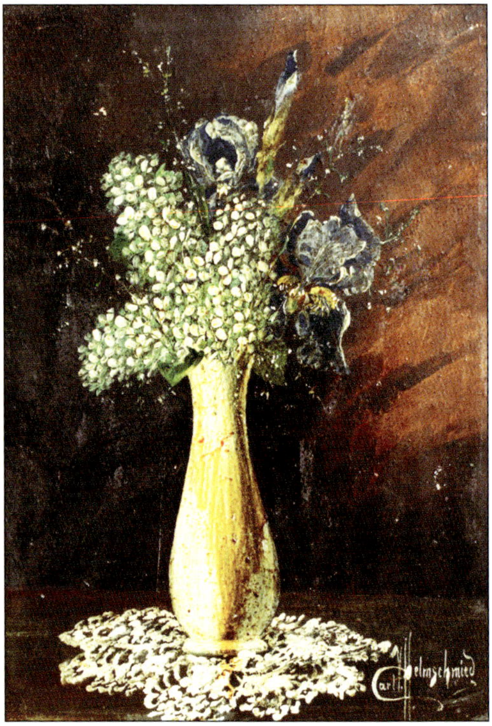

Carl Helmschmied. Carl Helmschmied was born in Austria in 1863. After his graduation, he sailed to New York and traveled to New Bedford, Massachusetts, where he was employed designing opalware. Two years later, he moved to Trenton, New Jersey, to work as a china decorator, only to return to New Bedford to work for the Mount Washington Glass Company. In 1886, Helmschmied came to Meriden and worked for the C.F. Monroe Opal and Crystal Decorating Works. He became a stockholder, the superintendent, and the company's lead designer for 16 years. In 1903, Helmschmied left the company and opened his own factory, the Helmschmied Manufacturing Company. The business was successful for a time but was later downsized to a small studio in his home. Helmschmied died in Meriden in 1934.

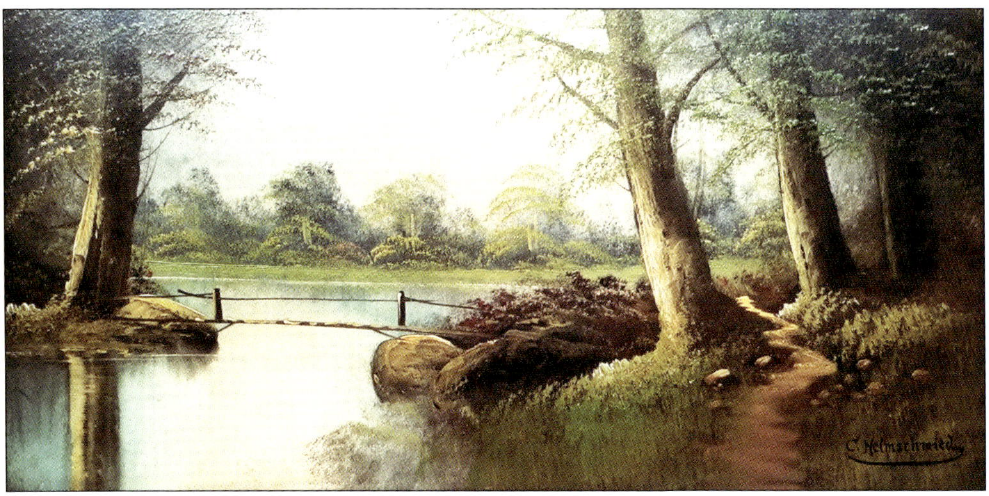

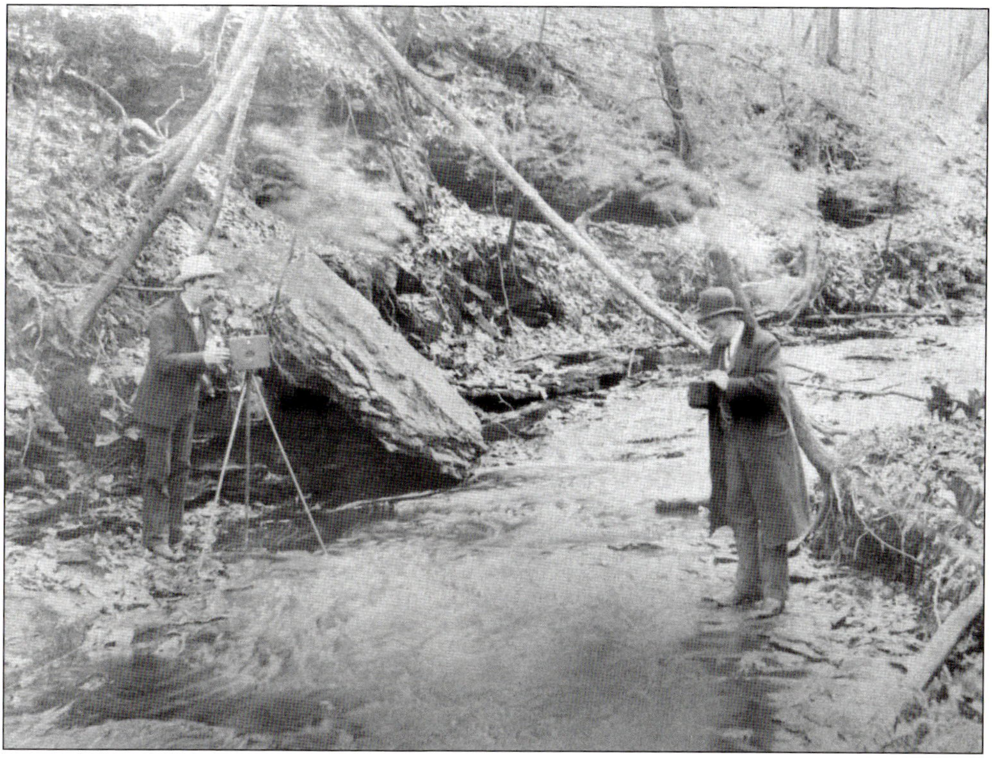

Photography as a Pastime. This c. 1900 image by C.I. Parker shows two men, Burton Hubbell on the left and presumably Levi Coe on the right, as they exchange composition tips about photographing this Meriden waterway. Although both men enjoyed photography as a pastime, Hubbell made it his profession while Coe spent a lifetime in Meriden politics and servicing several societies. (Courtesy of Brian Cofrancesco.)

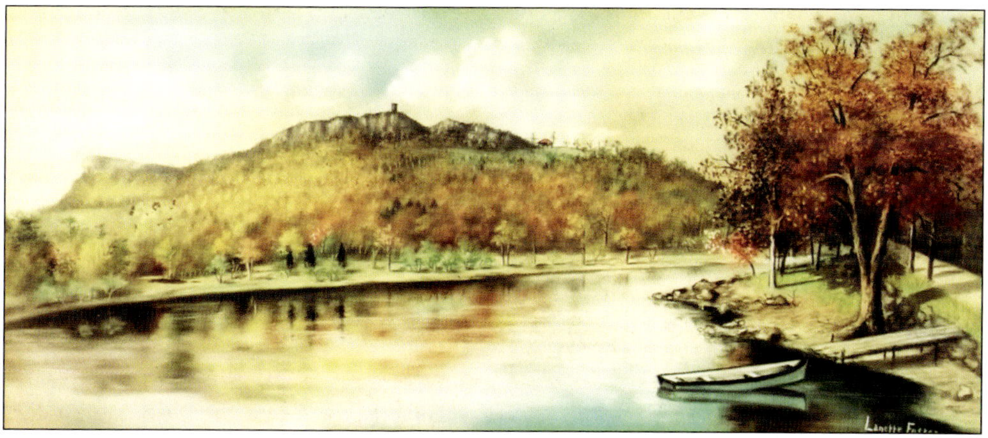

Lanette Foster. Lanette Foster, wife of J. Herbert Foster, resided in Meriden for a number of years. She was fond of nature and was a very skilled painter. In 1902, she and her husband moved to Mexico where he started the Meriden Rubber Planting Company. Over her lifetime, Foster's work was highly acclaimed by both New York and Mexican publishers. She died in 1907. (Courtesy of the Meriden Historical Society.)

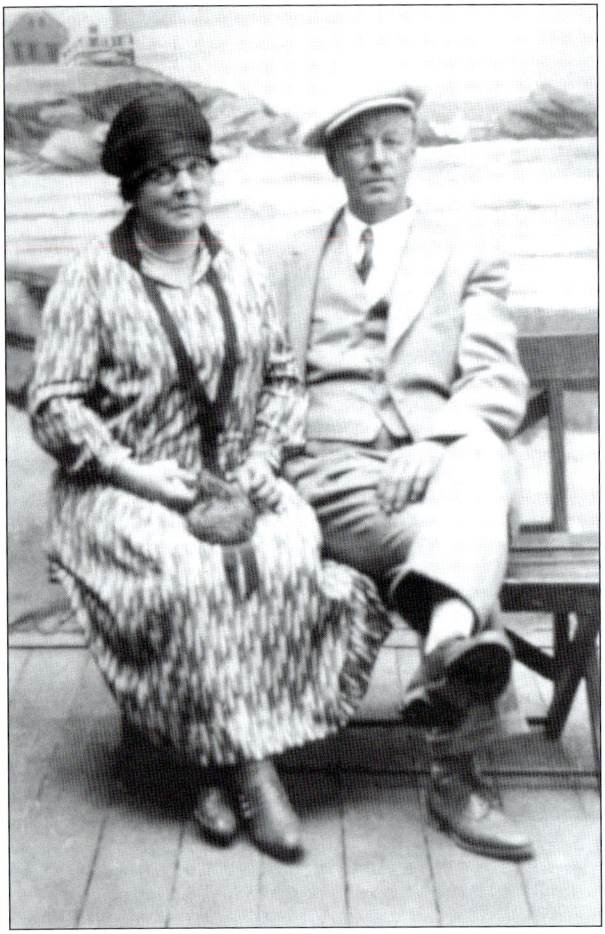

Albert E. Lewis. Albert E. Lewis was born in Birmingham, England, in 1872 and came to Meriden just five years later. Later, after a brief residence in New Britain, he found employment with the Bradley & Hubbard Manufacturing Company. Noted for his artistic talents, he was regarded as a very capable painter who utilized oils with great technique. Pictured here with his wife, Louise, Lewis died in 1939. (Courtesy of Allen and Neda Weathers.)

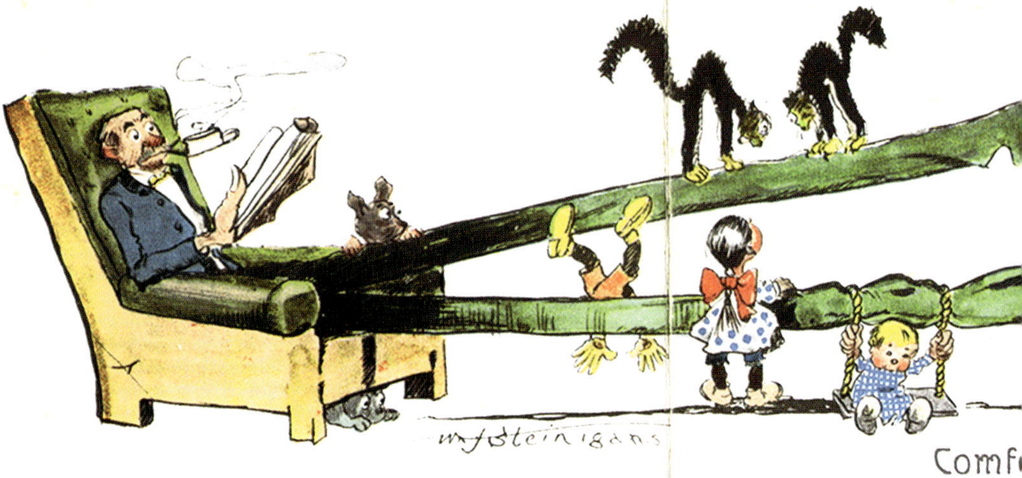

William John Steinigans. William John Steinigans was born in 1878. By 1901, he was working in Meriden as a clerk, but within four years, he had moved to New York City to be a cartoonist for Joseph Pulitzer's *New York World* newspaper. Steinigans is best remembered for continuing Gene

HARVEY C. VOORHEES. Harvey C. Voorhees was a prominent Meriden artist and photographer. During the 1891 Connecticut State Fair, he was awarded five first premium awards in the areas of Best Collection of Photographs, Best Crayon Artist, Best Large Photograph, Best Photograph in Natural Color, and Best Platinotype. In January 1902, he left Meriden for Boston, where became a member of the Massachusetts bar and a successful author of legal literature.

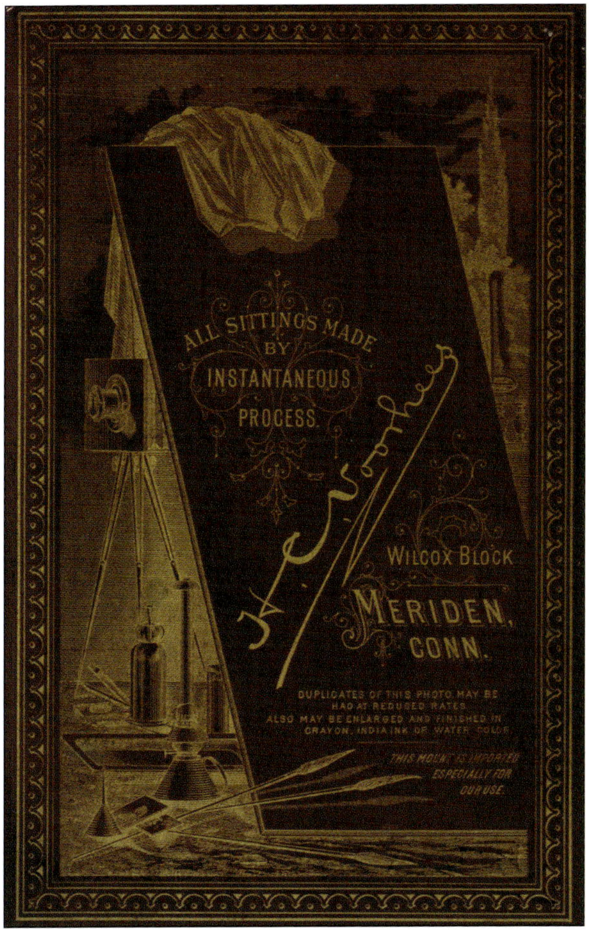

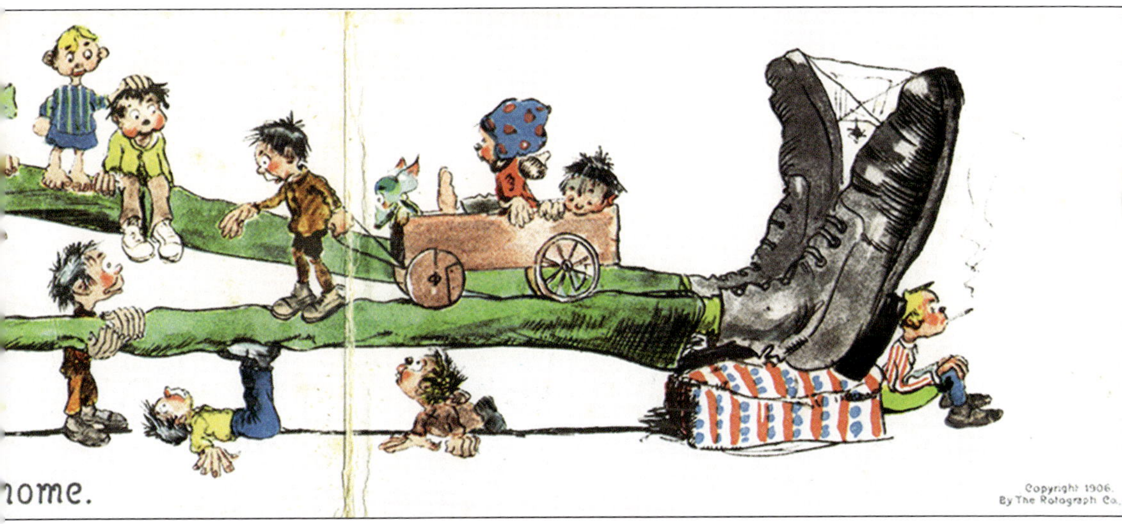

Carr's cartoon *The Bad Dream That Made Bill A Better Boy* from 1905 until 1911. He also created humorous postcards. Steinigans moved to California in 1913 for health reasons and passed away just five years later at the age of 39.

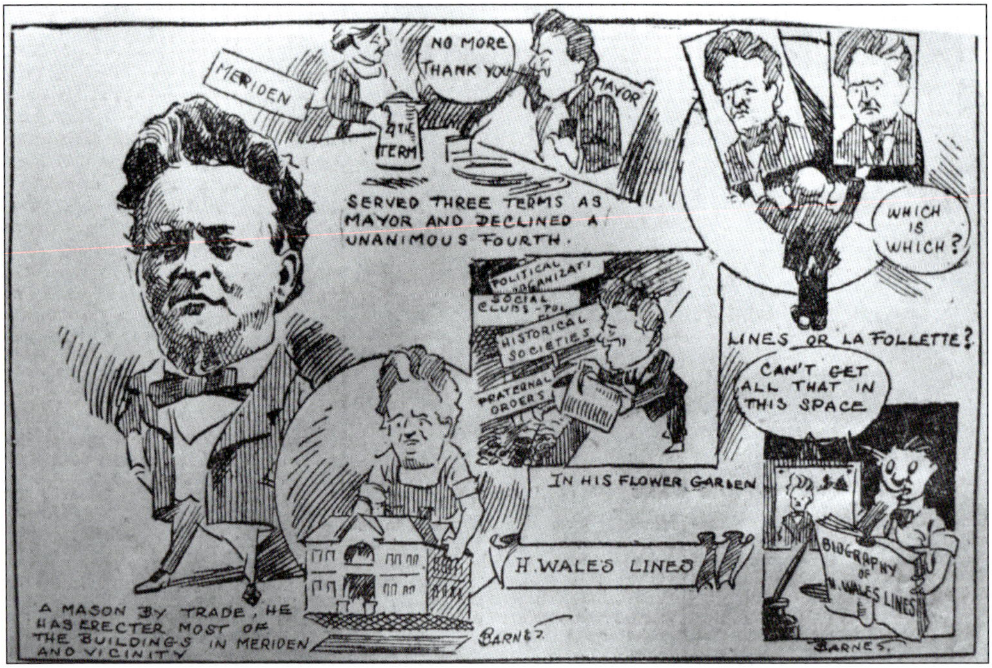

Caricature in 1912. In 1912, the *Meriden Daily Journal* published a series of 74 caricatures of well-known local citizens. These brilliant pen-and-ink renderings were done by the talented cartoonist Barnes (first name unknown). Local political cartoons, like this caricature of contractor H. Wales Lines, were commentaries on specific people or events, usually offering subtle criticism. (Courtesy of the Meriden Historical Society.)

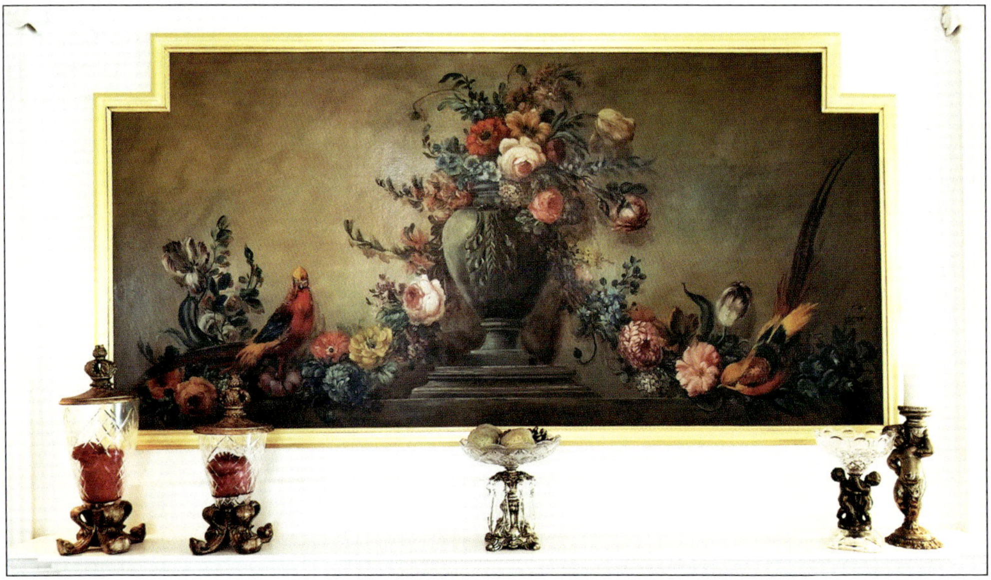

Meriden Home Overmantel. This unsigned 1918 overmantel painting is characteristic of the artwork that was being created in Meriden in the early 1900s. Still installed in a prominent local home today, this exquisite six-foot work combines the sensibilities of the Romanticism style with an astute technical prowess found in only a handful of local artists. Evidence suggests that this may have been painted by Meriden artist Charlotte Lilla Yale.

Two

An Artist Colony Emerges

On November 21, 1906, Meriden's first art exhibition opened its doors to the public in the upstairs lecture hall of the Curtis Memorial Library. It was the idea of a group of local artists led by Indianna Thomas and Julia Lansing Hall. Exhibition attendees paid an admission fee of 10¢, and the profits were donated to the library. The affair was such a great artistic and social success that Thomas was urged to hold another exhibition the following year.

To add a new dimension and prestige to the second exhibition, famous out-of-town artists were invited to show their work alongside local artists. The growing interest in these exhibitions and the amount of work to coordinate them convinced Thomas that it was time to formally organize a group of Meriden artists.

Thomas hosted three organizational meetings at her home on December 5, 11, and 18, 1907, and members voted to form the Arts and Crafts Association of Meriden. The following officers were elected: president, Edward Bradstreet; vice president, Charlotte Lilla Yale; secretary and treasurer, Robert B. Seidensticker; and corresponding secretary, Emma Rutherford. On March 11, 1908, the first general meeting of the Arts and Crafts Association of Meriden was held in Library Hall where George M. Curtis presented a lecture on art.

The members of this small organization were energetic and broad-minded, working hard to celebrate art and embed the association in Meriden's civic life. They gave $6–$10 each year to schoolchildren to purchase art posters and held free public exhibitions of paintings and etchings. When Meriden's new high school was built, the association gave a seven-foot-tall cast of Sophocles, which adorned the assembly room for years. In 1914, the association contributed $25 to a fund for the beautification of Winthrop Square, a park opposite the Winthrop Hotel on Colony Street in downtown Meriden. When new electric streetlights were installed in the city, a committee of association members advocated—although unsuccessfully—for an installation that was both practical and artistic. Members worked tirelessly to preserve the city's shade trees, sponsored art magazines subscriptions for the library, and sent money to France for the Artist Assistance Fund at the onset of World War I. As the war continued, the association saw many of its members enlist in military service, and in 1917, it dispersed with its annual activities.

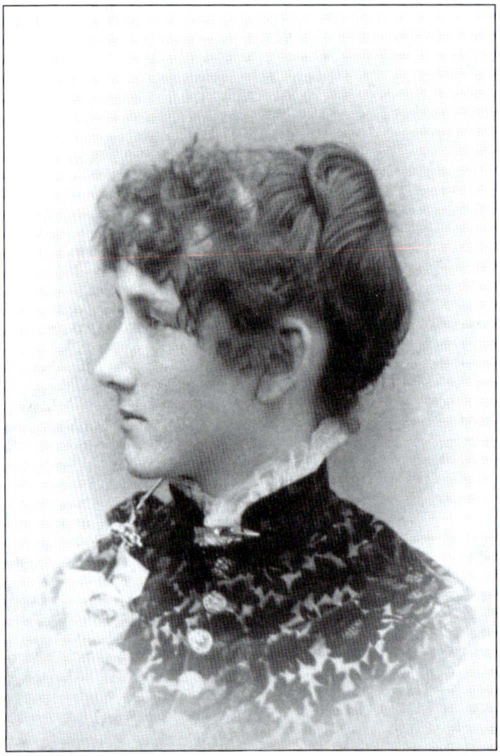

INDIANNA THOMAS. Indianna Thomas (left) was born in Middletown, Connecticut, on December 27, 1865. She was a graduate of the first Meriden High School class in 1883 and was well-known in Meriden artistic circles, having interests in both art and music. As an arts advocate and benefactor, she was the founding leader of the Arts and Crafts Association of Meriden. Thomas died in Meriden on January 10, 1948.

WILLIAM RETTENMEYER. William Rettenmeyer (below, left) was born in New York City in 1862 and was a silversmith at Tiffany and Company. In 1893, Rettenmeyer came to Meriden and designed the first sterling novelties for the E.A. Bliss Company. Throughout his life, he was also an avid painter, predominately working in watercolors. He was a charter member of the Arts and Crafts Association of Meriden and designed this logo (below, right) for the new organization. Rettenmeyer died in 1963. (Both, courtesy of the Meriden Historical Society.)

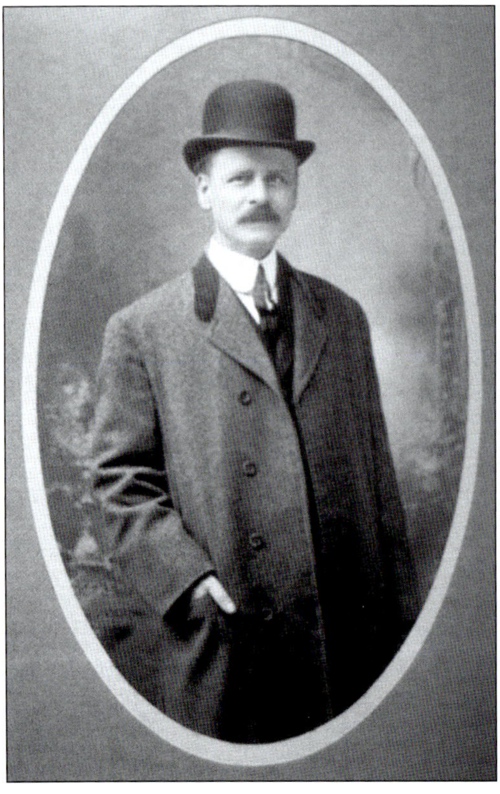

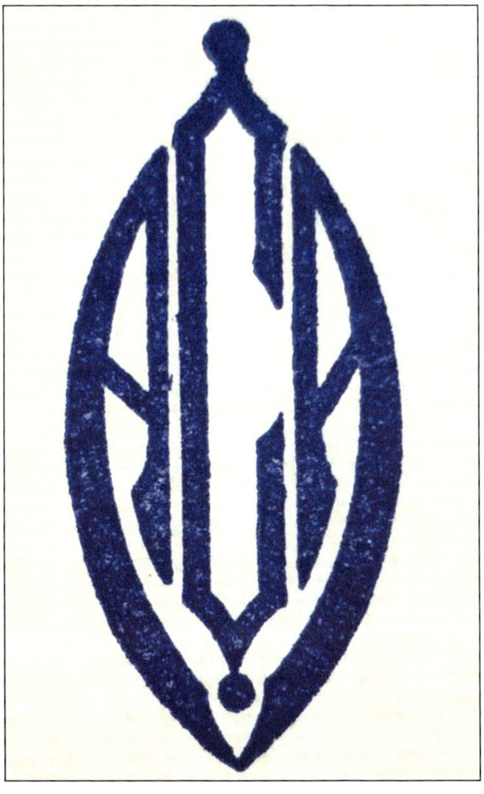

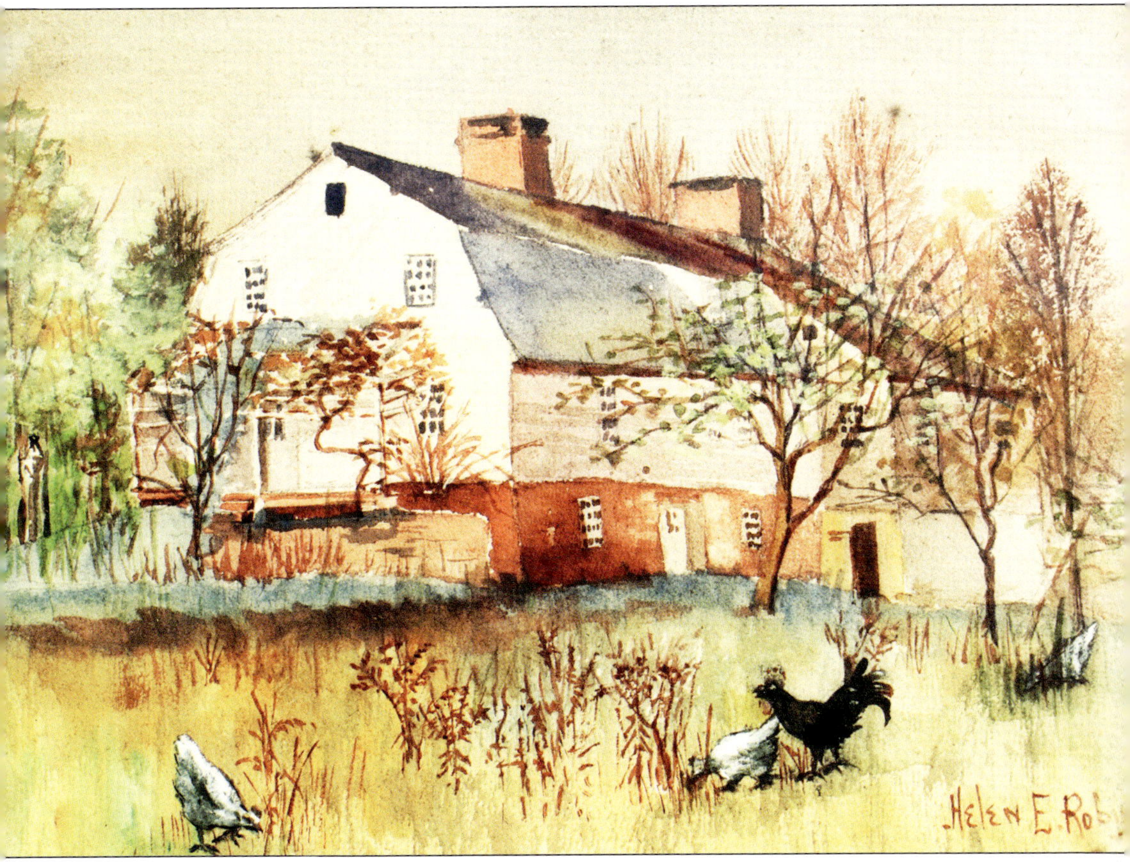

Helen Roby. Helen Roby was born in 1858 and lived most of her life in Detroit, Michigan. Around 1878, Roby left Detroit for Paris, France, to study art for three years. Roby came to Meriden in 1897 to take care of her brother S.J. Roby and his family when his wife died. While in Meriden, Roby befriended Indianna Thomas, who became her Meriden agent and coordinated a 1907 exhibit of her watercolor paintings at the "Old Clark Farm" (Solomon Goffe House Museum), where Roby was a tenant. The exhibit was one of the inspirations for formation of the Arts and Crafts Association of Meriden. Around 1912, Roby's brother remarried, and she moved back to Detroit. Unfortunately, her studio in Detroit had burned down and she lost several of her paintings. Some 12 years later in 1924, Roby returned to Connecticut and built a cottage in Madison. She spent summers there with her sister Elizabeth. Roby died at the Curtis Home in Meriden in 1957 at the age of 98. (Courtesy of Gallery 53.)

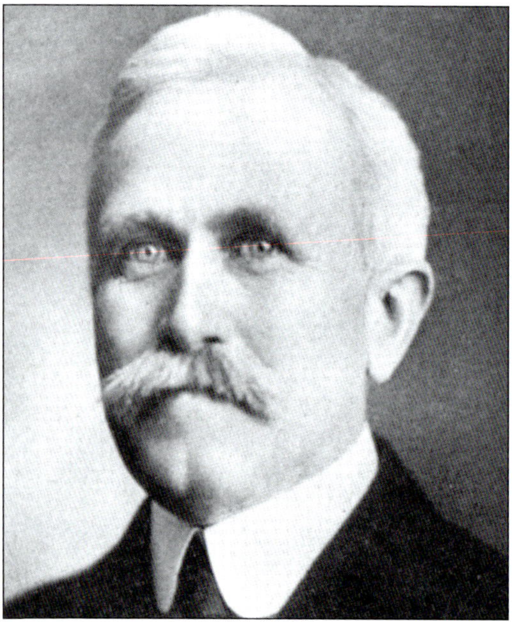

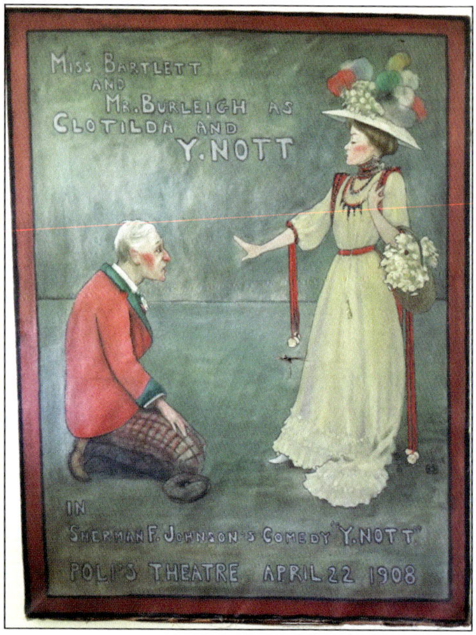

Edward Dudley Bradstreet. Edward Dudley Bradstreet was born on November 11, 1878. He attended Meriden schools and, despite an early bicycling injury, he remained consistent and graduated from Yale University in 1901. Later, he studied at the Art Students League in New York City. In 1906, he made three large posters that hung in Mosher's Drug Store window to announce local plays featuring a Frank L. Burleigh, Edith Bartlett, and Bradstreet himself. The plays were *Home Life*, *Reproduction of First Town Meeting*, and *Y Nott*. Bradstreet was the first president of the Arts and Crafts Association of Meriden. He later traveled to Vienna to study art until the start of World War I. One of his pieces, an oil painting of his friend and noted sculptor Louis Gudebrod, is in the permanent collection of the National Portrait Gallery in Washington, DC. Bradstreet died of pneumonia on January 14, 1921, at the age of 42.

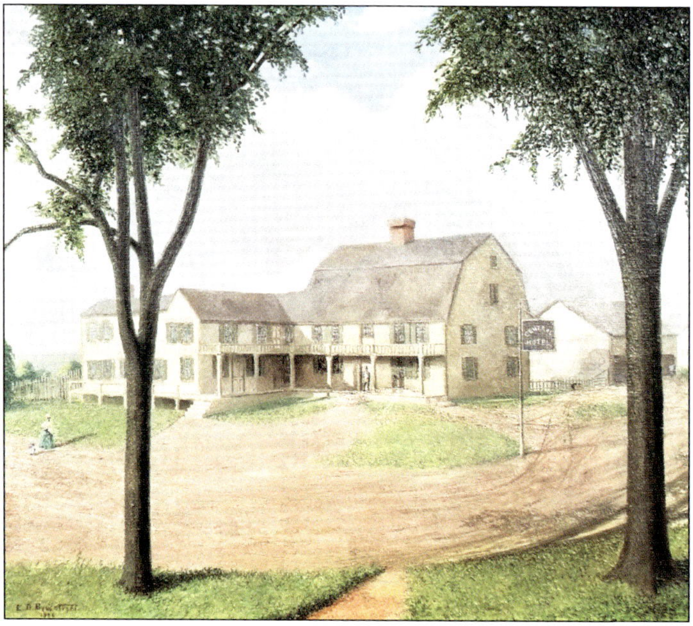

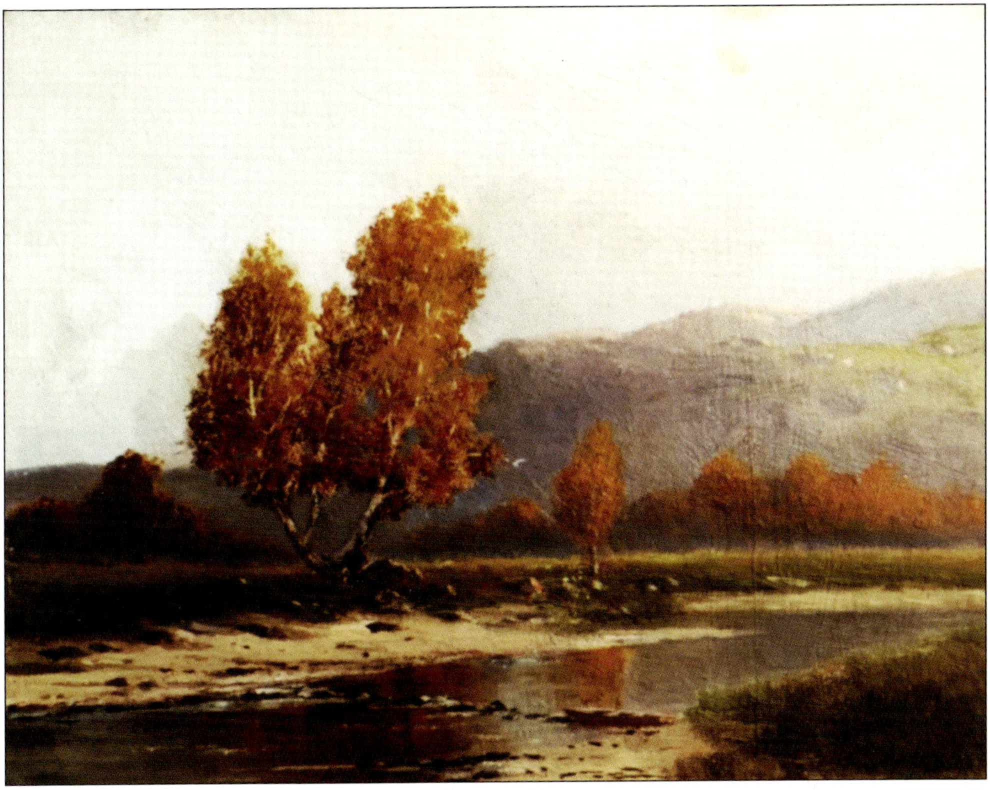

Charles G. Havens. Charles G. Havens, otherwise known as C.G. Havens, was born in 1848 and was a pressman for the Meriden newspapers for over 35 years. Havens was also a versatile artist, well-trained in pastels and oils as well as in photography. As a founding member of the Arts and Crafts Association of Meriden, his work received many accolades and awards. Havens died in Hartford in 1916.

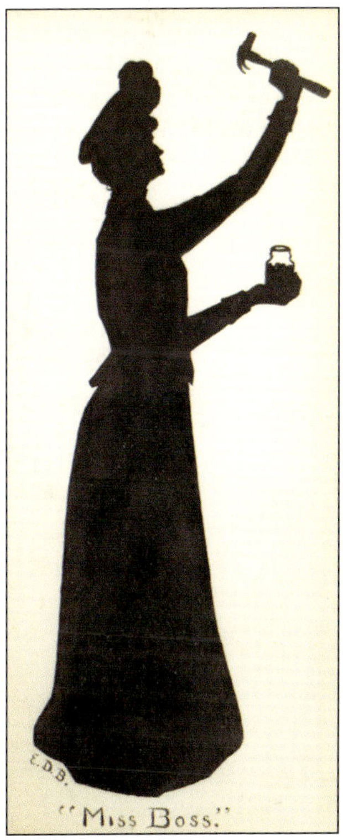

Silhouette of Indianna Thomas. The first American photographer was the silhouettist. Early patrons would go to these artists for a studio sitting and an inexpensive portrait. This caricature is a silhouette of Indianna Thomas, the founder of the Arts and Crafts Association of Meriden, and was created by then president of the organization, Edward Bradstreet. (Courtesy of Gallery 53.)

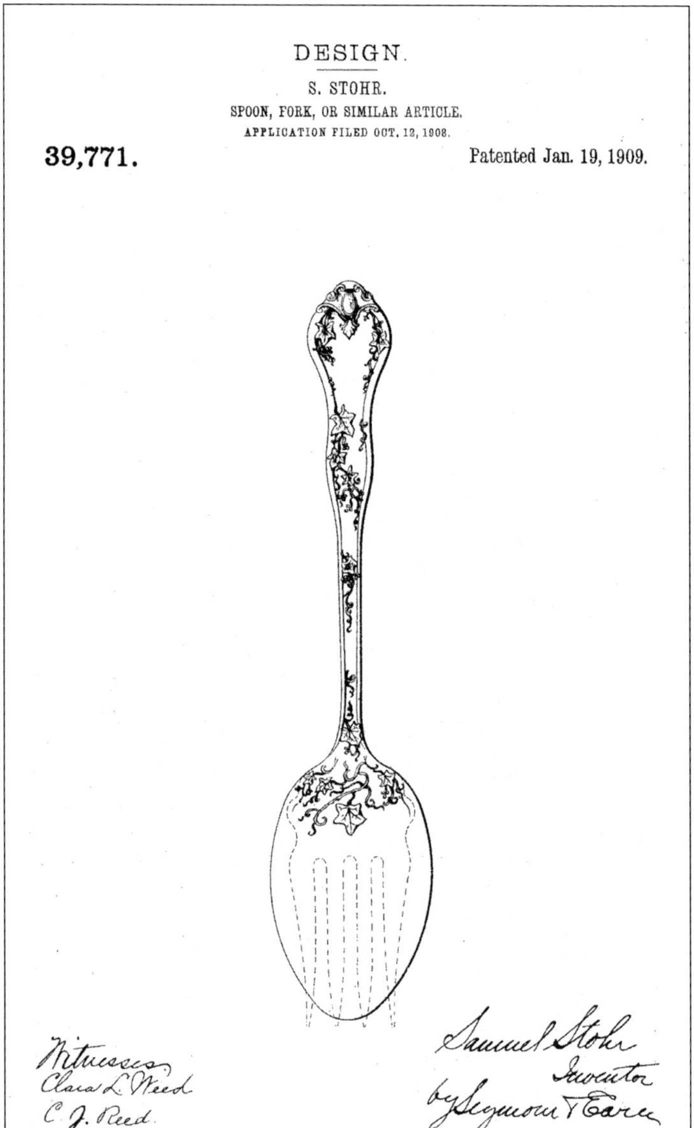

SAMUEL STOHR. Samuel Stohr was born in New York City in 1869 during America's Gilded Age. From ages 15 to 25, he was employed at Tiffany & Company in New York City before moving to Meriden in January 1897 to work at the Meriden Britannia Company. Stohr worked his way up to the position of head designer in the sterling silver department of the newly formed International Silver Company, a position he held until his death. With several patents for silver designs and flatware, Stohr was described "as one of the best designers in this class of work in the country." Later in life, Stohr worked as an art instructor at Meriden's German-American School and was a charter member of the Arts and Crafts Association of Meriden where he regularly exhibited his own silver-crafted artwork. Stohr died unexpectedly in 1932 after being struck by an automobile.

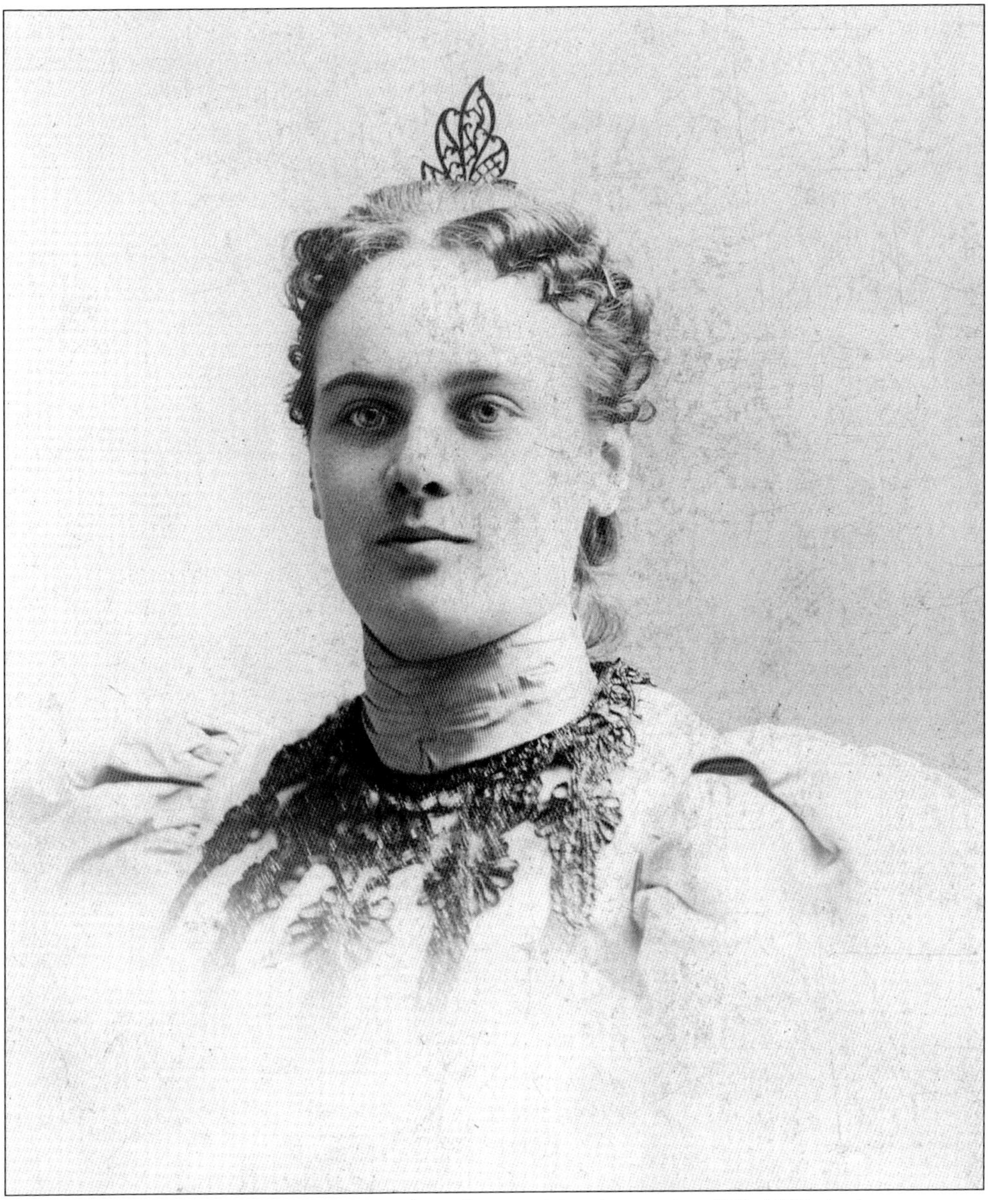

NELLIE FOSTER NAGEL. Nellie Foster Nagel was born in Meriden on April 23, 1873. At the young age of nine, she won an art prize at the state fair for a pencil rendering. She graduated from Meriden High School in 1891 and later from Pratt University, also taking courses at Columbia University, New York University, and City College of New York. Her teaching career ranged from working in a one-room school in Wallingford to being a drawing supervisor for the New York City school district before returning to Meriden to teach in the public schools from 1907 to 1915. In 1939, she was appointed the first woman to serve on the Meriden Board of Education. Nagel's work was shown in several of the top galleries in New York City as well as through the Connecticut Academy of Fine Arts. She headed the Arts and Crafts Association of Meriden and also belonged to the New Haven Paint & Clay Club and the New Britain Art League. Other honors included membership in the National Association of Women Painters and Sculptors and a listing in *Leading Women of America*. Nellie Nagel died in 1955.

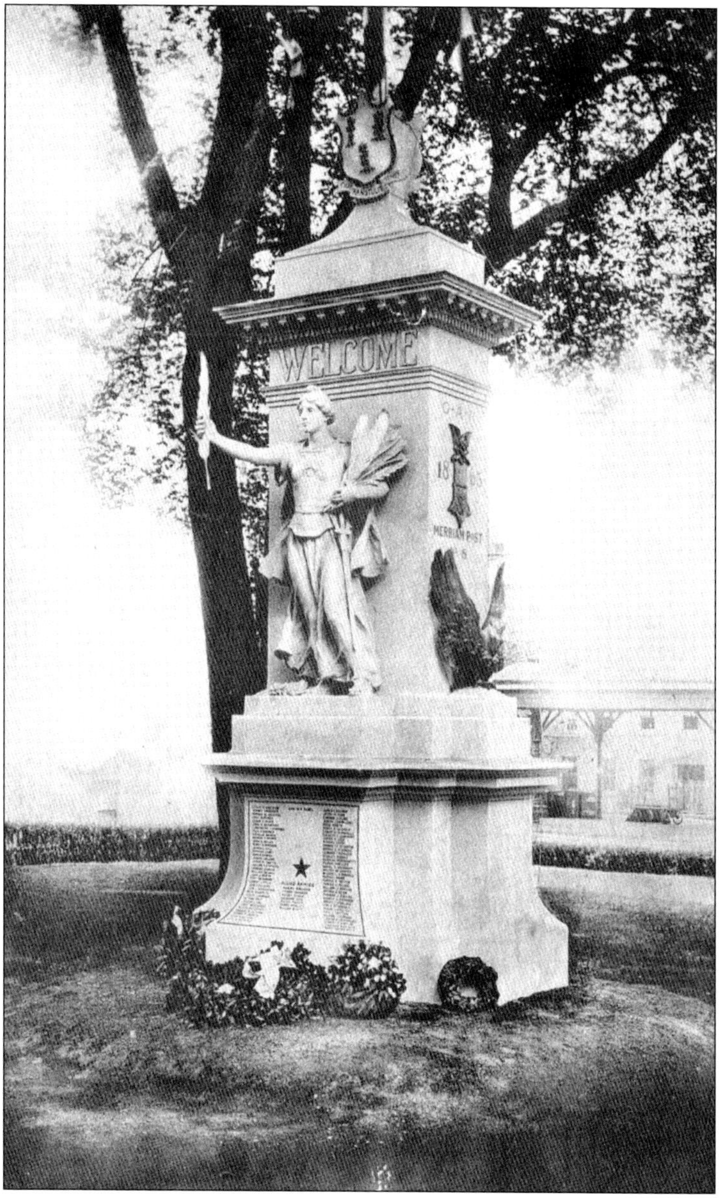

Louis Gudebrod. Louis Gudebrod was born in Middletown, Connecticut, in 1872. He came to Meriden at the age of 14 and worked nearby at the New Britain Terracotta Company for two years. He moved to New York City to continue the same type of work, but after visiting a sculptor's studio, he knew immediately that he wanted to study sculpture. He attended the city's Art Students League and later Yale University. Gudebrod then went to Paris from 1897 to 1900 where he was a pupil and assistant to the acclaimed Augustus Saint-Gaudens. Gudebrod worked with him on a bust of Union army general William Tecumseh Sherman and later the famous equestrian statue of General Sherman at Grand Army Plaza at the entrance to New York City's Central Park. While in Paris, Gudebrod continued to paint in the Realist style, although the current societal taste favored Impressionism and artists like Claude Monet. Upon his return to Meriden, Gudebrod continued to represent the city with his international approval as an artist. He married artist Julia Manley in 1961, the same year that he died.

Ethel Easton Paxson DuClos. Ethel Easton Paxson DuClos was born in Meriden in 1885. She first studied with Meriden artist Charlotte Lilla Yale and later at the Corcoran Art School in Washington, DC. In 1909, she began her studies at the Pennsylvania Academy of the Fine Arts under the tutelage of famed American Impressionism painter William Merritt Chase. Later, she traveled to Brazil and was one of the first American Impressionists to paint there. Upon her return to the United States, she taught art in Meriden, New York, and Vermont. She was represented at the Metropolitan Museum of Art in New York City and the New Britain Museum of American Art in Connecticut. She authored four books and wrote articles for a number of magazines, including the *Women's Home Companion* and *American Magazine*. DuClos died in Essex, Connecticut, in 1982.

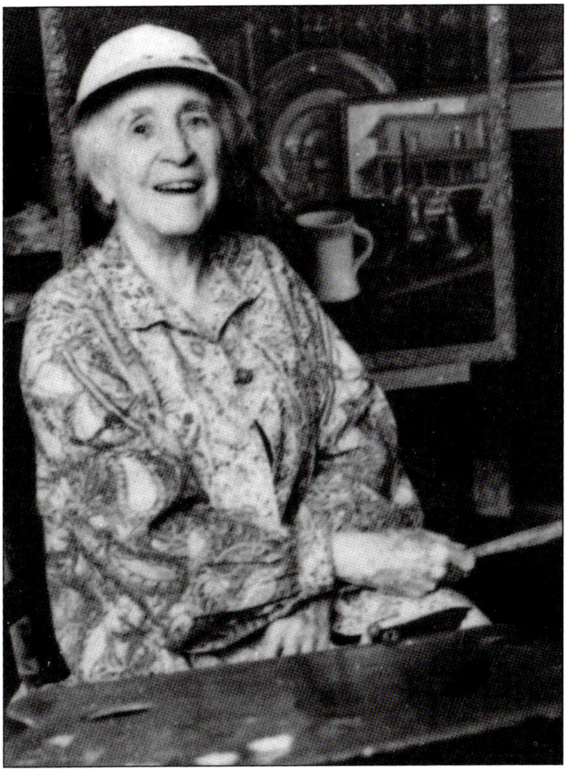

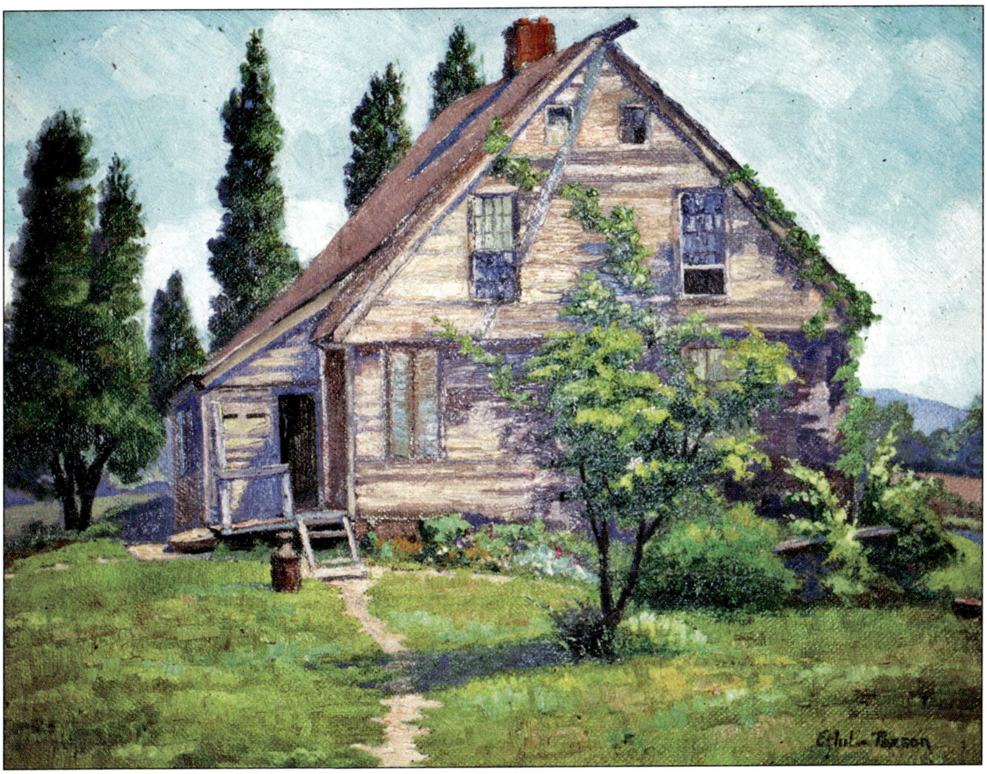

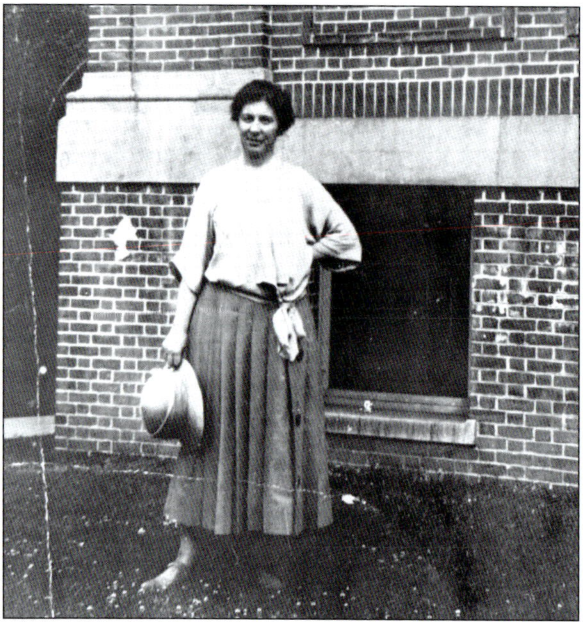

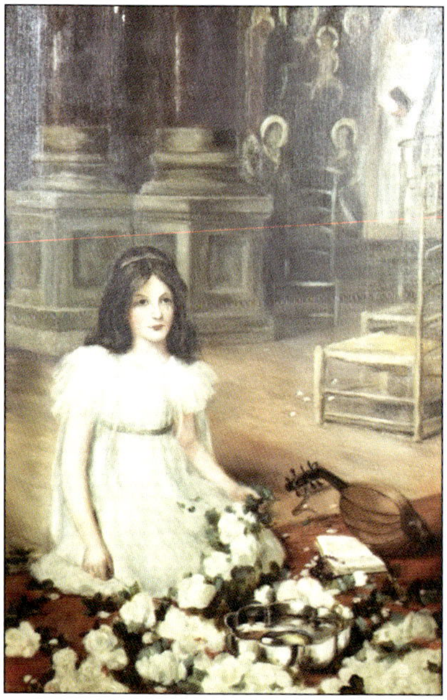

ROSEMARY BRADY. Rosemary Brady was born in Meriden in 1874 and graduated from Meriden High School in 1893. She studied art with Meriden artist Charlotte Lilla Yale and later furthered her craft by taking courses at Columbia University and Yale University. She was a popular teacher in the early days of art being taught in Meriden schools, beginning her teaching career at Church Street Elementary School before transferring to the new Meriden High School on Pleasant Street, teaching there until her retirement in 1938. She was a charter member of the Arts and Crafts Association of Meriden and a member of the National Retired Teachers Association. Some of her private pupils included Jean Tamburine and Charlotte Sternberg. Brady died on August 24, 1961, and is buried in St. Patrick's Cemetery in Meriden. (All, courtesy of the Meriden Historical Society.)

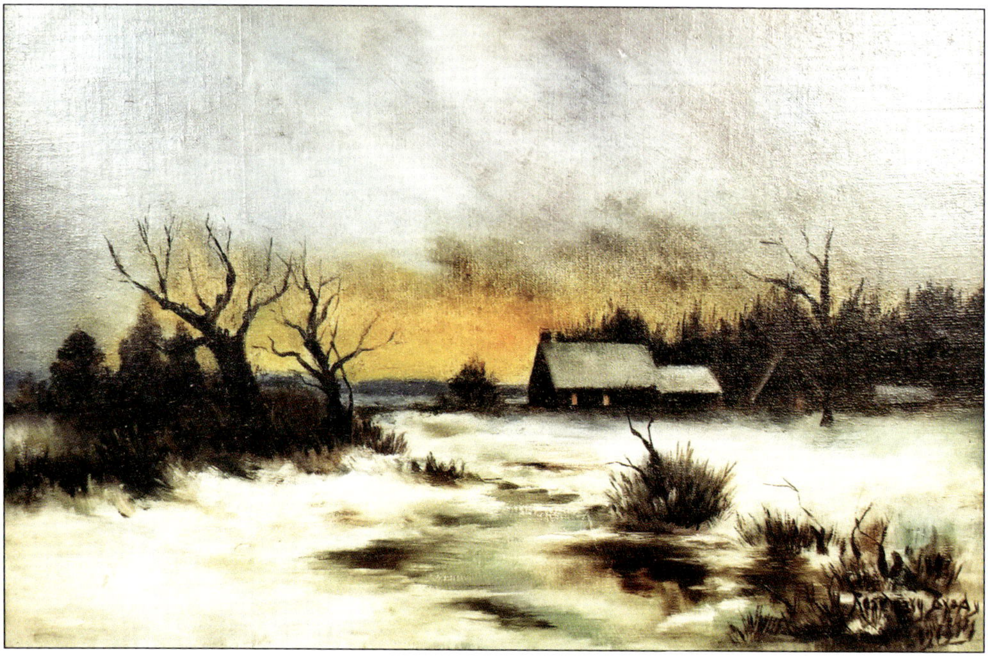

HENRIK HILLBOM. Born in Sweden in 1863, Henrik Hillbom studied with goldsmith Otto Lindeberg at a technical school in Stockholm. He later immigrated to New York where he worked for the Whitney Manufacturing Company for a short time before leaving to study painting with Benjamin Constant in Paris. He returned to New York and worked as an illustrator for the political journal *Harper's Weekly*, creating art like this *Sweets for the Holidays* drawing published in 1891. Later, he worked as a silver designer for the Wallace Manufacturing Company in Wallingford, Connecticut, while making a name for himself in the Meriden arts community as a landscape painter. Hillbom was one of the formative members of the Arts and Crafts Association of Meriden and was featured in many of its exhibitions. Hillbom died in 1948 at the age of 84.

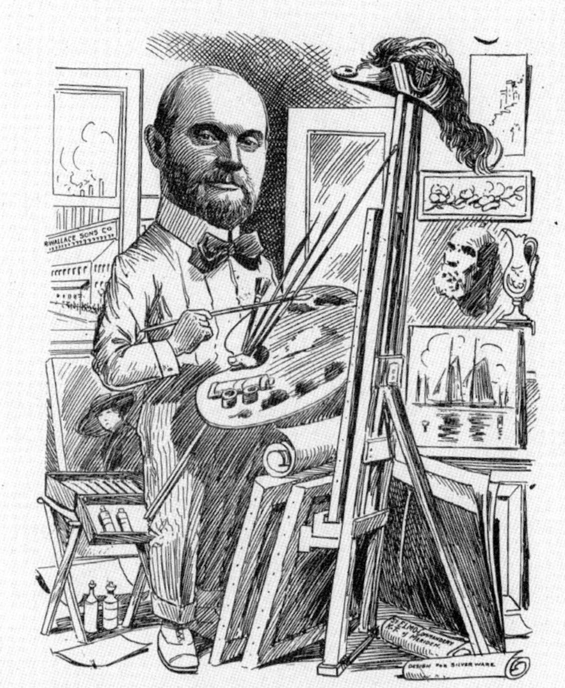

HENRIK HILLBOM

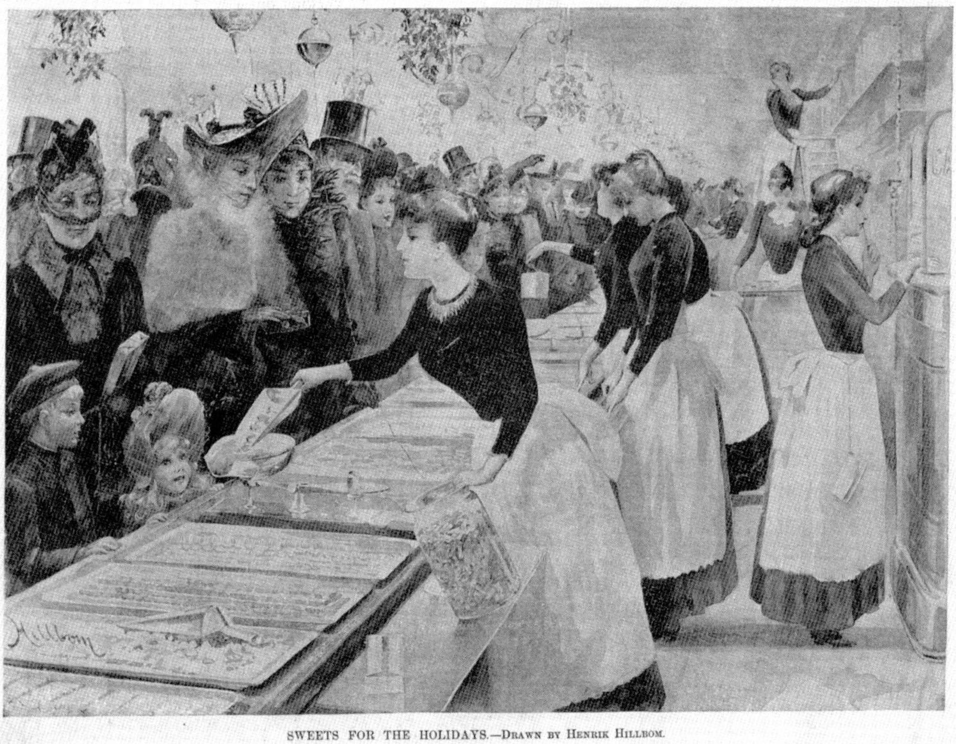

SWEETS FOR THE HOLIDAYS.—DRAWN BY HENRIK HILLBOM.

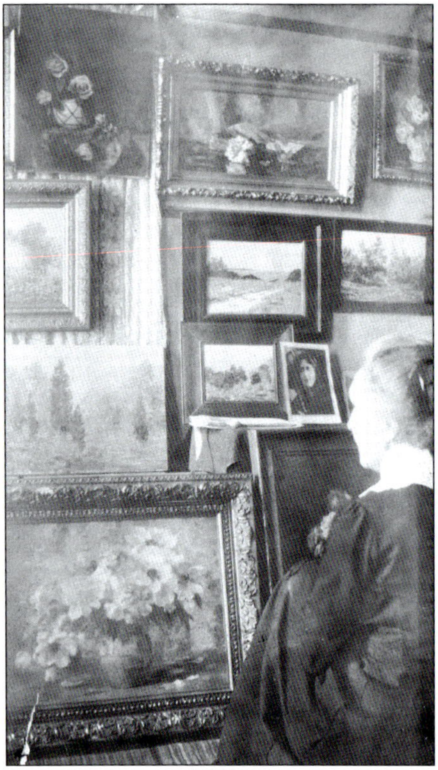

A Visit to an Artist Studio. Ethel Paxson began studying with Charlotte Lilla Yale when she was about 10 years old. Each three-hour lesson cost 50¢. Paxson and Yale's unique teacher-student bond and mutual respect for each other's art continued throughout their lifetimes. This 1916 interior photograph shows Yale viewing the many paintings exhibited in the studio of her former student, Paxson.

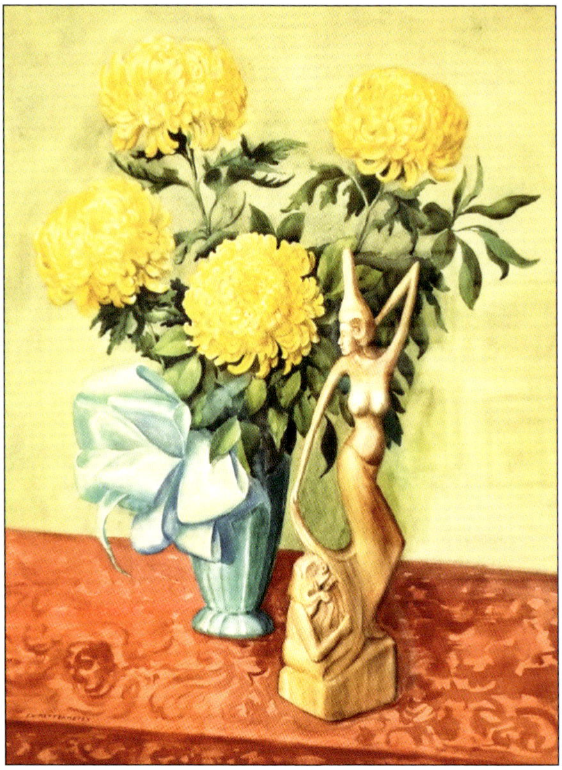

Frederick Rettenmeyer. Frederick Rettenmeyer was born in Meriden in 1891. He enjoyed painting in oil and watercolor and studied with Meriden artist Charlotte Lilla Yale as well as Harry Ballinger and Emil Gruppe of Gloucester, Massachusetts. A jewelry designer by trade, Rettenmeyer became the president of the Napier Company. He was a member of the New Haven Paint & Clay Club, the Lyme Art Club, and the Arts and Crafts Association of Meriden. Rettenmeyer died in 1965.

Three

The Business of Art

As Meriden became a manufacturing mecca and metropolis for producing silver wares in the mid-19th century, there was an uptick in the local workforce. The Meriden Britannia Company led the way in hiring artists for design and production positions, strategically combing art with commerce to ensure its products were both practical and visually appealing. C.F. Monroe Opal & Crystal Decorating Works and the Helmschmied Manufacturing Company had similar strategies, employing artisans to embellish their decorative chinaware with incredible motifs. In response, young artists from across the country flocked to Meriden with the hopes of finding work as designers and decorators in the "Silver City."

With a growing community of artists who practiced their crafts not only in the factories but recreationally in their private lives, new businesses opened across the city. John F. Butler Painting Supplies and J. Lacourciere Company sold art supplies, paint, and framing materials to recreational artists.

The local printing industry also leveraged art to boost commerce. Prior to the 19th century, printed publications were typically illustrated using etchings and engravings on copperplate. Innovations during the Industrial Revolution—wood engraving, lithography, and photomechanical reproduction—enabled printing companies to increase their use of images and the speed at which they reproduced them. Across the country, there was a proliferation of newspapers, journals, magazines, and books, prompting new printing companies to open their doors in communities like Meriden.

This boom in the manufacture of artistic wares and printed items, coupled with an influx of young talent who produced art professionally and recreationally, demonstrated the genius of the Meriden Britannia Company's business strategy that commerce and art went hand in hand.

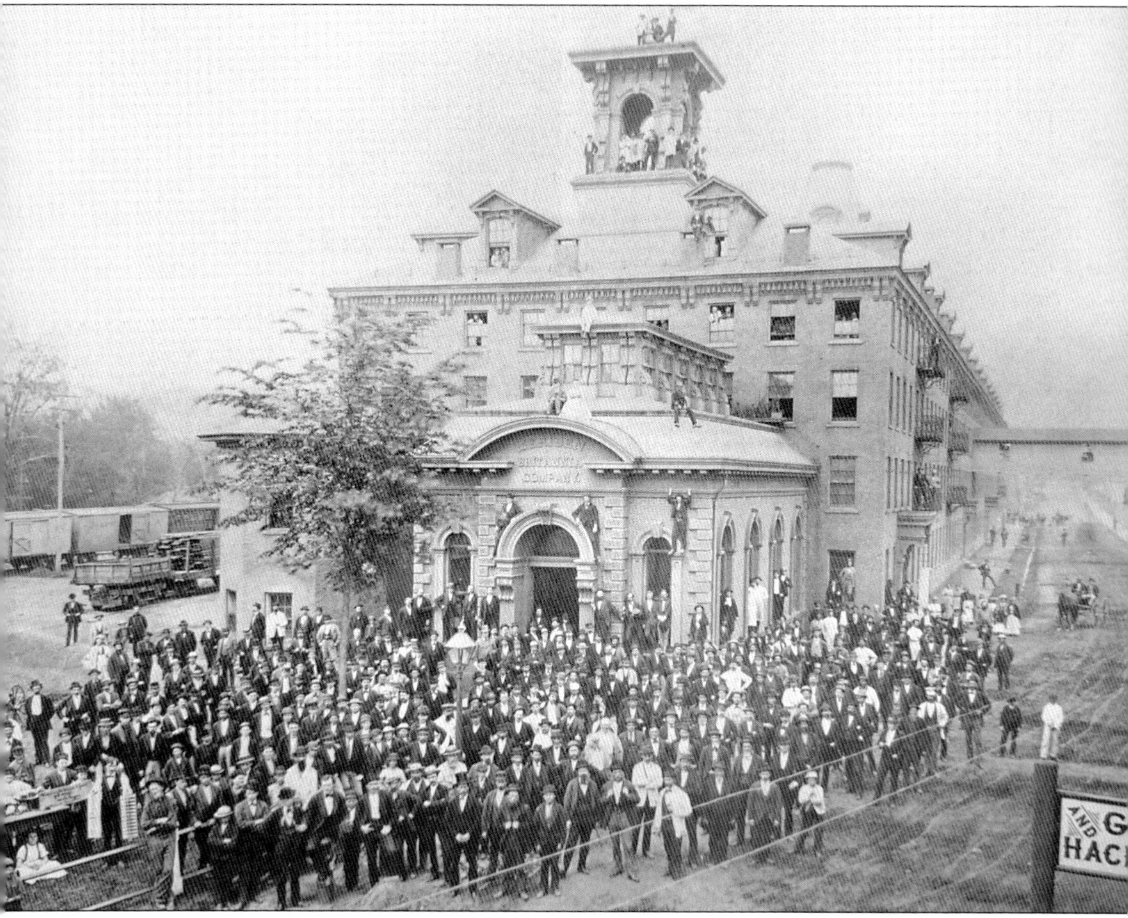

MERIDEN BRITANNIA COMPANY. The Meriden Britannia Company was formed in 1852 and manufactured housewares made of Britannia metal. As the company's success grew, artists of all talents were hired to assist with the new electro-silverplating design process. By 1876, the Meriden Britannia Company was one of the leading silverware manufacturers in the country and won the first-place medal for silverwares at the Centennial International Exposition in Philadelphia that year. According to Sotheby's in New York, "The publicity of the award and the impression the firm made on the fair's eight-million visitors was continued by the catalogues and other intensive marketing; by the end of the 1870s the Meriden Britannia Company was considered the largest silverware company in the world." In 1898, the company merged with other silver manufacturers to form the International Silver Company, which was also headquartered in Meriden. Today, the Meriden Britannia Company's designs are in many museum collections around the world. (Courtesy of the Meriden Historical Society.)

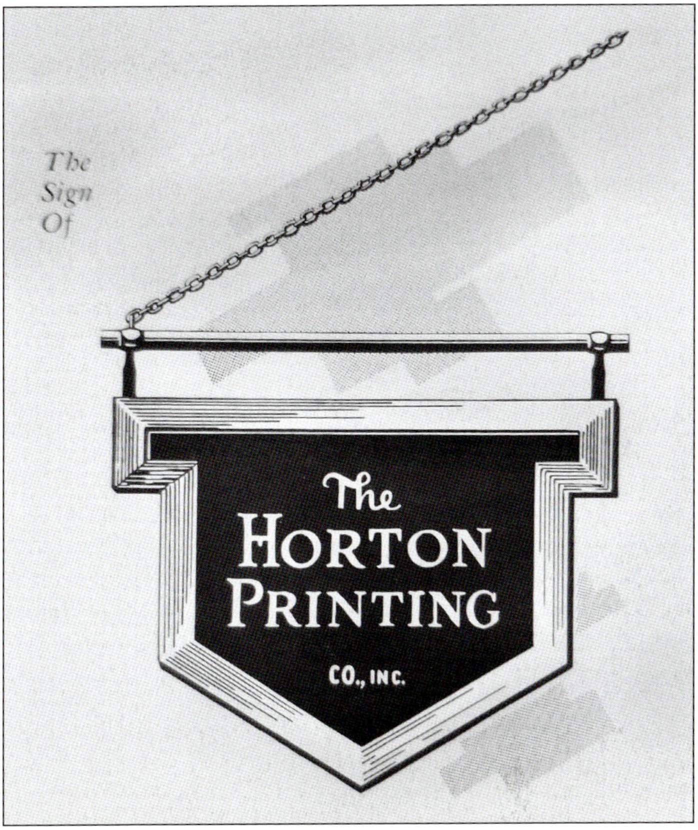

The Horton Printing Company. One of Meriden's first printing businesses was the Horton Printing Company. It was started in 1867 by Elisha A. Horton and carried on for many years as a general print shop. In 1893, it was reorganized and, over time, developed a specialty in printing large-edition, artistic commercial booklets. The company really flourished with its reproduction of business letterheads, a chief form of advertising.

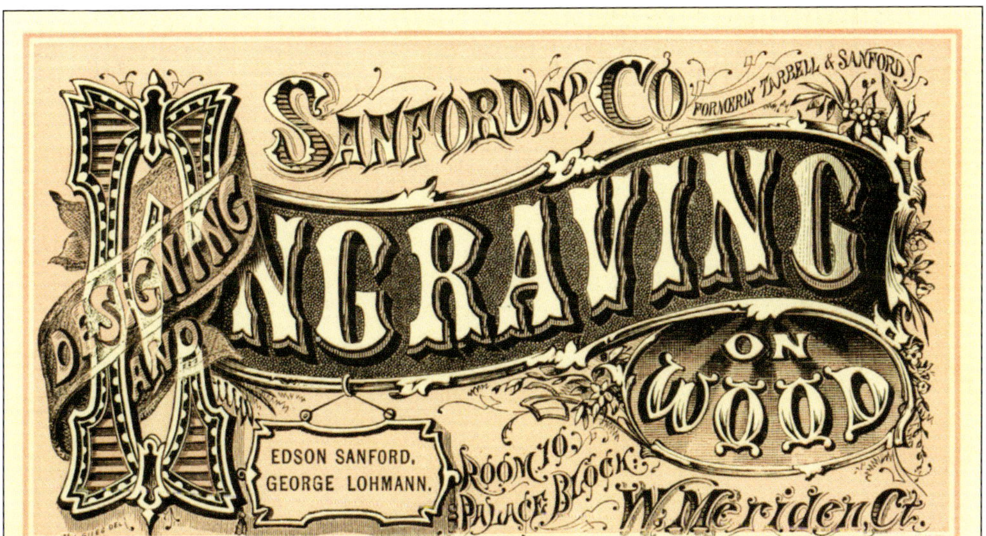

Sanford and Company. Edson Sanford was born October 18, 1826, in Monroe, Connecticut. Upon moving to Meriden, he began Sanford and Company, an engraving business that operated for over two decades. Engaged in mostly commercial work, the business illustrated catalogs for the likes of the Meriden Britannia Company, the Charles Parker Company, Edward Miller & Company, Bradley & Hubbard Manufacturing, and others. Sanford died sometime after 1910.

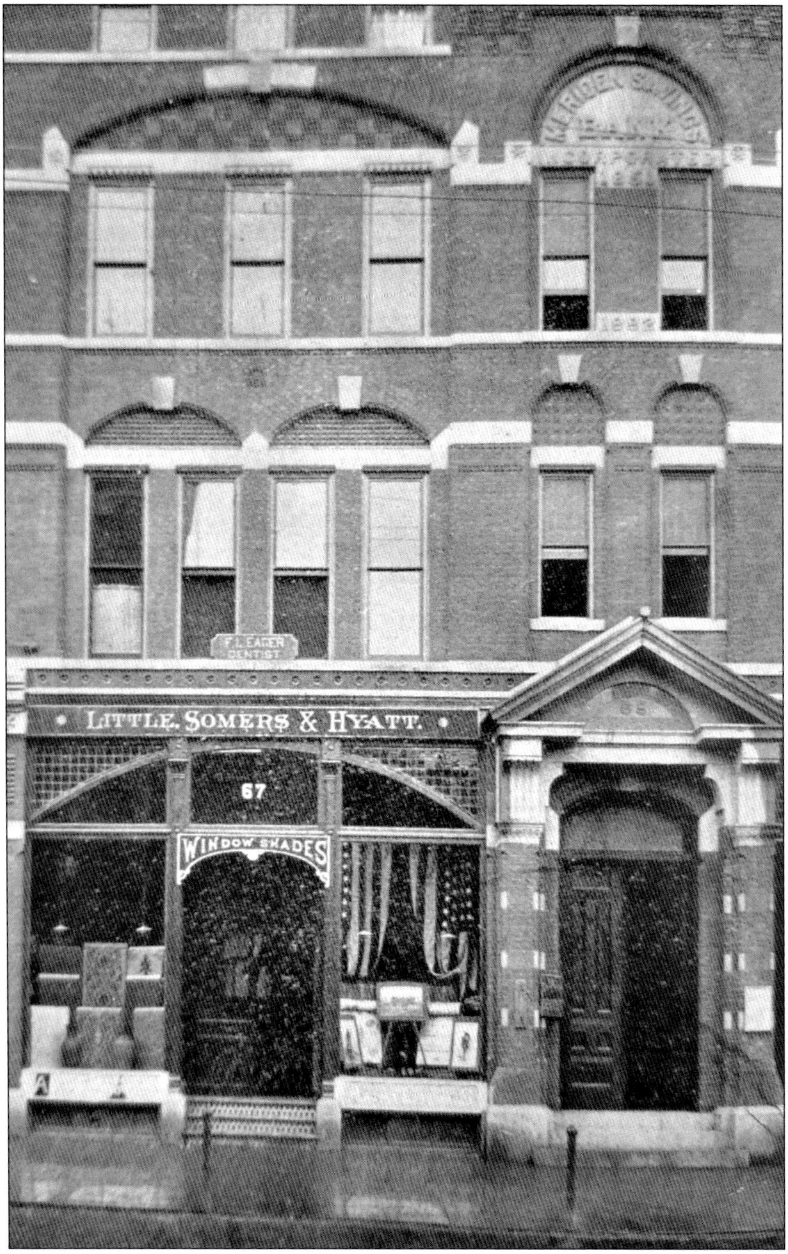

LITTLE, SOMERS & HYATT. Little, Somers & Hyatt was one of the largest and best-known businesses in the painting and decorating trade. The business was started in 1872 by Hubert Little, and in January 1883, he partnered with John Somers under the name Little & Somers. Ten months later, the longtime chief of the Meriden Fire Department, Isaac B. Hyatt, became a partner, and the name was changed to Little, Somers & Hyatt. In 1887, Somers withdrew from the business and joined the Chapin Paint Company and later the Chicago Varnish Company, though Little and Hyatt kept Somers in the business name. By its incorporation in 1904, Little, Somers & Hyatt offered wall coverings and painters' supplies and specialized in house signs and fresco paintings. The company also carried a large stock of artist materials. The business operated successfully for decades but finally closed in 1957. (Courtesy of the Meriden Historical Society.)

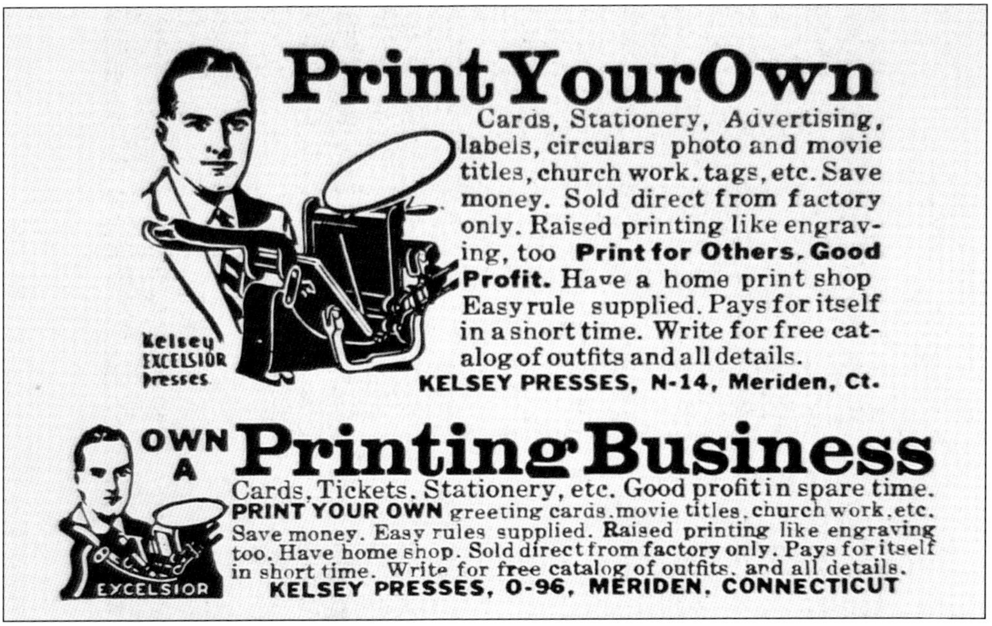

THE KELSEY PRESS COMPANY. The Kelsey Press Company, manufacturers of printing presses, was established in Meriden in 1872 and was a highly successful printing enterprise for over a century. From this acclaimed September 1938 advertisement, the business was deemed as having "the ad that launched a thousand printing shops." Both inventor Thomas Edison, and Cyrus H.K. Curtis, founder of the *Saturday Evening Post* and the *Ladies' Home Journal*, used Kelsey presses.

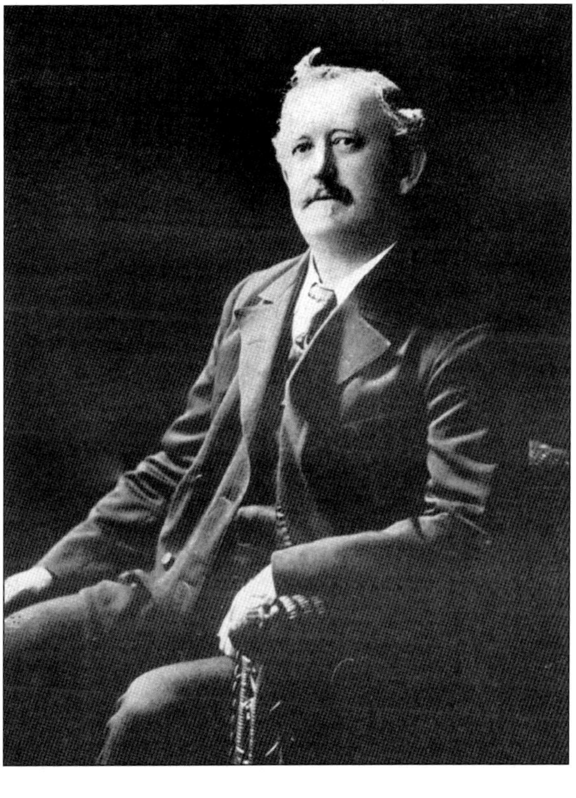

AUGUST SCHMELZER COMPANY. August Schmelzer emigrated from Germany to Meriden in 1870. Three years later, he opened a stationary store, and 11 years after that went into the wood and coal business. In the early 1900s, he began photographing Meriden and sending his images back to Germany to be hand-colored and reproduced as postcards. Today, these early postcards are highly collectible. Schmelzer died in Meriden on October 13, 1927.

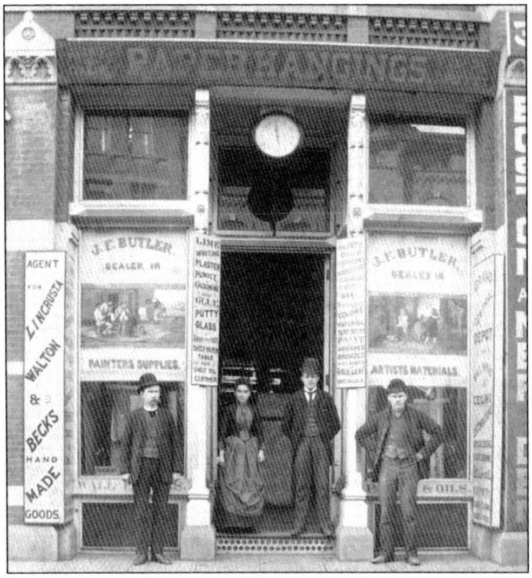

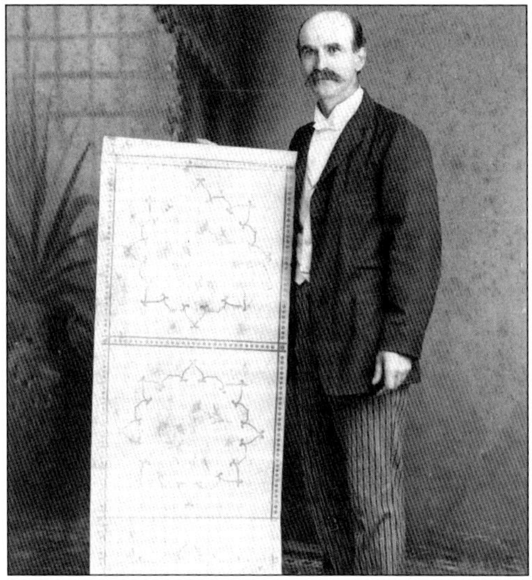

JOHN F. BUTLER PAINTING SUPPLIES. John F. Butler, an Irish immigrant, moved to Meriden at a young age. He enlisted in the Navy after the start of the Civil War and later began working for Bela Carter's painting and decorating business. He became Carter's business partner and amassed enough capital to open his own business, John F. Butler Painting Supplies, on Colony Street in 1876. This remarkable establishment provided the city with a complete line of wallpapers, paints, artist supplies, drafting equipment, and a picture framing service. For years, it was believed to be the oldest paint store in the country. Following Butler's death in 1905, this business remained in the family until 2001 and eventually closed its doors in 2011. (All, courtesy of the Meriden Historical Society.)

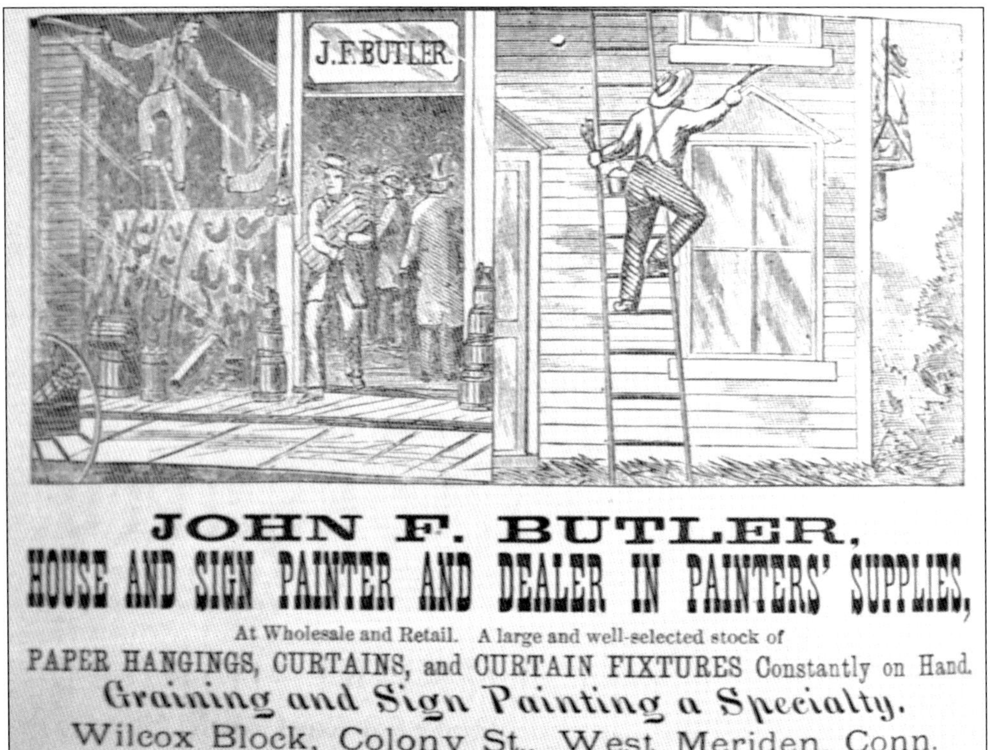

The Wm. W. Wheeler Company. William Wheeler came to Meriden to work for his older brother, Frank Wheeler's, commercial photography studio. Around 1876, the younger Wheeler had learned enough of the business to open his own shop in the city, the Wm. W. Wheeler Company, which specialized in line engraving and photographing manufacturers' samples for their catalogs. In his later years, Wheeler authored two books, *Life: A Novel* and *Rest*. Wheeler died in 1916.

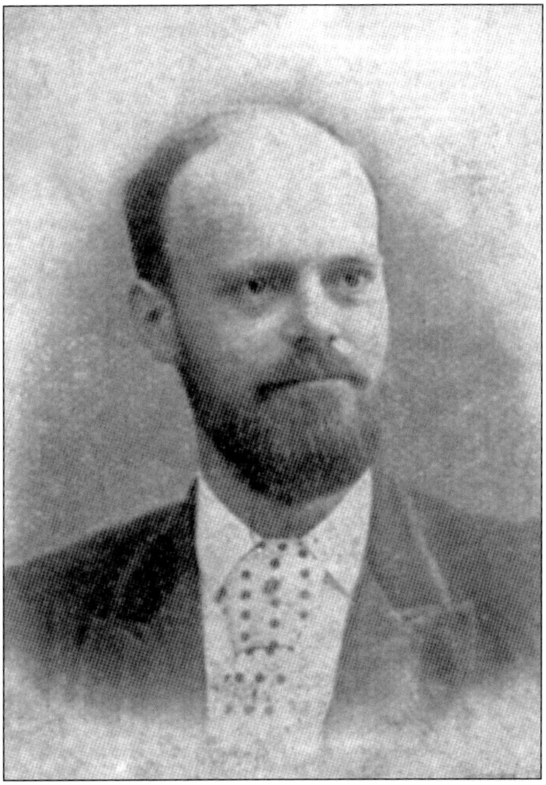

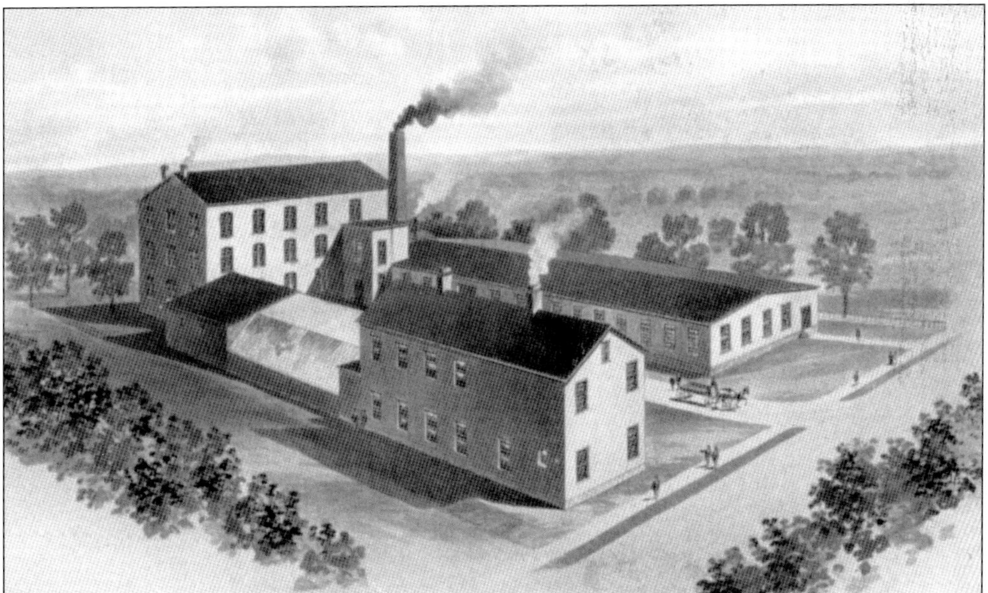

The Meriden Gravure Company. The Meriden Gravure Company was founded in 1888 by industrialists Charles Parker and James F. Allen. Driven by the needs of the local silver industry, the Meriden Gravure Company was a successful printing outfit known for developing an early expertise in high-quality image reproduction. It was in operation for over a century until 1989 when its Meriden facility closed down and all operations moved to Vermont.

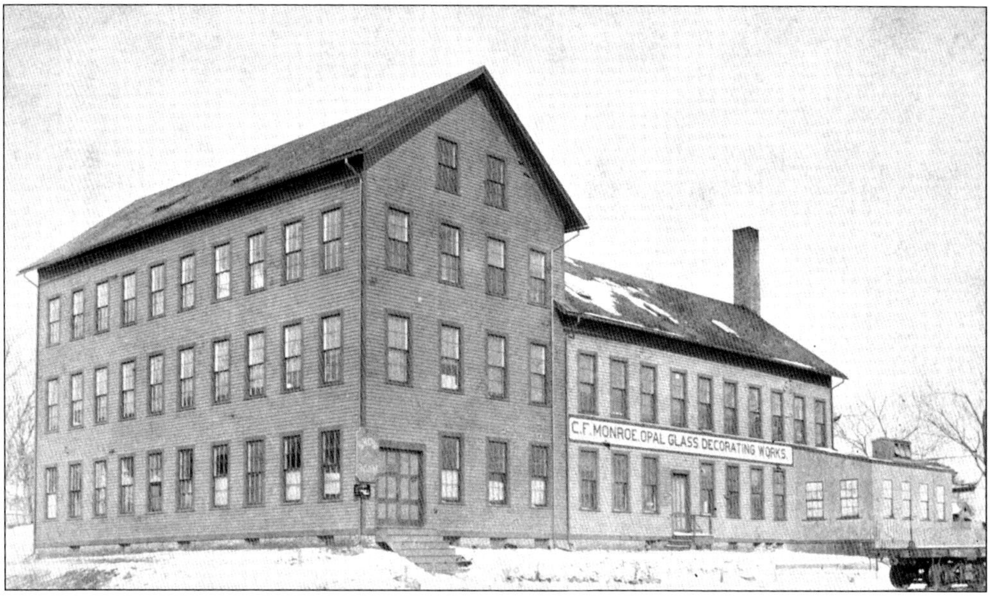

C.F. MONROE OPAL AND CRYSTAL DECORATING WORKS. Established in 1892, C.F. Monroe Opal and Crystal Decorating Works was a successful manufacturer of hand-decorated vanity items. With the addition of a glass-cutting department and the production of sterling silver and metal goods, the company employed 200 artists, engravers, and designers. As the Victorian era came to an end and public opinion began favoring the Art Deco style, the company went out of business in 1916.

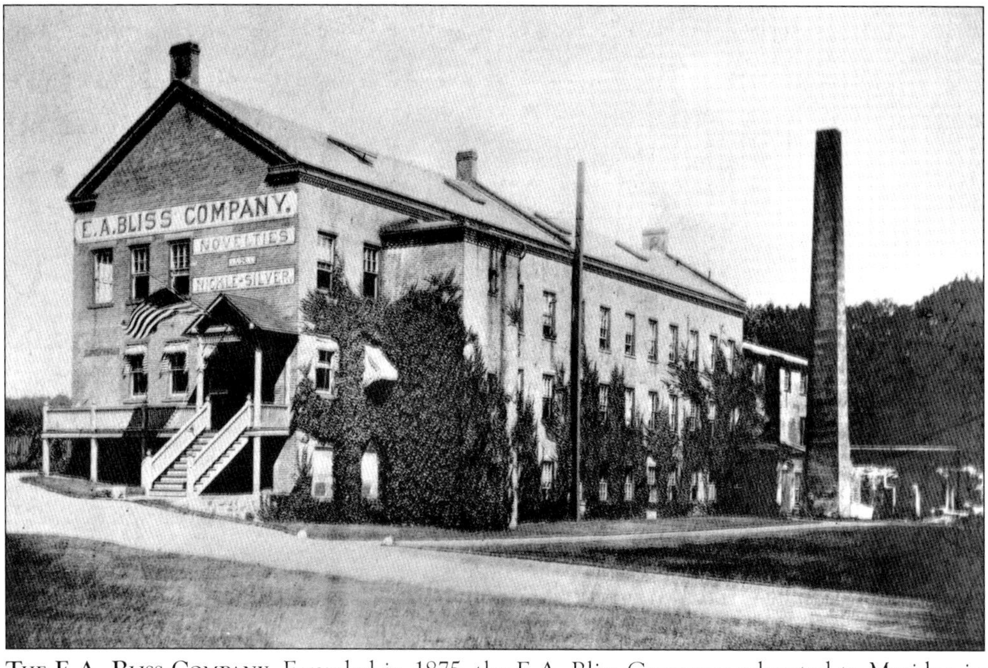

THE E.A. BLISS COMPANY. Founded in 1875, the E.A. Bliss Company relocated to Meriden in 1890. The company produced a variety of jewelry and novelties and, by 1890, added a line of silver designs. Artists from all over the world were employed by E.A. Bliss to produce the finest of sterling silver designs. By 1922, the company's name was changed to the Napier Company, and it continued producing its artistic wares.

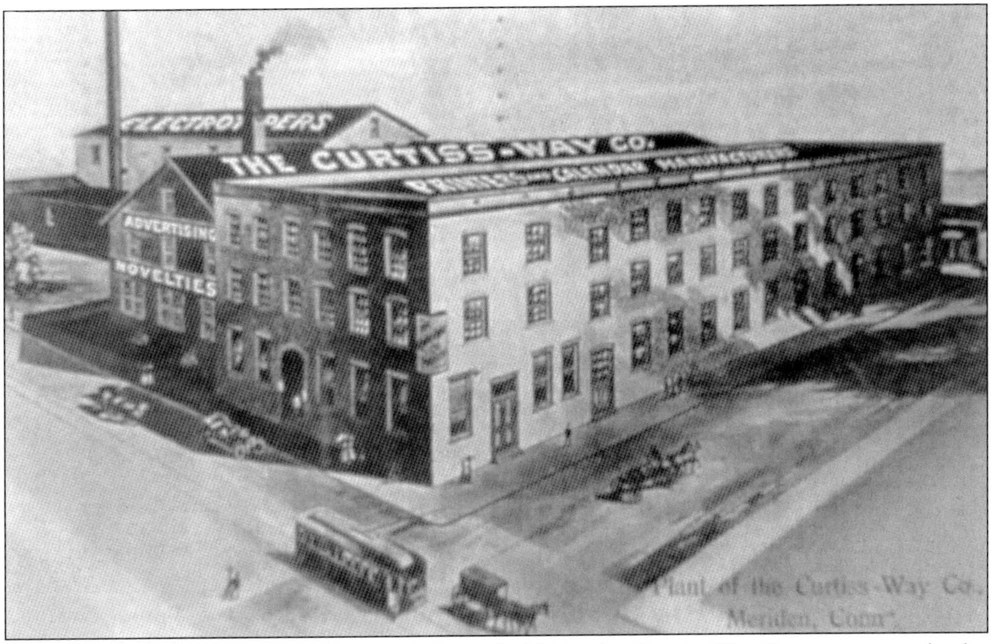

CURTISS-WAY COMPANY. From 1888 until the early 1960s, the Curtiss-Way Company was a leader in Meriden printing. In 1896, the business was acquired by James A. Curtiss, who reorganized it and made it an art printing, bookbinding, and electrotyping firm. Upon hiring William H. Way as its superintendent in 1902, it was renamed the Curtiss-Way Company. The following year the company was advertised as the largest producer of calendars in New England. Later, the company broadened its services to include the publishing of comic books.

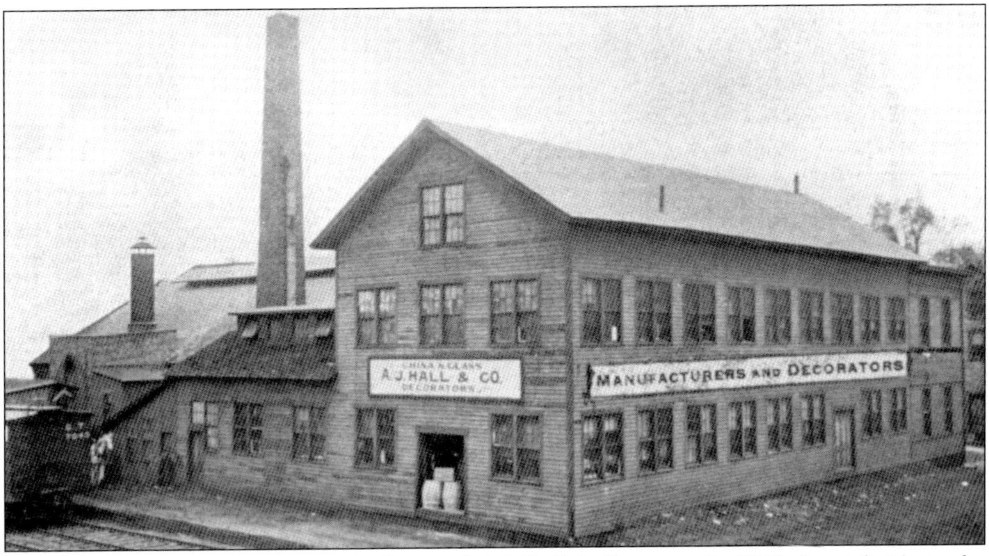

A.J. HALL & COMPANY. Arthur J. Hall started A.J. Hall & Company in 1899. Specializing in the manufacturing of decorated fine glass and china wares, this company employed several talented artisans over the years, including Walter Wilson and Frederick Matzow. In 1906, the company merged with the Goodwin and Kintz Company of Winsted, Connecticut, closing the doors of its Meriden company. Hall later managed the New York office of the J.D. Bergen Company, a Meriden-based producer of cut-glass wares.

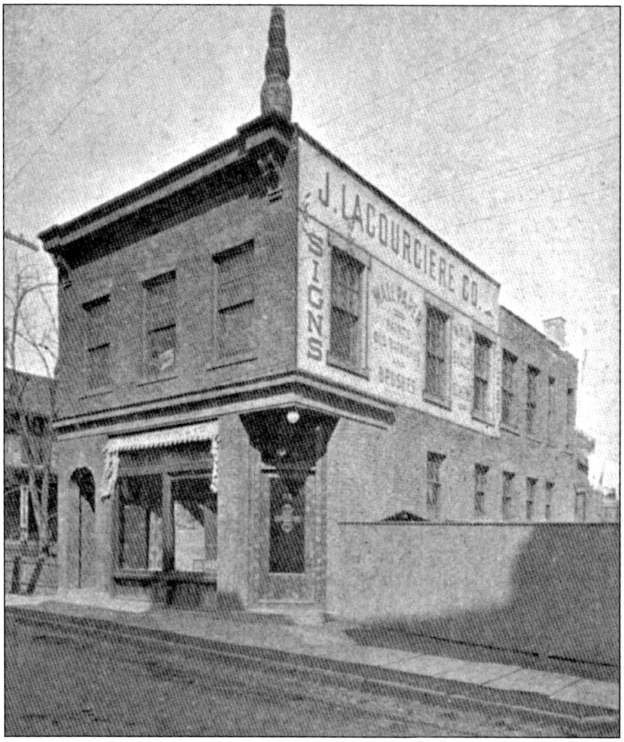

The J. Lacourciere Company. Joseph Lacourciere, president and treasurer, and J. Alfred Lacourciere, secretary, were partners in the J. Lacourciere Company. Established in the late 19th century, the business was known for art decorating, paint supplies, wallpaper, and sign painting. It employed from 15 to 20 men at all times and carried the finest of reputations in the city.

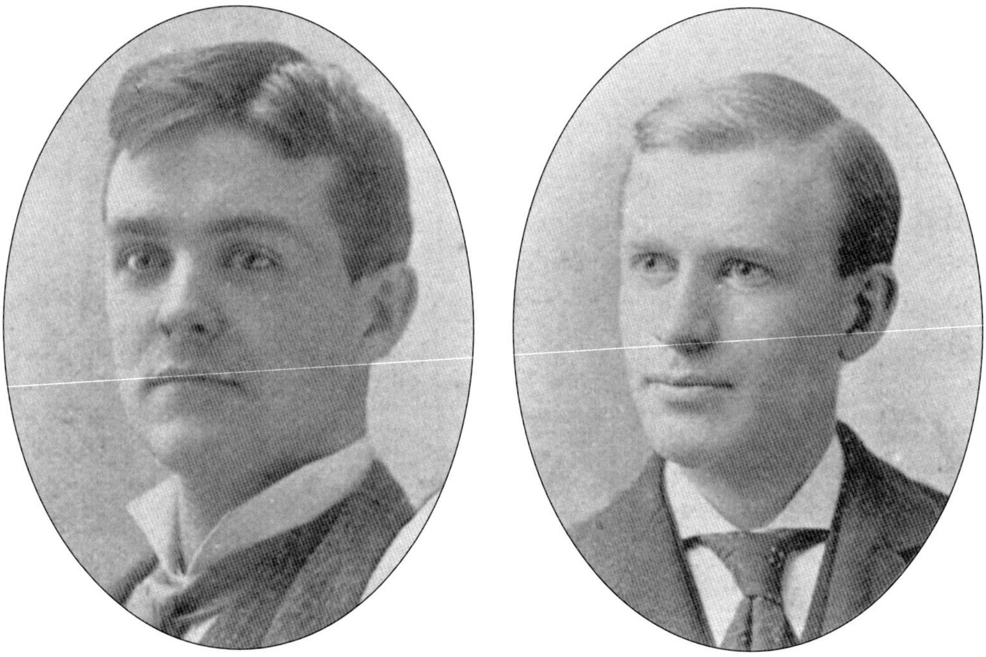

Haley & Akers. John P. Haley (left) and John Akers (right), both natives of New Jersey, came to Meriden and firmly established Haley & Akers as a reputable and competitive portrait photography studio. However, in the summer of 1900, the partnership dissolved, and Akers left Meriden for an opportunity in Bridgeport. Haley continued to run the studio and, three years later, found a suitable business partner in Ernest W. Pigeon.

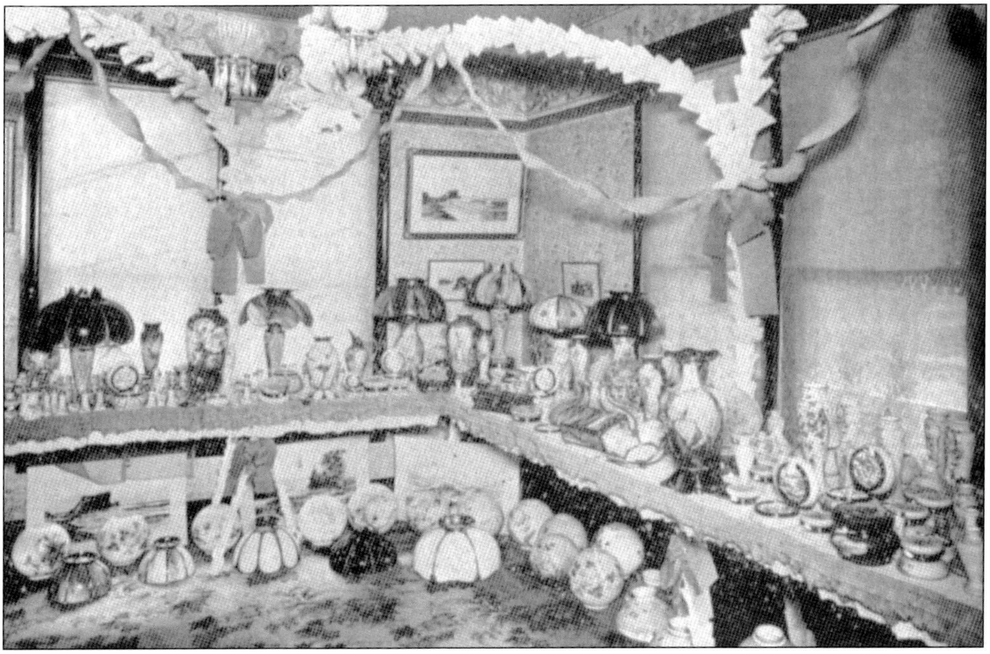

Helmschmied Manufacturing Company. In 1903, Carl Helmschmied departed the C.F. Monroe Opal and Crystal Decorating Works to open his own factory, seen here in the back of his home on Reservoir Avenue. Known as the Helmschmied Manufacturing Company, he produced and sold artistic colonial glass pieces, handcrafted metal ornaments, novelty vases with shades, and other decorated wares. The company was dissolved by 1908.

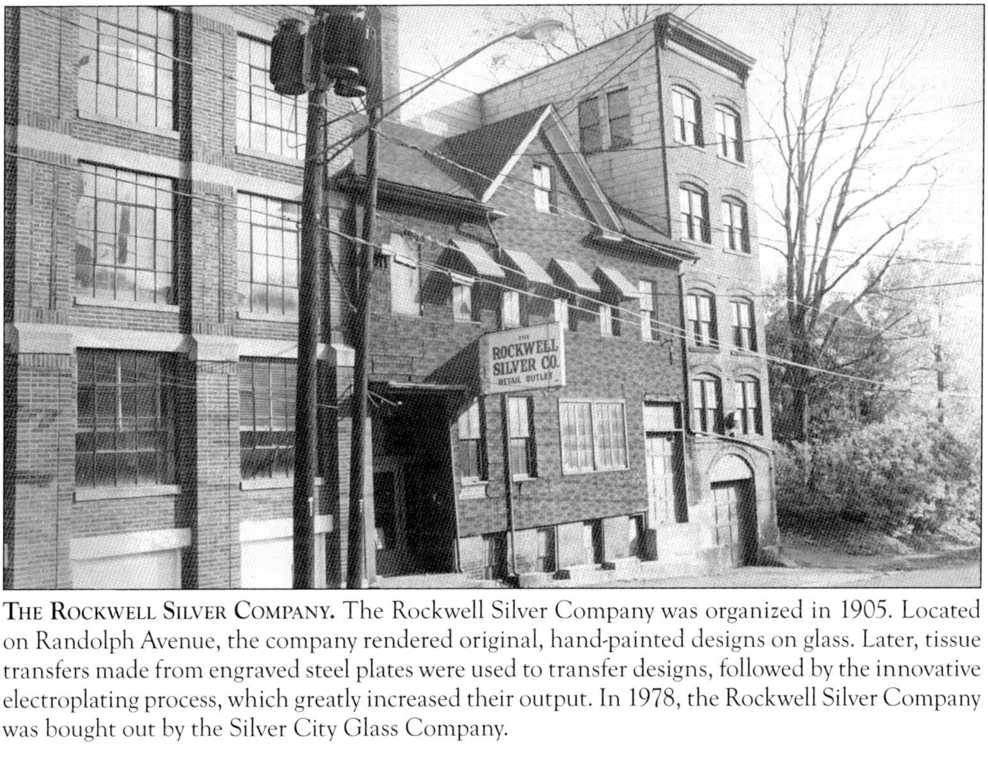

The Rockwell Silver Company. The Rockwell Silver Company was organized in 1905. Located on Randolph Avenue, the company rendered original, hand-painted designs on glass. Later, tissue transfers made from engraved steel plates were used to transfer designs, followed by the innovative electroplating process, which greatly increased their output. In 1978, the Rockwell Silver Company was bought out by the Silver City Glass Company.

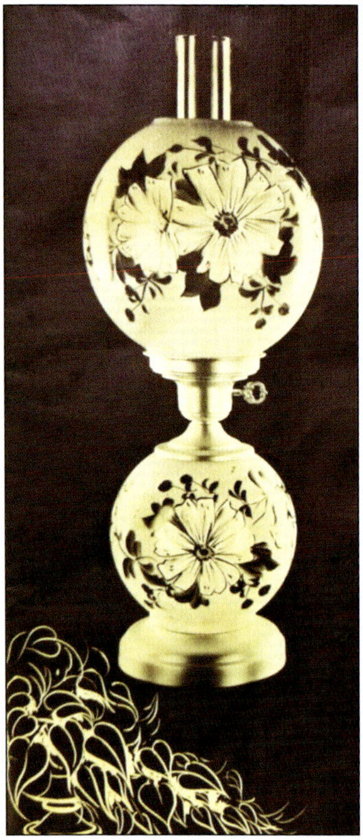

Kiss Lamp Company. The Kiss Lamp Company began in 1907 when founder Aaron Kiss came to Meriden from Long Island, New York. Born in Hungary, Kiss acquired metalworking skills and hand-craftsmanship techniques from his Hungarian artisan ancestors. The company made 170 different lamp models and sold its pieces to many popular stores, such as G. Fox and Company and Foucault's Furniture and Appliance, as well as in a retail shop at their factory.

Tredennick Paint Company. The Tredennick Paint Company was at the forefront of manufacturing black-out paint, a special cover used by the military for camouflage during World War II. In March 1949, the company opened its Meriden plant as a retail outfit with a complete line of paints and painting accessories. A similar outfit was also maintained in Wallingford, Connecticut.

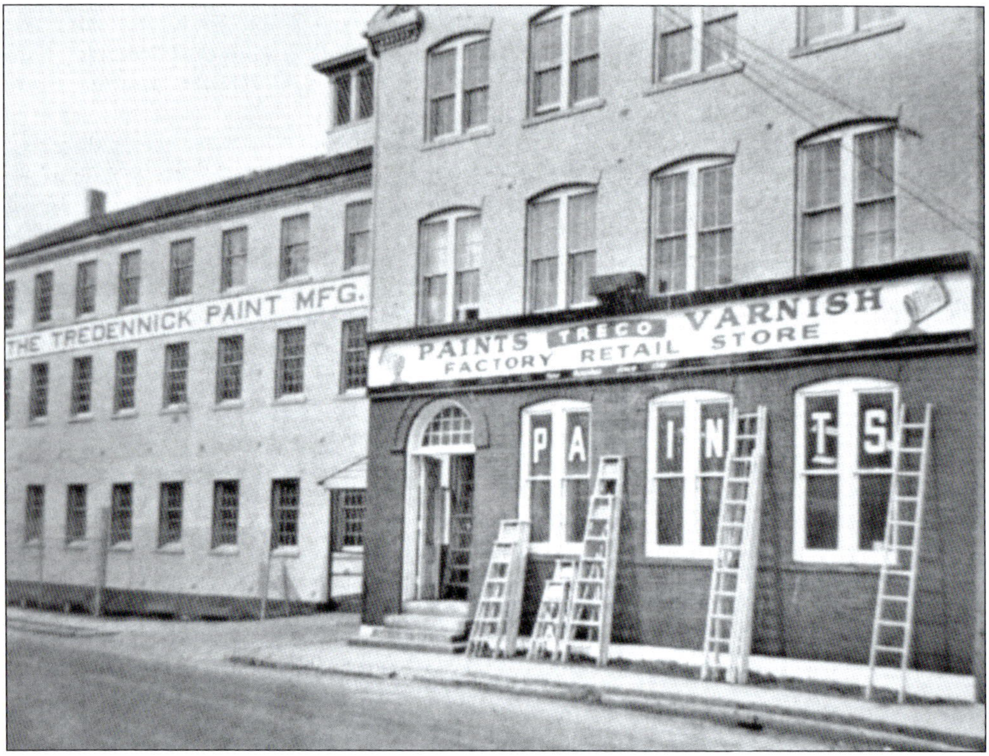

Four

THE HANDEL LAMP COMPANY

The Handel Lamp Company and its forerunners produced an array of high-quality, decorative household items from 1885 until 1936. Founder Philip Julius Handel acquired an aptitude for business at a young age, leaving school at age 14 to embark on a career in manufacturing. He trained as an apprentice at the Meriden Britannia Company and was soon employed by the Meriden Flint Glass Company, where he worked for five years developing the skills and knowledge necessary to start his own glassworks company. While working at the Meriden Flint Glass Company, Handel met Adolph Eydam, a prominent local glassworker and his future business partner.

The two formed the Eydam and Handel Company in 1885, employing local artists who demonstrated a level of technical proficiency not typical in central Connecticut's arts communities. These artists created exquisite, hand-painted household goods, with each artist incorporating his or her unique flair. No two products were exactly the same, a hallmark that established the Eydam and Handel Company from other mass manufacturers of the era.

After eight years in business together, Handel bought out Eydam and renamed the company P.J. Handel. By 1907, Handel products were in peak demand, and the company was rapidly expanding, with new styles being introduced regularly and patents being taken out on exciting new design concepts. Philip Julius Handel died suddenly on July 7, 1914, at the age of 48, leaving his widow, Fanny Hirschfeld Handel, as the company's president. She ran the Handel Company for five years before William F. Handel, Philip's cousin, took over management.

The company saw tremendous growth under new leadership. In the years after World War I, the economy was booming, and the Handel Lamp Company had assembled an impressive group of artists and craftsmen. Joseph Palme was hired as one of the company's many talented designers, joining Albert Parlow, Henry Bedigie, Frank Gubisch, and others. Many of these artists sold their own artwork on the side, earning them local notoriety and adding even more value to the Handel products. For years, the company was ranked as one of the greatest lamp makers in the world.

The Handel Lamp Company was forced to close its doors in 1936 as a result of the Great Depression. Today, Handel lamps are considered second only to those manufactured by Tiffany & Company in price and desirability.

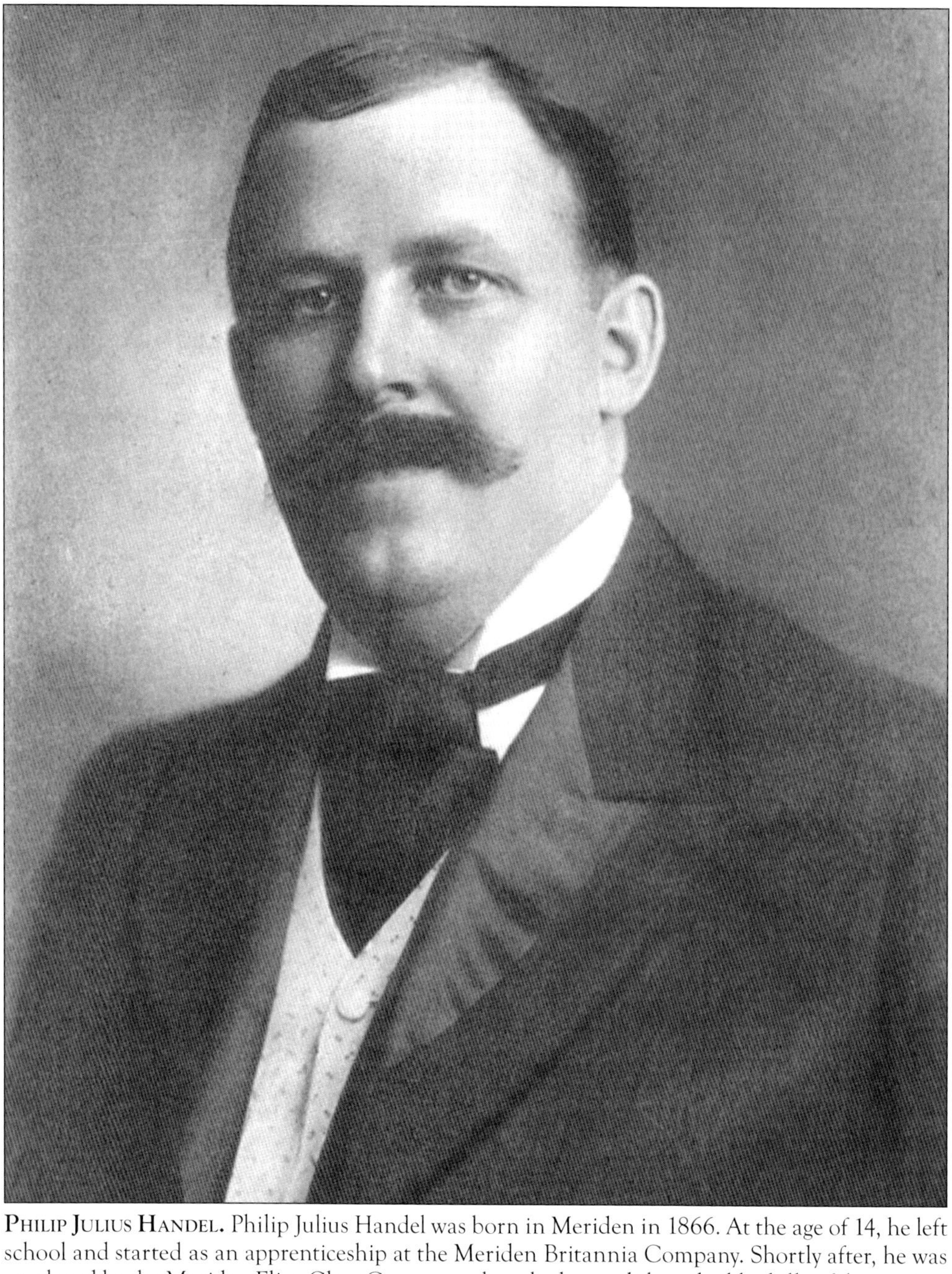

PHILIP JULIUS HANDEL. Philip Julius Handel was born in Meriden in 1866. At the age of 14, he left school and started as an apprenticeship at the Meriden Britannia Company. Shortly after, he was employed by the Meriden Flint Glass Company where he learned the valuable skills of decorating, design, and working with glass. There he met Adolph Eydam, a prominent glassworker in Meriden. In 1885, the two formed a business partnership specializing in decorated glassware. Handel bought out Eydam in 1893, and the company became known as the P.J. Handel Company and later the Handel Lamp Company. By the early 1900s, the Handel Lamp Company was flourishing, and its products were in high demand. The company maintained a factory in Meriden and a showroom in New York City. Philip J. Handel was very active in the local community, particularly with the Masons, the Home Club, and other fraternal organizations. He passed away in 1914 at the age of 48.

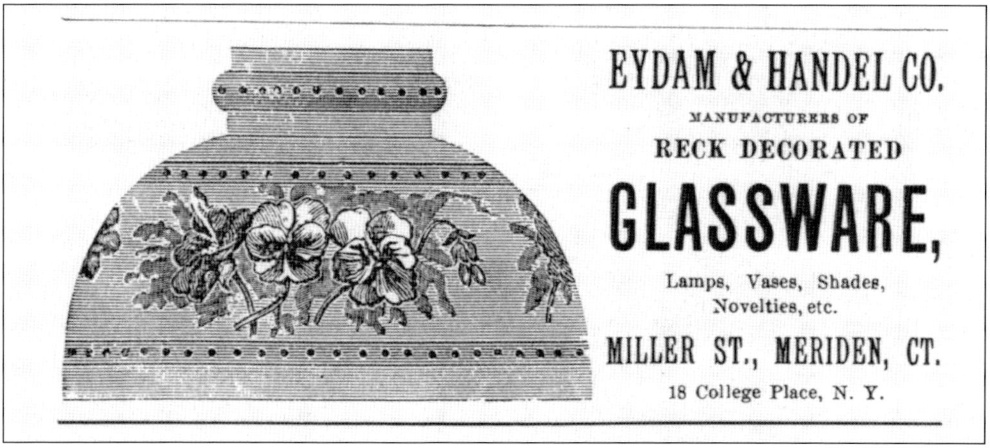

EYDAM AND HANDEL COMPANY. In 1885, nineteen-year-old Philip Handel and friend Adolph Eydam formed a business partnership and created the Eydam and Handel Company in Meriden. Specializing in glass decorating and lamp manufacturing, the company flourished, culminating in the opening of a retail showroom in New York City. In 1892, less than eight years after the start of Eydam and Handel's collaboration, their partnership ended. Handel bought out Eydam's share of the company and managed it for the next 22 years.

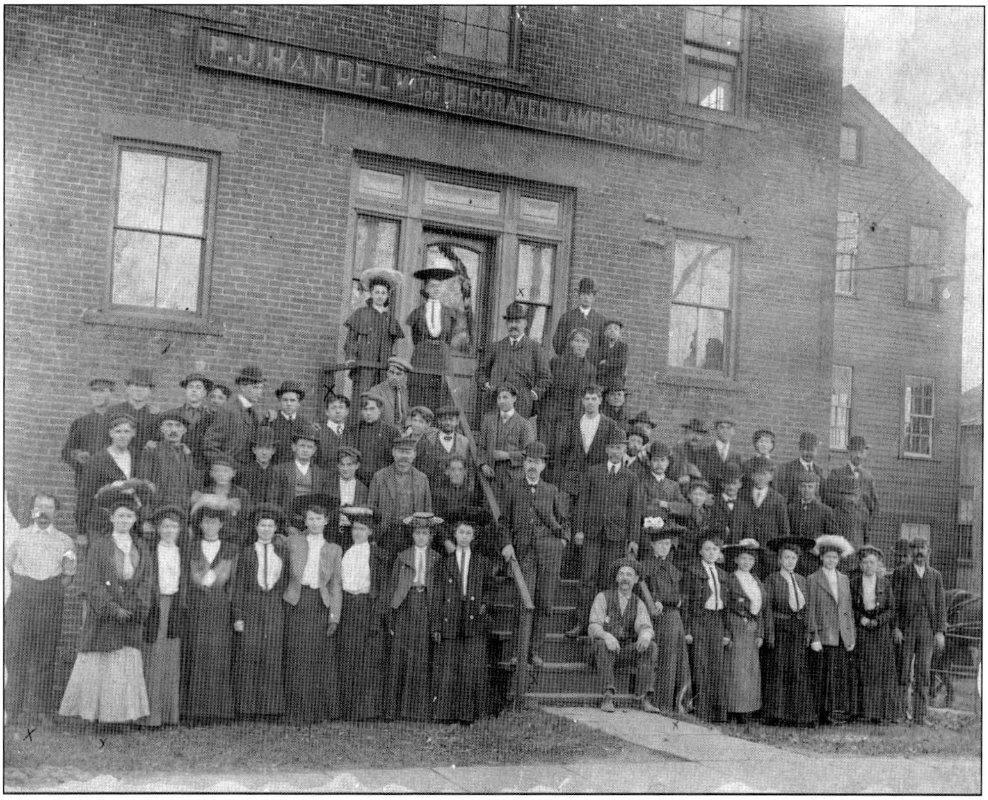

THE P.J. HANDEL COMPANY. This four-story brick factory building that once stood at 381 East Main Street was home to the P.J. Handel Company, later known as the Handel Lamp Company. This c. 1902 image shows Philip Julius Handel (center) and the impressive group of artisans and designers he employed to create the company's signature lamps. (Courtesy of the Meriden Historical Society.)

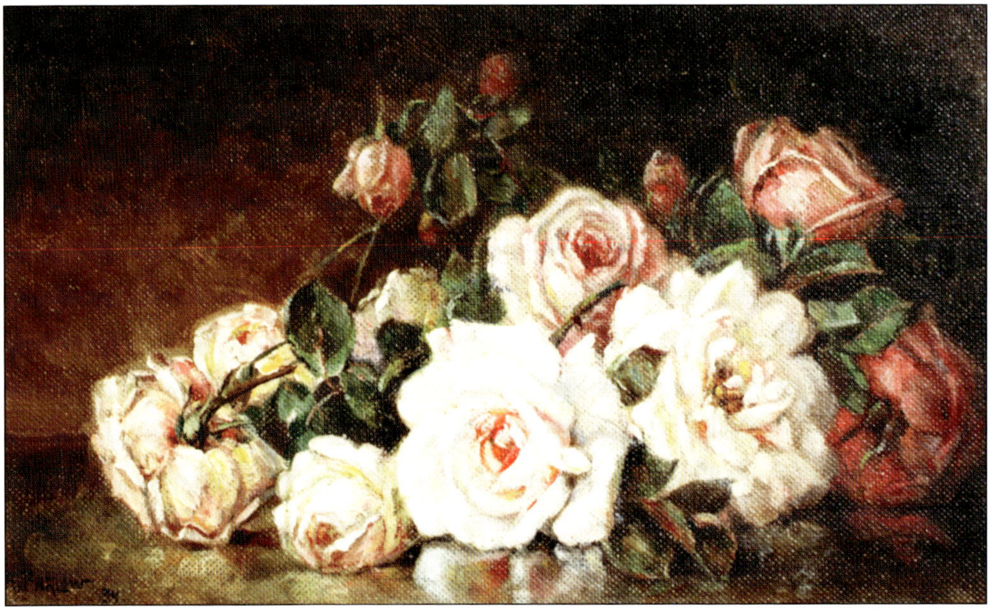

Albert Parlow. Albert Parlow was born on Cape Cod in Sandwich, Massachusetts, on March 13, 1866. Two years later, his family moved northwest to the seafaring town of Bedford. Parlow grew up fascinated with the local whaling lore and of the whalers returning from their voyages. Parlow first designed for the Lenox China Company, "the oldest and most famous manufacturer of fine china in the United States" (The Meriden Historical Society). Concurrently, he was asked to decorate a set of china for Queen Victoria of England. Years later, Parlow came to Meriden where he was employed as a chief designer of lamps and lighting fixtures at the Handel Lamp Company. He was an outstanding artist and a prolific designer, becoming the firm's secretary and chief decorator in 1903; he retained those titles until the late 1920s. Parlow was one of the few artists who was allowed to sign his last name on Handel lamps, signing as A. Parlow or AParlow. Albert Parlow died in Old Saybrook, Connecticut, on April 15, 1969, at the age of 103.

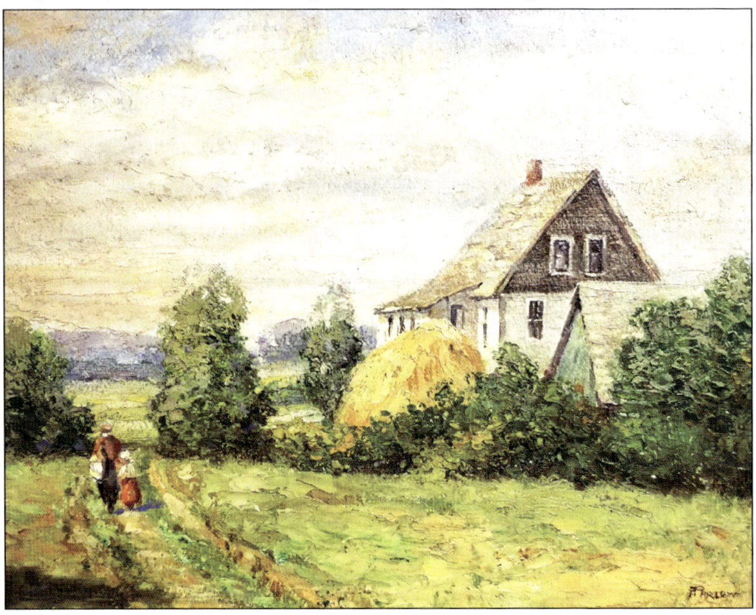

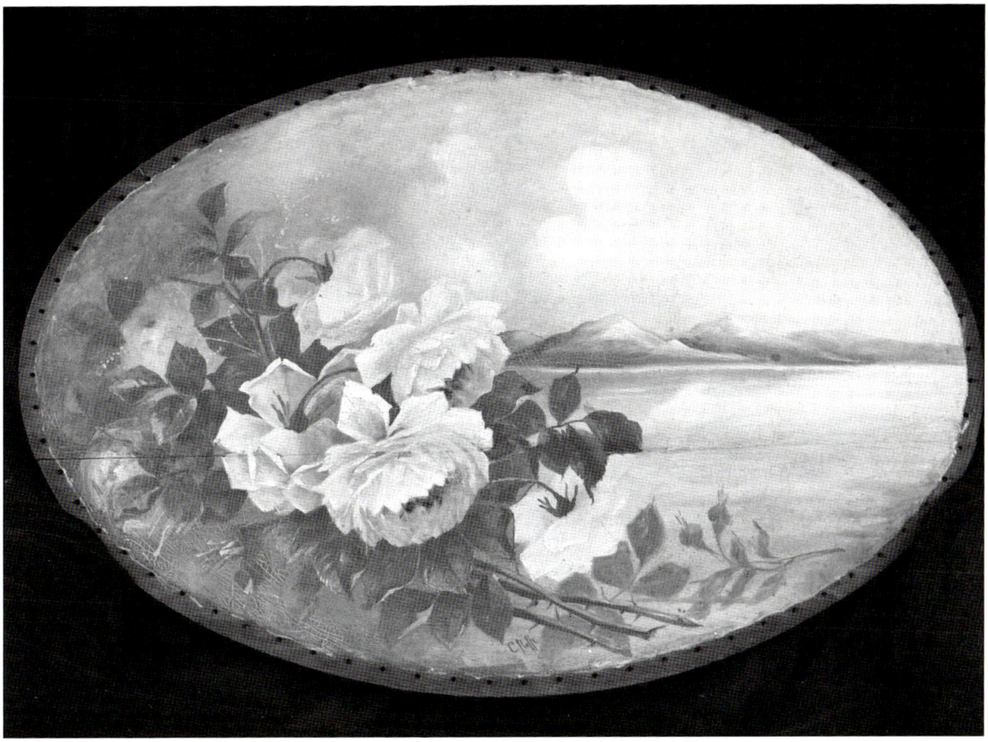

KARL PUFFE. Karl Puffe was born in Steinshonau, present-day Czechoslovakia, in 1858. With only $16 in his pocket, he boarded a ship to America in 1892 with hopes of a promising future for him and his family. Upon arrival, they came to Meriden where Puffe found employment as a prominent glass decorator with the Handel Lamp Company for over 30 years. Puffe died in 1927.

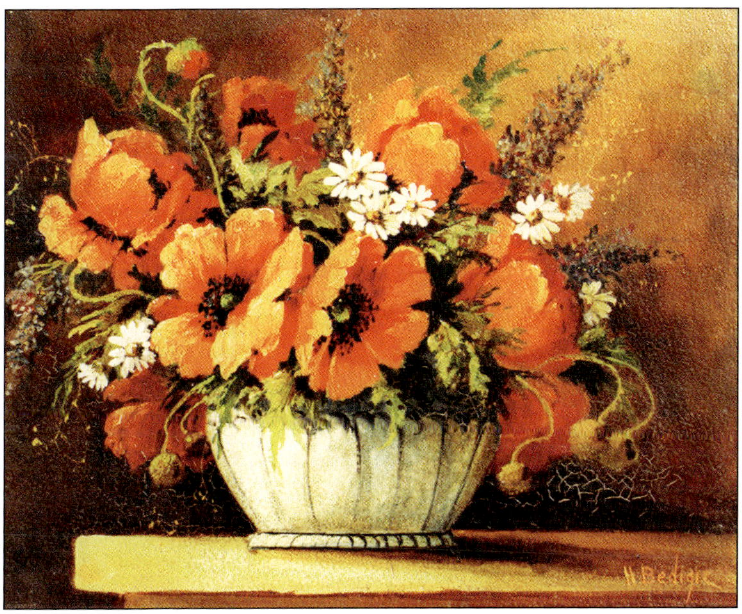

HENRY A. BEDIGIE. In 1905, Henry A. Bedigie of New York came to Meriden to accept a job as an artist at the Handel Lamp Company, a post he held for over 30 years. One of Philip Handel's premier lampshade painters and a top designer, Bedigie often depicted seascapes in his lamp art. Bedigie died in Meriden on May 13, 1945. (Courtesy of Allen Weathers.)

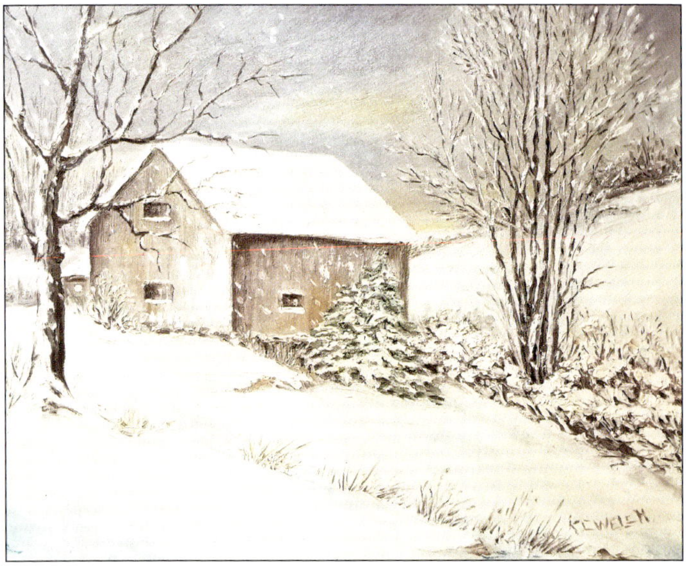

Katherine Casey Welch. Katherine Casey Welch was born April 6, 1893, in Meriden. After graduating from high school, she was employed as a decorator with the Handel Lamp Company. Welch proved to be a highly skilled decorator, and only she and colleague Robert Godwin were trusted to use the delicate and meticulous technique of gold tracing on the company's lampshades. In 1919, she left Handel to start a family.

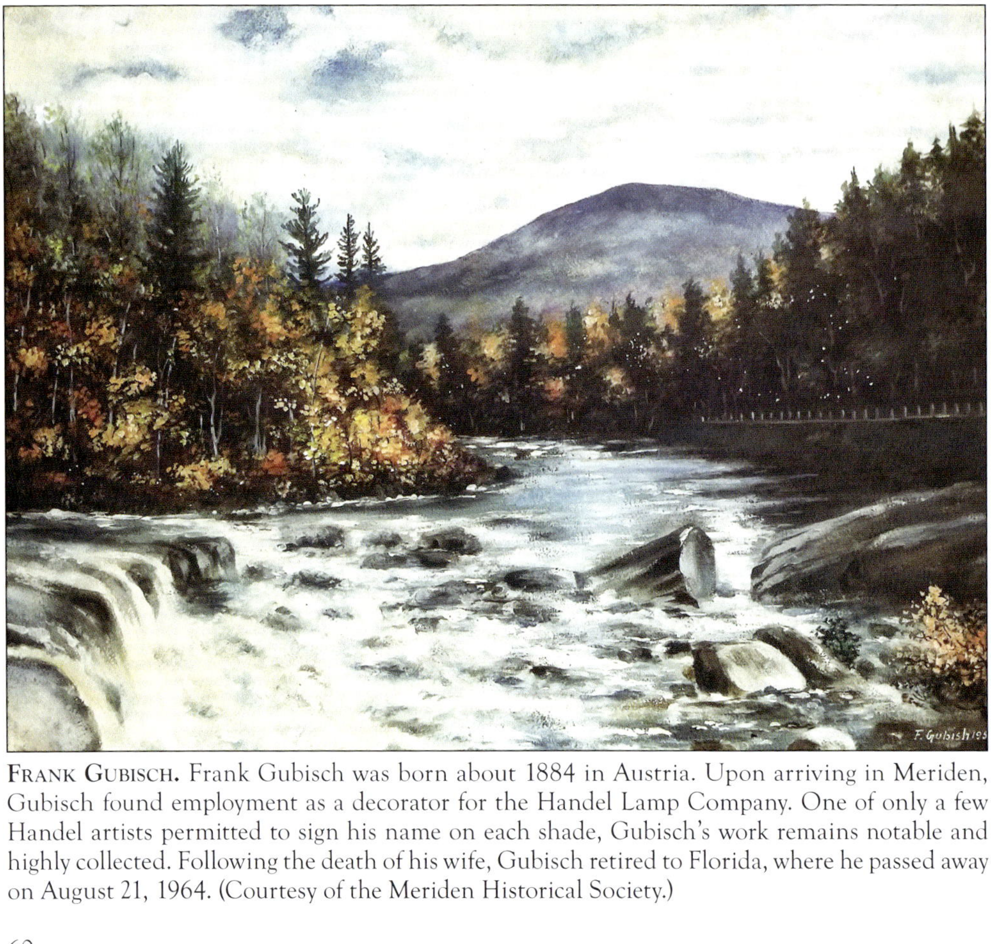

Frank Gubisch. Frank Gubisch was born about 1884 in Austria. Upon arriving in Meriden, Gubisch found employment as a decorator for the Handel Lamp Company. One of only a few Handel artists permitted to sign his name on each shade, Gubisch's work remains notable and highly collected. Following the death of his wife, Gubisch retired to Florida, where he passed away on August 21, 1964. (Courtesy of the Meriden Historical Society.)

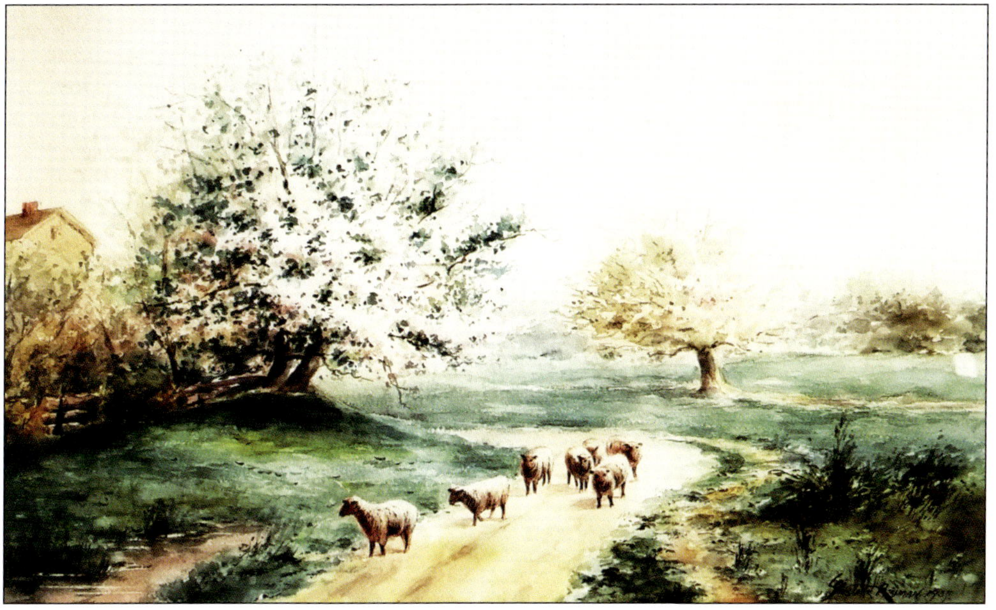

Gustav Reiman. Gustav Reiman was born in Brooklyn, New York, in 1867. He came to Meriden in 1873 and worked as a decorator for the C.F. Monroe Opal and Crystal Decorating Works. He later painted and/or modeled for the A.J. Hall Company, the Handel Lamp Company, and the Bradley & Hubbard Manufacturing Company until his retirement around 1937. Predominately a landscape painter, Reiman's oil paintings and watercolors are characterized by their unique compositions and finely rendered details. According to Clarence T. Wilks, a former A.J. Hall employee, Reiman "was by far the most accomplished artist in the area." Reiman had exhibited his art locally with the Arts and Crafts Association of Meriden and at the New Haven Public Library. He was the father-in-law of the well-known Meriden photographer Samuel Perkins. Reiman died in Meriden on December 9, 1948. (Both, courtesy of the Lorenzo F. Suzio Collection.)

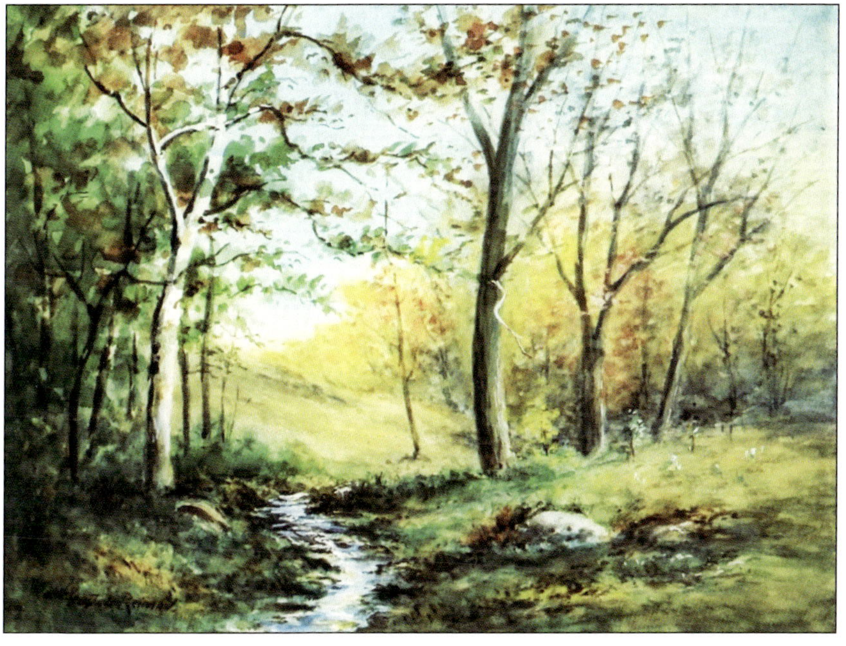

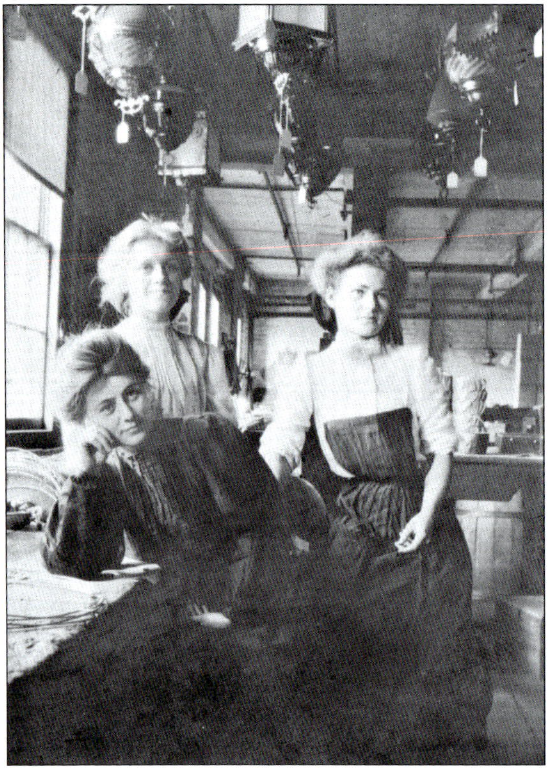

Women Decorators of Handel. At the turn of the 20th century, Meriden was home to innumerable factories and the artistic products of many of these companies fueled Meriden's fame as a manufacturing center. The Handel Lamp Company, for example, employed artists of the highest caliber to decorate their wares, several of whom were women. The advent of World War I, in particular, created new employment opportunities for women.

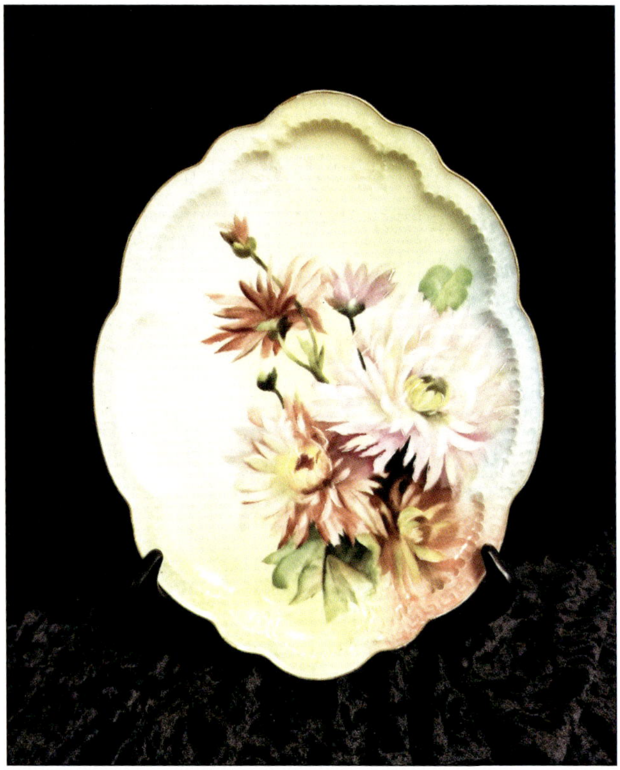

Ernest Lewis. Ernest Lewis was born in Meriden in 1886. He studied art at the New York School of Applied Design and at the Art Students League of New York. He was a trained sculptor, having studied under famed Meriden sculptor Louis Gudebrod. Lewis was chief designer for the Handel Lamp Company and aside from his designs for Handel, he was known for his 20-foot mural, *The Driving of the Golden Spike*, for the General Motors Company. Ernest Lewis died in 1973.

Emil Melchior. Emil Melchior was born in Yalesville, Connecticut, in 1872 and came to Meriden as a young child. In his adulthood, Melchior was employed as a decorator at the C.F. Monroe Opal and Crystal Decorating Works for several years before periods at the Handel Lamp Company and the Rockwell Silver Company. His artwork and designs at Rockwell were highly praised. Emil Melchior died in Meriden in 1928. (Courtesy of the Meriden Historical Society.)

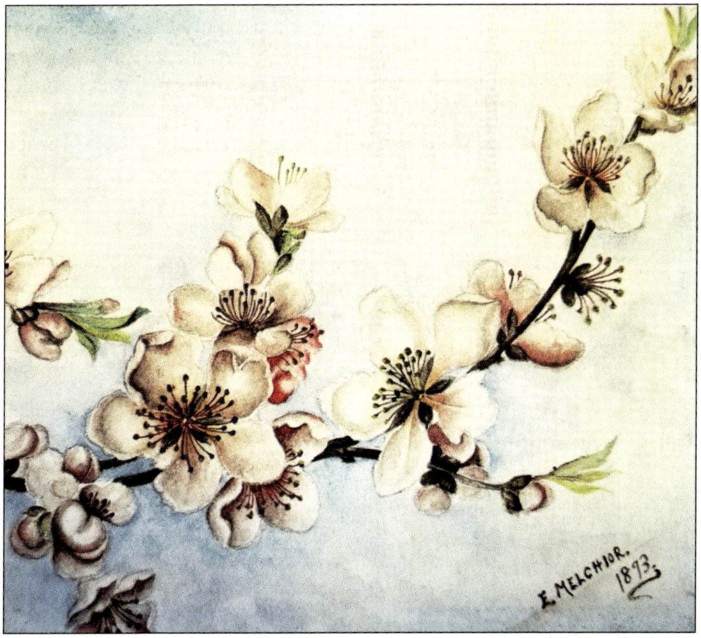

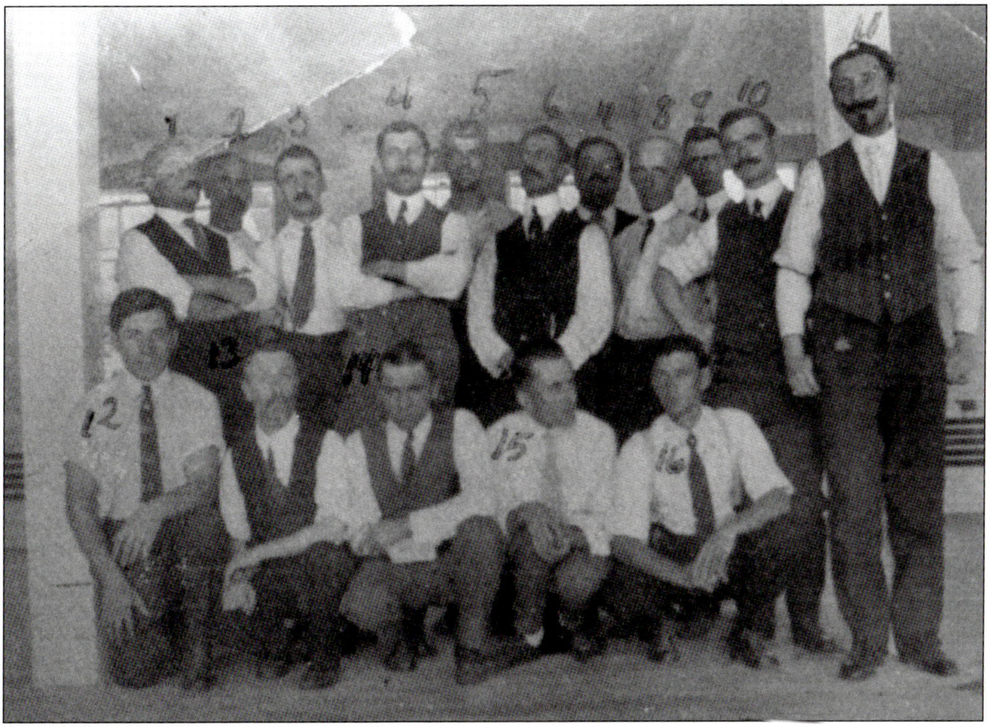

The Handel Lamp Company Decorators. The artists of the Handel Lamp Company were considered some of the top artisans in Meriden at the time. This photograph shows the company's decorators around 1916. They are, from left to right, (kneeling) Robert Godwin, Gustave Loehner, Peter Broggi, and William Clark; (standing) Edward Dunibar, ? Baumgarten, Jack Fitzgerald, Frank Gubisch, Julius Myers, Karl Puffe, Henry Bedigie, George Lockrow, William Runge, John Bailey, Hans Huebener, and Joe Devine. (Courtesy of the Meriden Historical Society.)

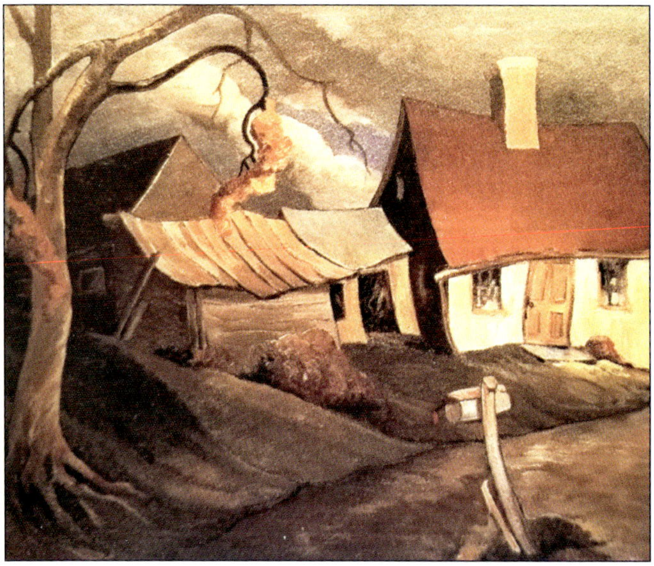

Peter Broggi. Peter Broggi was a highly skilled decorator for the Handel Lamp Company. He was also a skilled artist outside of work and a vital member of the Arts and Crafts Association of Meriden during its reorganization. Broggi was a World War I veteran who was active with the American Legion and remained with the organization throughout his lifetime. Peter Broggi died in Meriden in 1941. (Courtesy of the Meriden Historical Society.)

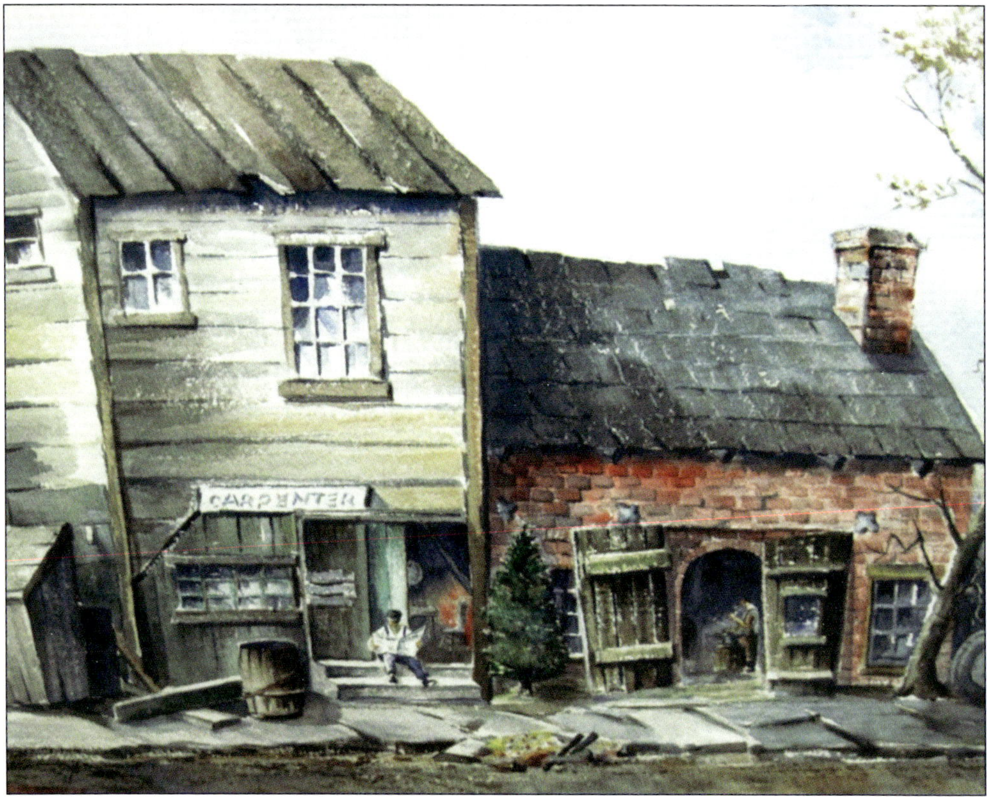

Ray Freemantle. Ray Freemantle was born in Meriden in 1894. Before his career as an artist for the Handel Lamp Company, he worked for both the *Meriden Record* and the *Meriden Daily Journal*. In 1925, Freemantle and his wife, Elsie, moved to Long Island where he was hired by Paramount Pictures to paint their lobby posters. After a stint in the US Navy, Freemantle made painting trips to South America, Mexico, the West Indies, and across the United States. In 1965, he and Elsie moved to Austin, Texas, and he later moved to Ohio after his wife's death. Freemantle died in 1977.

Joseph Palme. Joseph Palme was born in Bohemia, a part of Austria, in 1865. He relocated to the United States, in New York City, in 1909 before moving to nearby Mount Vernon, New York, where he specialized in making silver-on-glass pieces. He later worked for the Pairpoint Manufacturing Company. William Handel knew of Palme's work and personally asked him to come to Meriden and work for the Handel Lamp Company in 1918. Outside of work, Palme was at home in nature—often catching and mounting butterflies and insects as well as preserving bird's eggs—which was evident in his beautifully ornate designs depicting birds and flora. Perhaps his finest designs were his *Birds of Paradise* table lamps, some of Handel's most endeared and treasured pieces. Because of the captivating detail of Palme's lamps, only Palme or fellow Handel artist Peter Broggi were allowed to add the finish. Palme died in 1949.

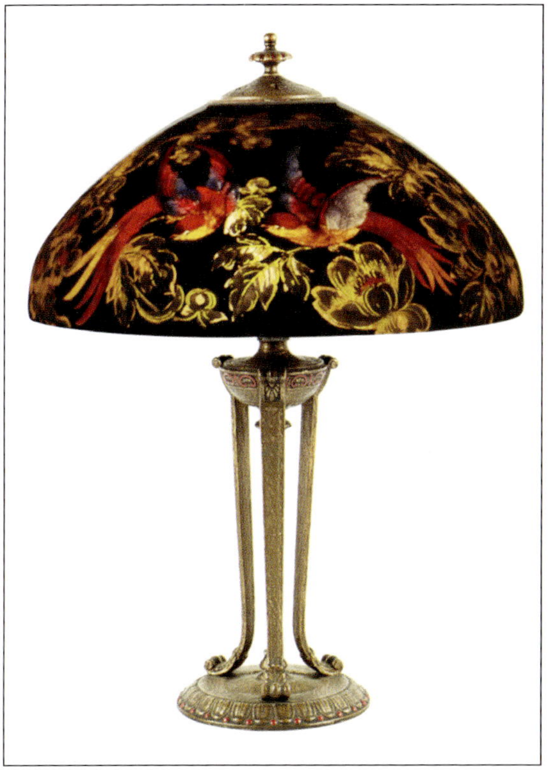

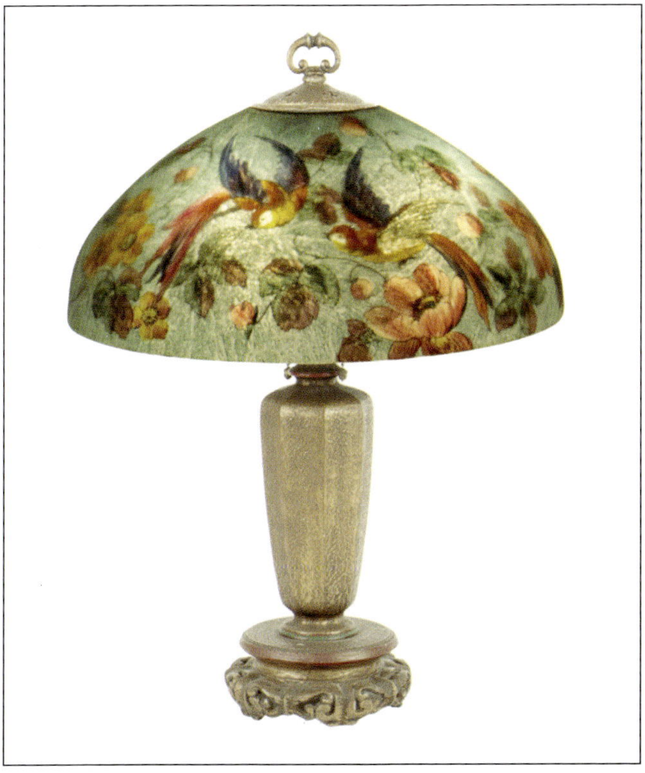

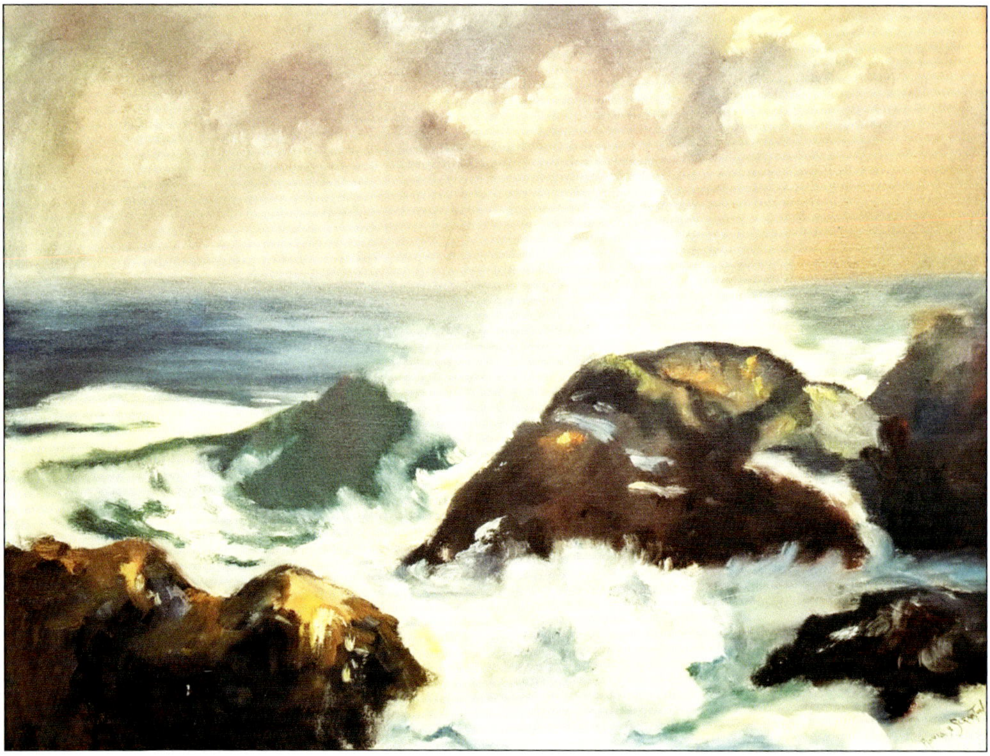

Flavia Scranton. Flavia Scranton was a pupil of Charlotte Lilla Yale and later became her assistant. Scranton put her talent to work for the Handel Lamp Company and the Rockwell Silver Company and further developed her artistic skills by studying with Harry Ballinger of Rockport, Maine. A longtime member of the Arts and Crafts Association of Meriden and art chairman of the Meriden Woman's Club, Scranton died the day before her 85th birthday in 1975.

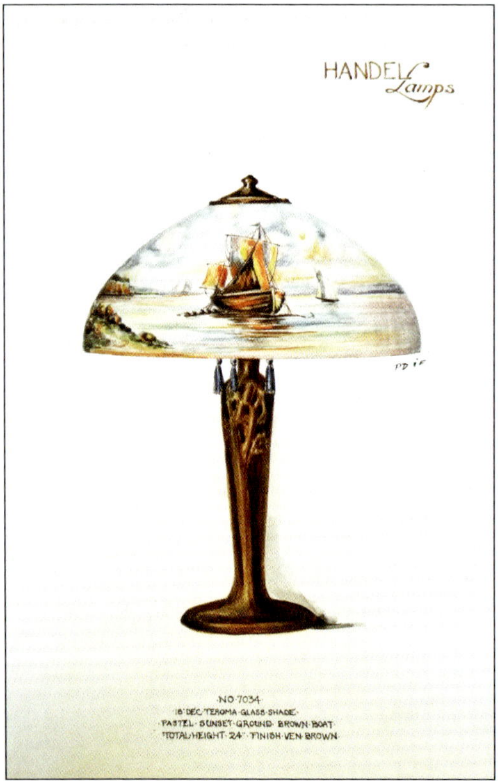

Reverse-Painted Lampshade in Watercolor. Headed by Ernest C. Lewis, Handel's Design and Art Department was responsible for creating watercolor renditions of the lamps for sales purposes, advertisements, and as instructional materials for the decorators. This particular reverse-painted lampshade design, numbered 7034, was completed by Lillian Mackay. (Courtesy of the Meriden Historical Society.)

Five

Artists of the Depression Era

The onset of the Great Depression in 1929 was a turning point and an awakening for many local artists. Leading companies never fully recovered from the stock market crash, leaving businesses and their employees facing uncertainty for years. Some artists had their wages cut, others were laid off, and several were displaced.

To stimulate economic recovery and uplift the American people, Pres. Franklin Delano Roosevelt and his administration created the Works Progress Administration (WPA), a federal New Deal agency that offered paying jobs to unemployed people. The job focused on public works and infrastructure projects with one specific WPA program—the Federal Art Project—supporting struggling artists through public art commissions. Three Meriden artists were selected to work for the WPA: John Backstrom, Isabella Ruth Doerfler, and Ernst Lohrmann. Through these commissions, the WPA rediscovered the critical importance of art to one's culture while also giving artists stability and opportunity.

After nearly a 10-year hiatus, the Arts and Crafts Association of Meriden reconvened in April 1933. Thanks to the efforts of Louise Connaway, the Macbeth Gallery of New York City offered to loan paintings for an exhibit in Meriden, which was ultimately sponsored by the Meriden Woman's Club and coordinated by Indianna Thomas. With an enthusiastic revival, the association reintroduced its arts activities and exhibits and remained active until the start of World War II.

Meriden suffered greatly from the Depression. The wholesale collapse of values, the plummeting demand for merchandise and distinct products, the staggering inventory losses, the inevitable increase in unemployment, and the psychological atmosphere paralyzed the country. As businesses collapsed, local artists like Frederick Matzow and Walter Wilson resorted to selling freelance art. Other artists found relief in collaborating with fellow artisans to minimize the cost of living. Yet despite these immense challenges, the Depression fostered new artistic talent and presented opportunities for Meriden's once employed artisans.

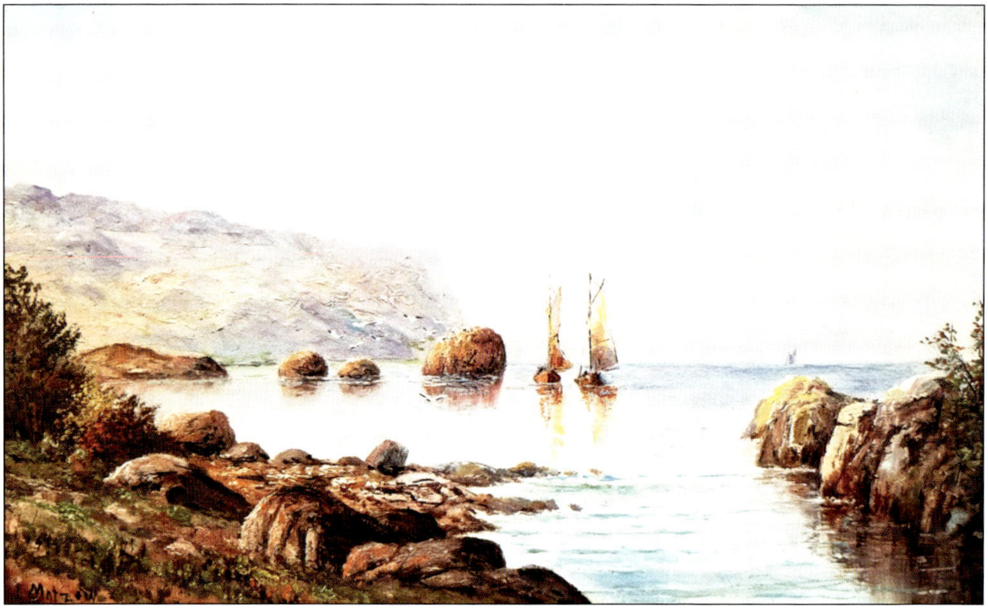

FREDERICK MATZOW. Frederick Matzow was born in Norway in 1862 and came to America at the age of 12. As an adult, Matzow traveled throughout the Northeast for years, giving live painting demonstrations at local businesses, which attracted crowds eager to witness his landscape painting skills. Referred to as "a lightning artist," he most often used oils and painted scenes in just 6 to 10 minutes. Matzow stopped in Meriden frequently, and his immense reception persuaded A.J. Hall, a successful art dealer, to permanently bring him to Meriden around 1912. After a few years as a Meriden resident, Matzow sought regular employment with the Handel Lamp Company as a decorator. When the company closed in 1936, Matzow moved downtown where he opened a painting studio with fellow artist John Backstrom. Matzow died in Meriden in 1938.

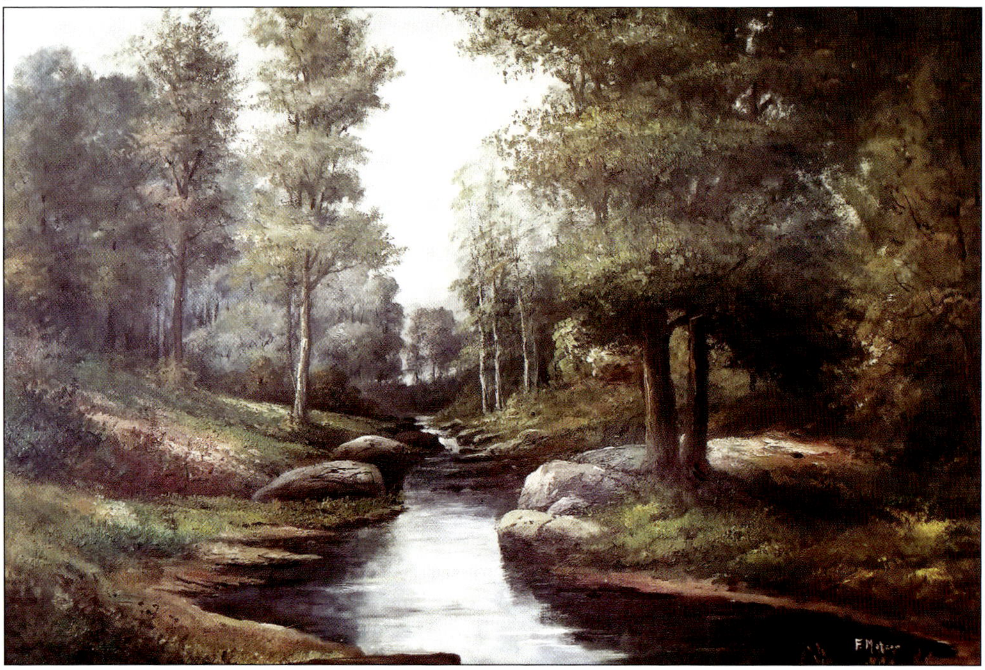

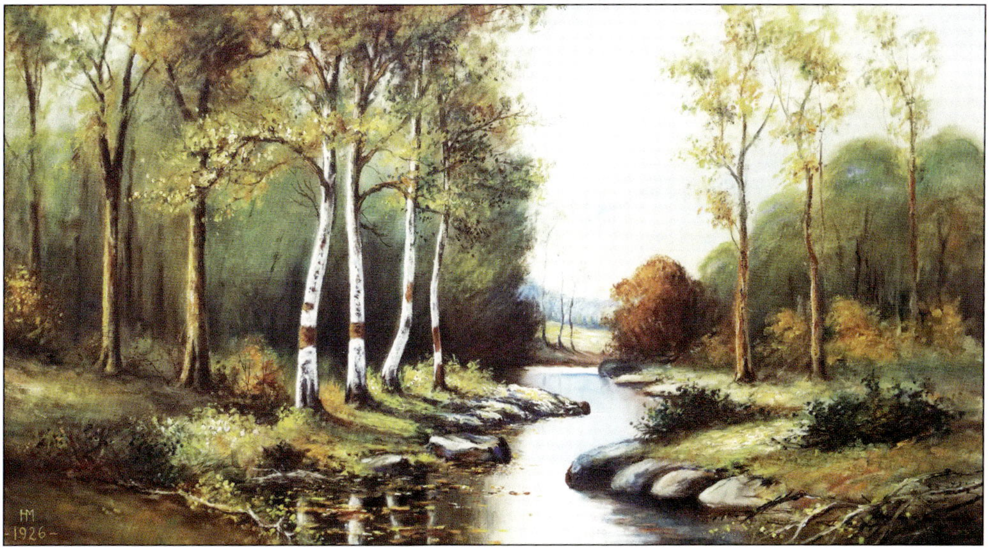

Henry J. Meinke. Henry J. Meinke was born January 27, 1909, in New Jersey. His family moved to Meriden when he was young, and he attended the local schools. Meinke befriended Meriden artist Frederick Matzow, who allowed him to observe his painting process. This tutelage inspired Meinke to further pursue instruction in art, and he graduated from Yale Art School in 1932. Meinke died in 1985. (Courtesy of Allen and Neda Weathers.)

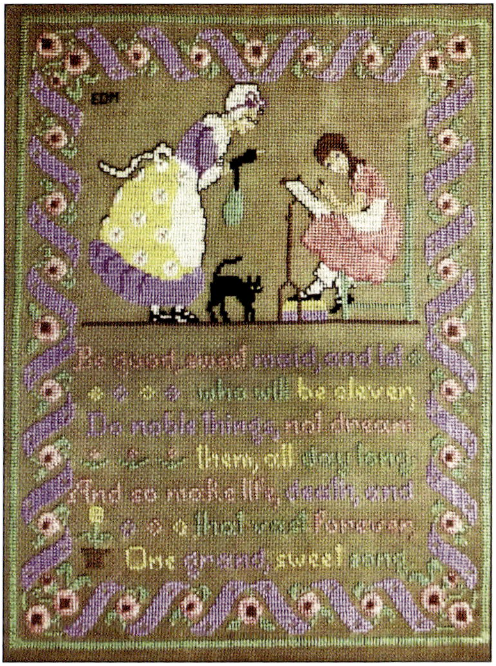

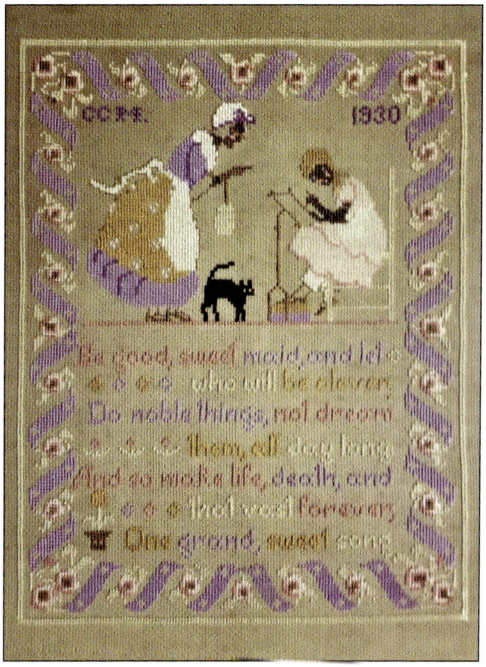

Depression-Era Needlepoint. These Depression-era needlepoints, initialed "EDM" and "CCM," were made in Meriden in 1930. They are beautifully embroidered pieces that feature similar scenes of women instructing children, with the color of the subjects' skin tones being one difference between the two. The medium of needlepoint offers a wide range of opportunities for self-expression, and creativity is often used to create pictures, pillows, seat cushions, and other beautiful items to decorate and accentuate a home. (Both, courtesy of Meriden Historical Society.)

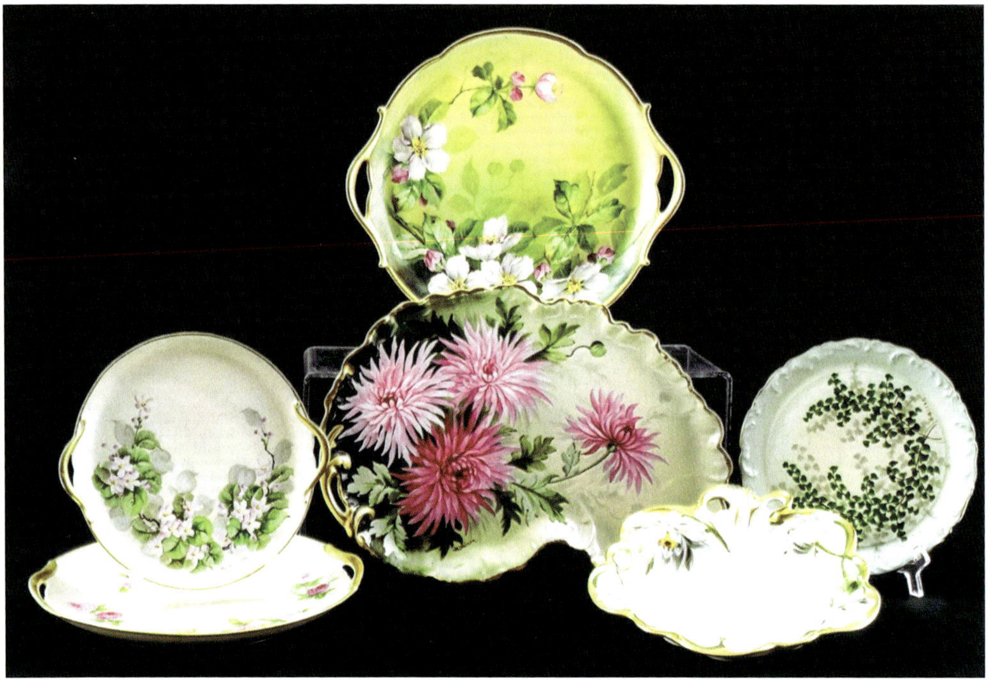

Walter Wilson. Walter Wilson was born in Manchester, England, in 1870 and came to Meriden some nine years later. As an adult, Wilson designed for the Handel Lamp Company and produced handsomely decorated china and glass pieces. After leaving Handel, he was the chief decorator for the A.J. Hall Company. From 1905 to 1917, Wilson was in business with local artist Joseph Hickisch managing a china-decorating studio of their own in Meriden. When the Hickisch partnership dissolved in 1917, Wilson moved his studio to his home in neighboring Southington, Connecticut, and reproduced some of the most popular chinaware patterns he originally created for Handel. Wilson continued painting until the day of his death on January 2, 1955, in Meriden. He was 82 years old. (Top, courtesy of Nest Egg Auctions; bottom, courtesy of Sherwin Borsuk.)

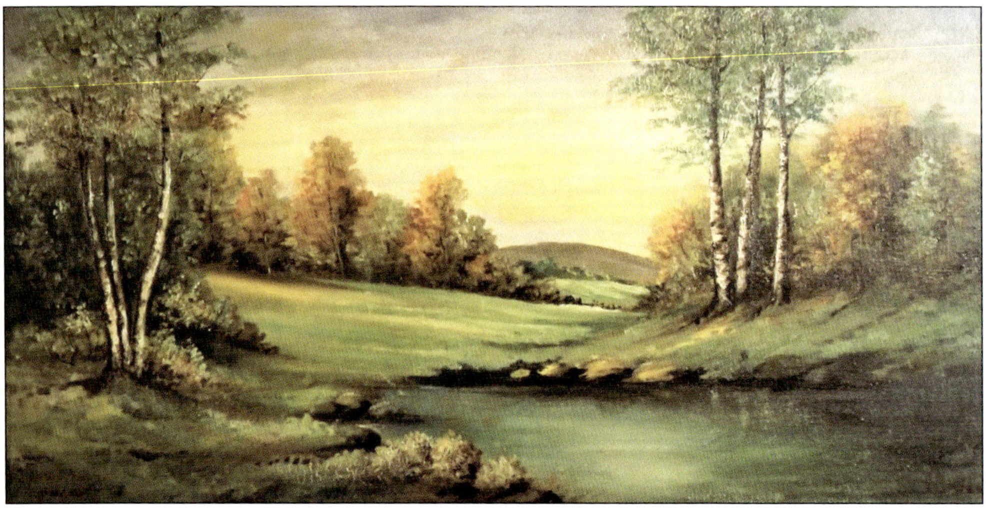

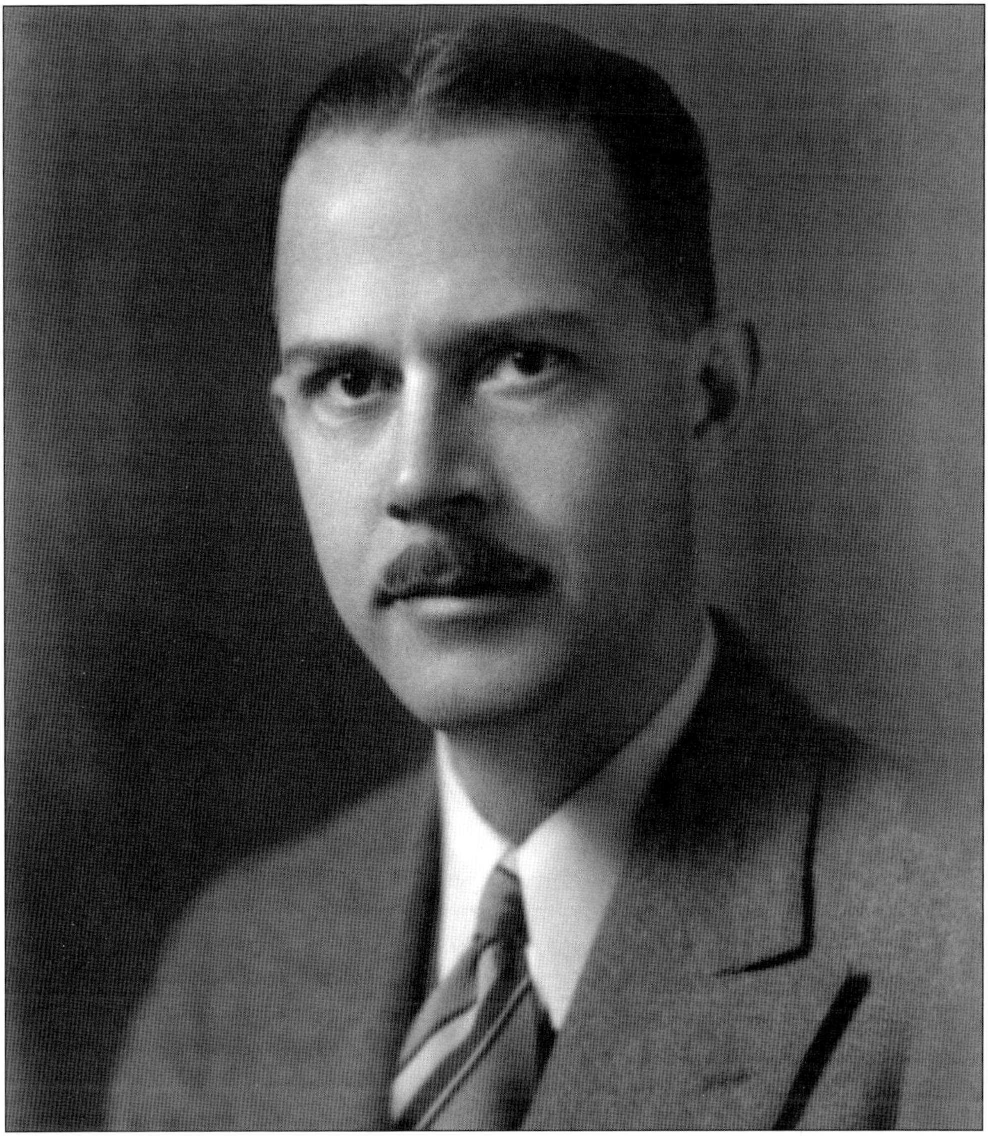

LORENZO HAMILTON. Born in 1895, Lorenzo Hamilton left his architectural mark on homes and public buildings that dot today's Meriden landscape. A 1914 graduate of Meriden High School, Hamilton went on to study at Phillips Academy in Andover, Massachusetts, and then Yale University. His dream of opening his own architecture firm became a reality in 1923, and over the next decade, he gained prominence as a local residential architect but was also the designer of several important civic structures. Beginning in 1929, he collaborated with Meriden sculptor Louis Gudebrod on the plan for one of Meriden's most poignant and prominent landmarks, Memorial Boulevard on Broad Street, once a training ground for Revolutionary War soldiers recruited to fight for the colonies. Among Hamilton's most significant projects were First Church of Christ Scientist in Bradley Park; Bradley Memorial Nurses' Home on Cook Avenue; the Bradley Home on Colony Street; the Hanover School in South Meriden; Wilcox Slate Trade School, then on Miller Street; Roger Sherman and John Barry Elementary Schools; and the renovated Wilcox Block on Colony Street. His last major local project prior to his death in 1955 was the World War II Veterans Memorial Hospital. (Courtesy of Marcus Hamilton.)

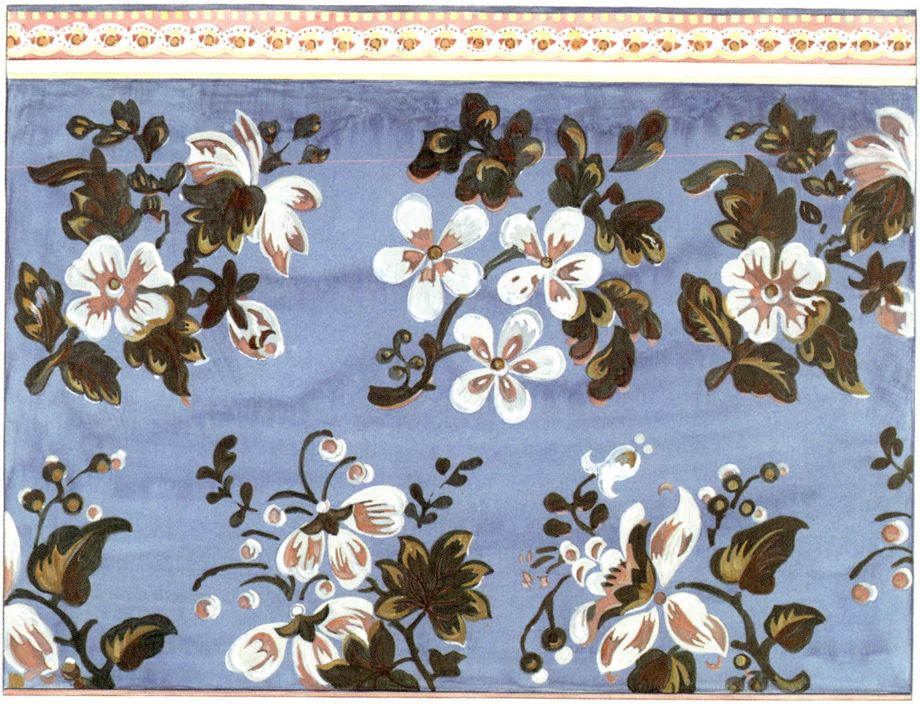

Isabella Ruth Doerfler. Isabella Ruth Doerfler was born in Meriden on July 23, 1883. She began painting at the age of 10 while attending Meriden's public schools. She graduated from the Yale School of Art and launched a career as a teacher, children's book illustrator, designer for publishing houses, and decorator of antiques. Doerfler was a member of the Arts and Crafts Association of Meriden and of the Association of Connecticut Artists and was considered to be "one of the best renderers of textiles in New England." In 1936, under the Works Progress Administration's (WPA) Federal Arts Project, she worked on the Index of American Design. Doerfler also completed 62 works for the WPA, and her pieces were sent across Connecticut to Undercliff Sanatorium in Meriden, the Soldiers' Home in Rocky Hill, Connecticut State Farm for Women in Niantic/ East Lyme, Norwich State Hospital in Norwich and Preston, Connecticut State College (University of Connecticut) in Storrs/Mansfield, and the West Hartford School System. During World War II, she worked in the mechanical drawing department of a defense plant. Doerfler died in the neighboring town of Berlin, Connecticut, on November 15, 1954, at the age of 71. (Courtesy of the National Gallery of Art.)

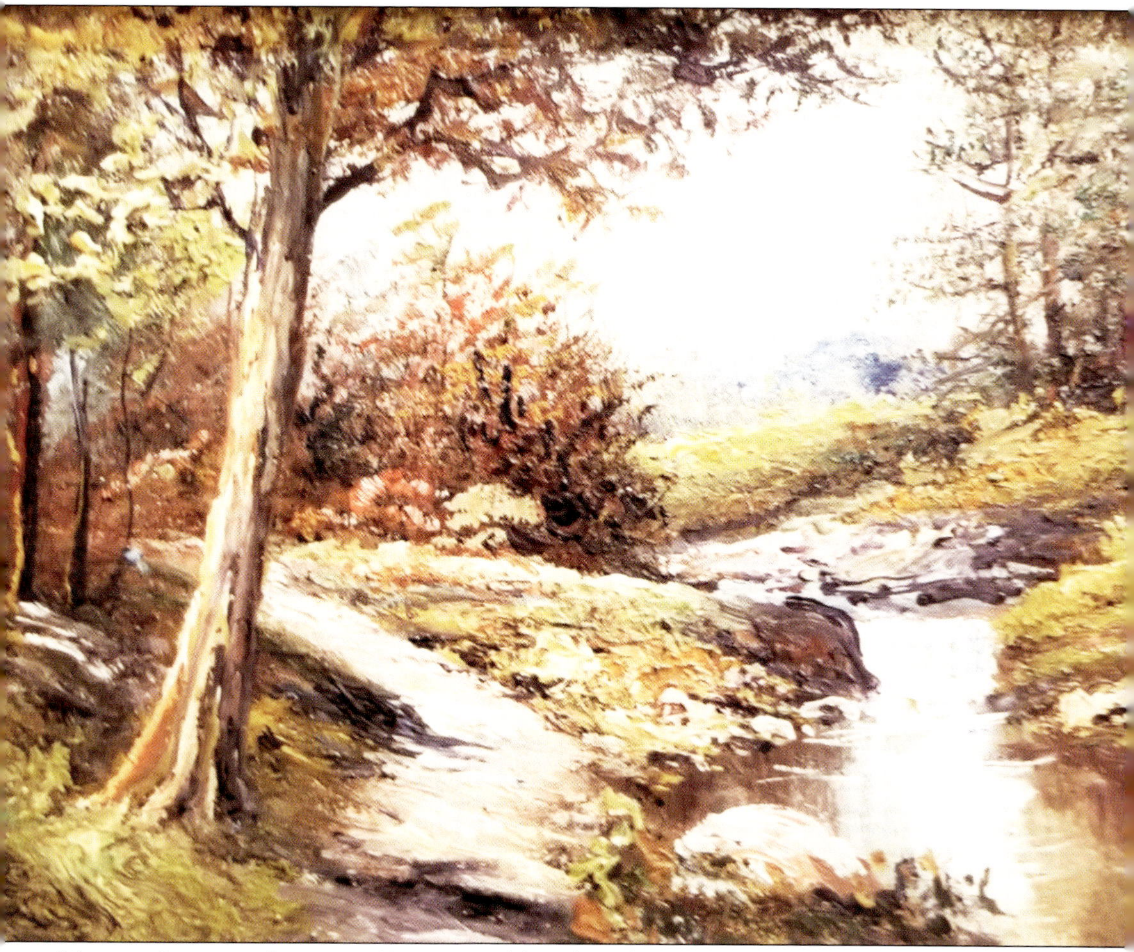

Meriden School of Landscape Painting. Although no definitive name exists, Meriden School of Landscape Painting has been used extensively in Meriden art and art history circles to describe locally situated artworks that seemed to merge two distinct painting traditions: the Hudson River School and American Impressionism. In the Hudson River School tradition, artists embraced the landscape as a meaningful subject just as industrialization was reshaping terrains and human connections to the environment, a scenario which Meriden was undergoing. American Impressionism was a style of art that was characterized by loose brushwork, vivid colors, and a wide array of subject matters, though many Impressionist pieces focused on landscapes. Both traditions had their origins in the 19th century but saw a renewed popularity, particularly in central Connecticut, in the 1920s and 1930s with artists such as Frederick Matzow and John Backstrom. These artists usually painted en plein air, or "out of doors," to capture the landscapes firsthand. This unsigned Depression-era painting is a model example of this Meriden School of Landscape Painting style.

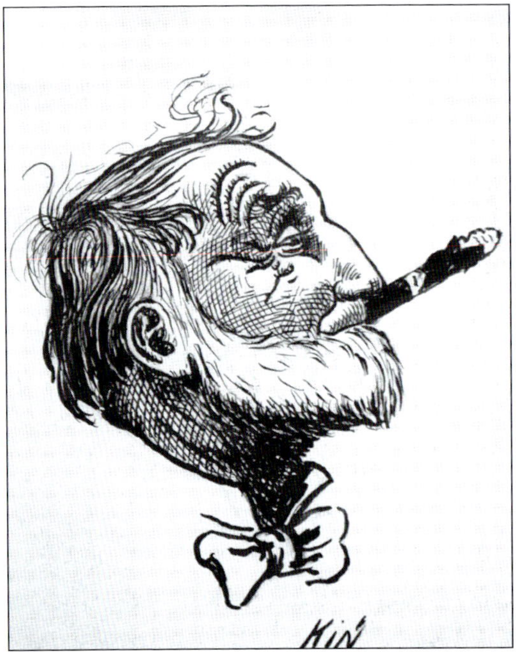

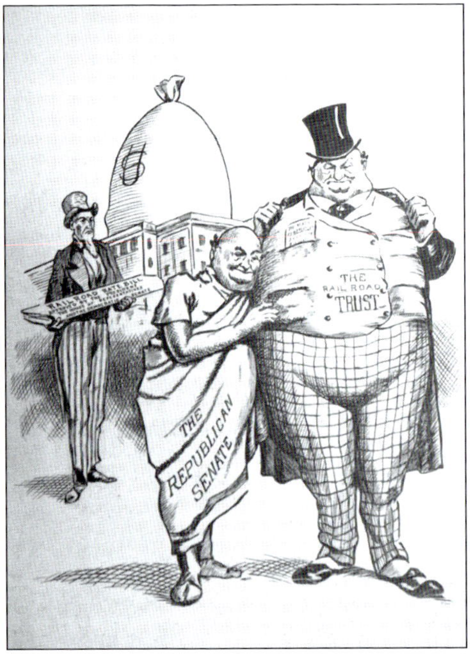

JOHN KINKADE. John Kinkade was born in New Britain, Connecticut, in 1887. As a child, he and his family moved to Meriden, where he was a model art student. He attended art school and then continued his creativity as an employee at International Silver Company, working at a factory in nearby Wallingford, Connecticut. These political cartoons demonstrate his masterful pen-and-ink technique. Kinkade died in 1979. (Both, courtesy of the Meriden Historical Society.)

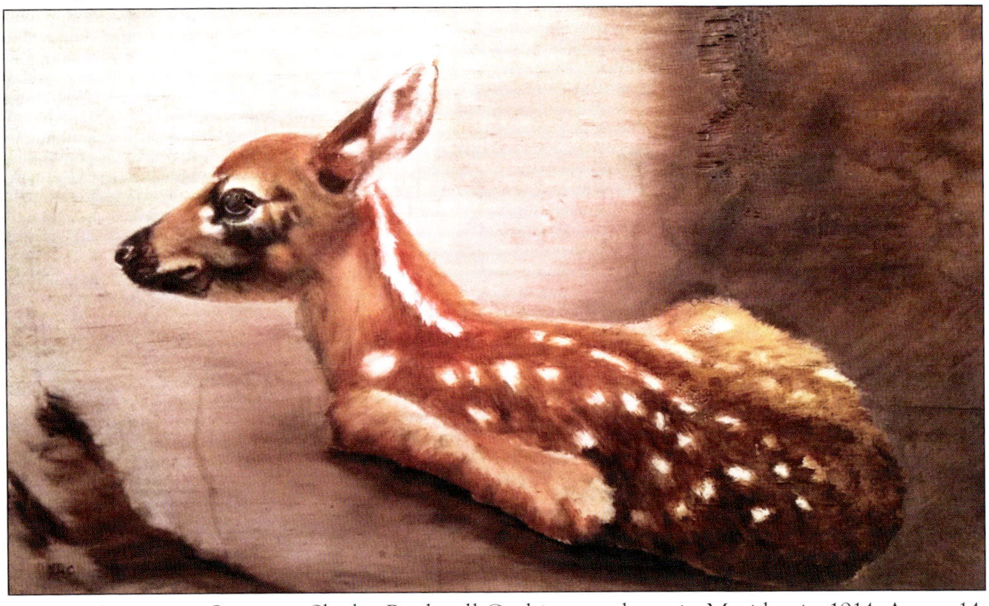

SHIRLEY ROCKWELL CUSHING. Shirley Rockwell Cushing was born in Meriden in 1914. At age 14, she began working as an artist for her family's glass art business, Rockwell Silver Company. She designed patterns and was skilled in brushwork on glass. After her retirement, Cushing expanded her artistic talents by creating wildlife paintings on wood and on canvas, like this image of a fawn on wood. Cushing died August 11, 2015, at the age of 101.

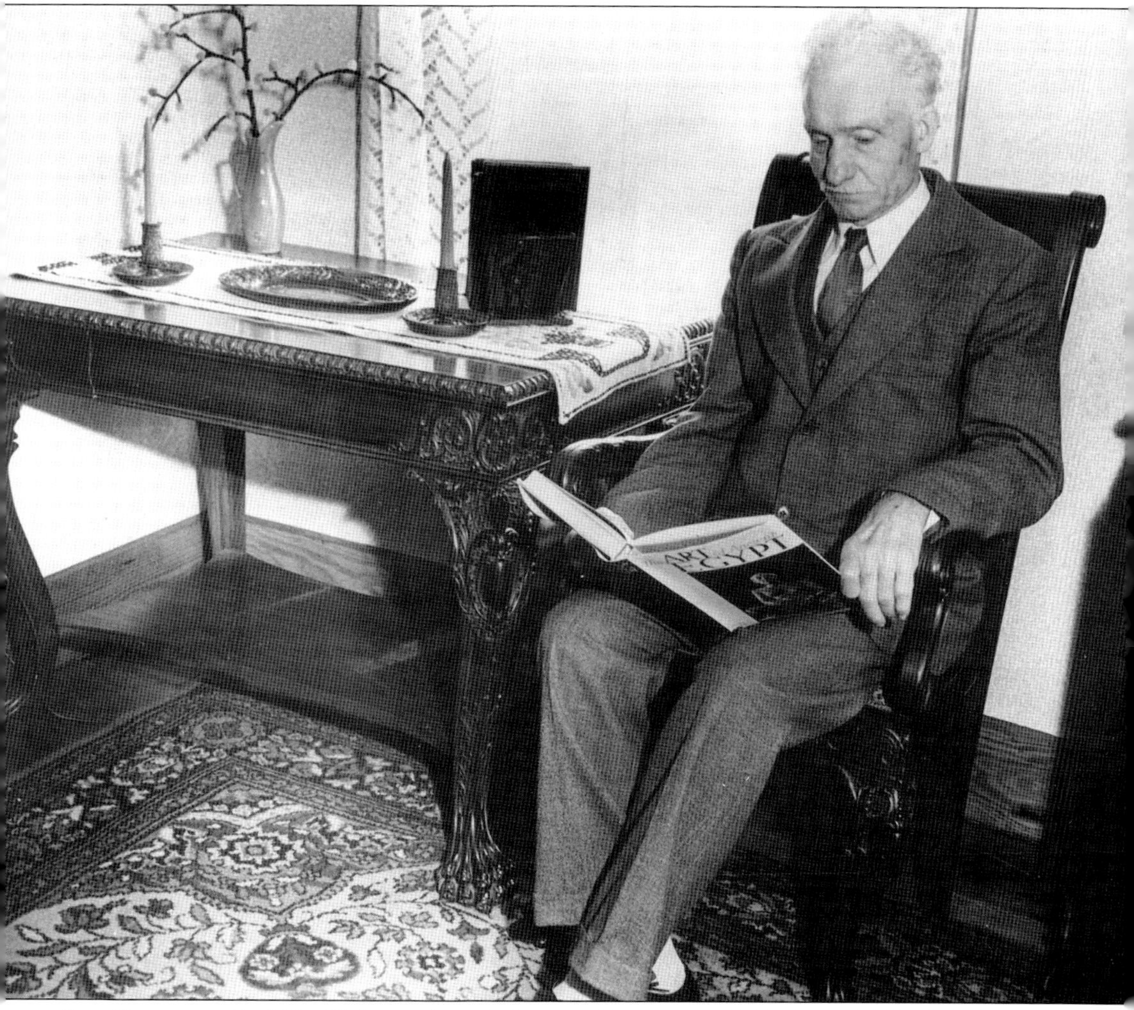

EMIL KOEFFINKE. Emil Koeffinke was born in Prussia, Germany, in 1868. At age 14, Koffinke began his apprenticeship as a woodcarver, creating horses and great chairs for carousels. In 1888, he left his homeland and came to the United States, settling in New Haven where he found employment in a piano factory carving the trim on pianos. From there, he transferred to the Aeolian Company in Meriden where he carved pianos and organs. He later worked at the Museum of Natural History in New York City for seven years. In addition, he spent time as a gun stock carver at the Winchester Repeating Arms Company in New Haven. Seen here in 1939 at the age of 71, Koffinke is seated in a mahogany side chair beside a library table that he carved himself, both of which are now in the collection of the Meriden Historical Society. Koffinke died in 1959 at the age of 90. (Courtesy of the Meriden Historical Society.)

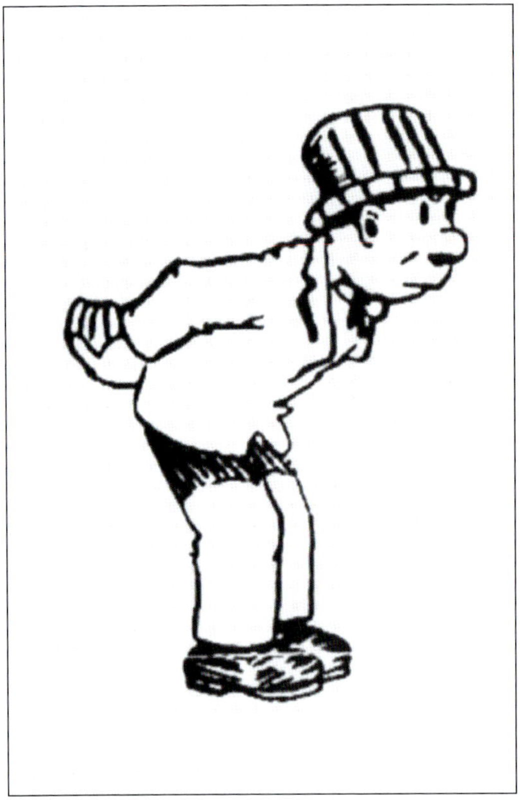

Frank Warren Hopkins. Frank Warren Hopkins was born in Utah in 1884 and became a prolific illustrator. His most well-known credits were early-1900s comic strips *Scoop the Cub Reporter* and *Snuggle Pups*. By the time he moved to Meriden in the late 1930s, Hopkins was a freelance artist and was no longer connected to the strips. Hopkins passed away in New Haven, Connecticut, on September 15, 1956.

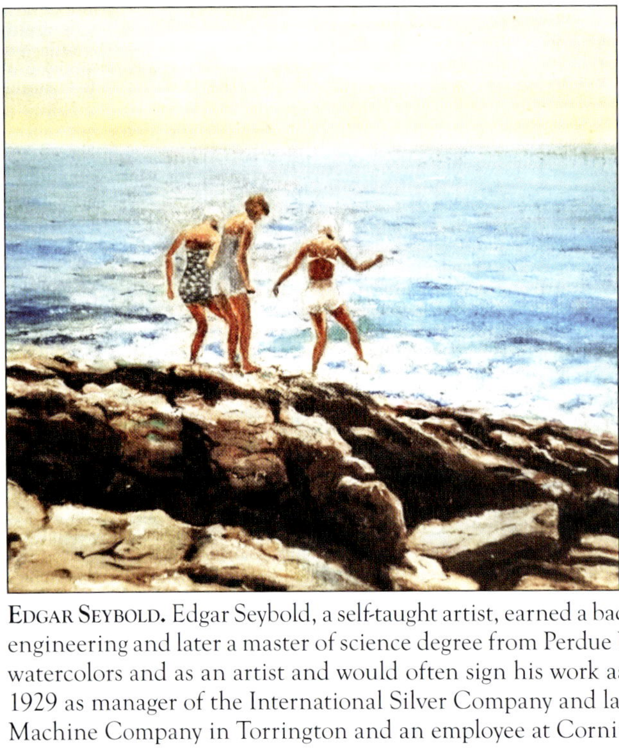

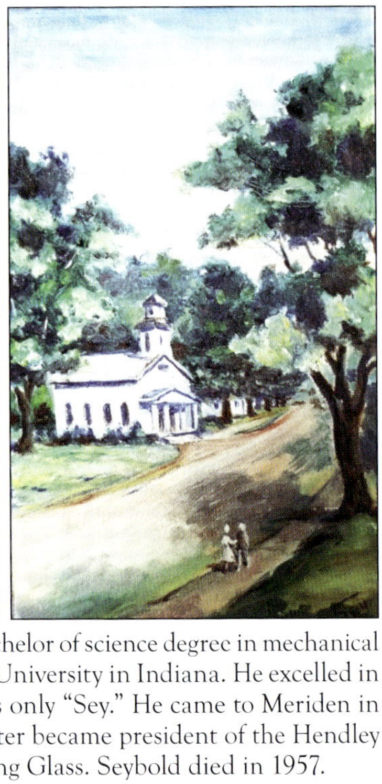

Edgar Seybold. Edgar Seybold, a self-taught artist, earned a bachelor of science degree in mechanical engineering and later a master of science degree from Perdue University in Indiana. He excelled in watercolors and as an artist and would often sign his work as only "Sey." He came to Meriden in 1929 as manager of the International Silver Company and later became president of the Hendley Machine Company in Torrington and an employee at Corning Glass. Seybold died in 1957.

Beulah Bowers. As a supervisor of art in the city's public schools for over 20 years, Beulah Bowers's influence on the Meriden art community was vast. Born in Massachusetts in 1895, she was well-traveled before settling into her Meriden position in 1939. She also served as president of a number of groups, including the Connecticut Arts Association and the Arts and Crafts Association of Meriden. Bowers died in 1975.

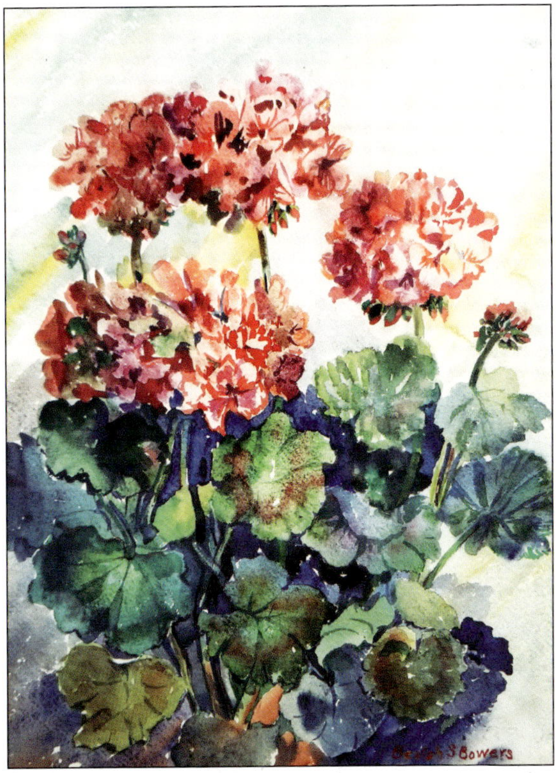

Arts and Crafts Association of Meriden Gavel and Block. This ceremonial gavel and block were made by Frederick Rettenmeyer and presented to the Arts and Crafts Association of Meriden in May 1945 when Beulah Bowers, supervisor of art for Meriden's public schools, was serving as president. Stored inside the base of the block is an ornate, hand-decorated pamphlet recounting the history of the association. (Courtesy of Gallery 53.)

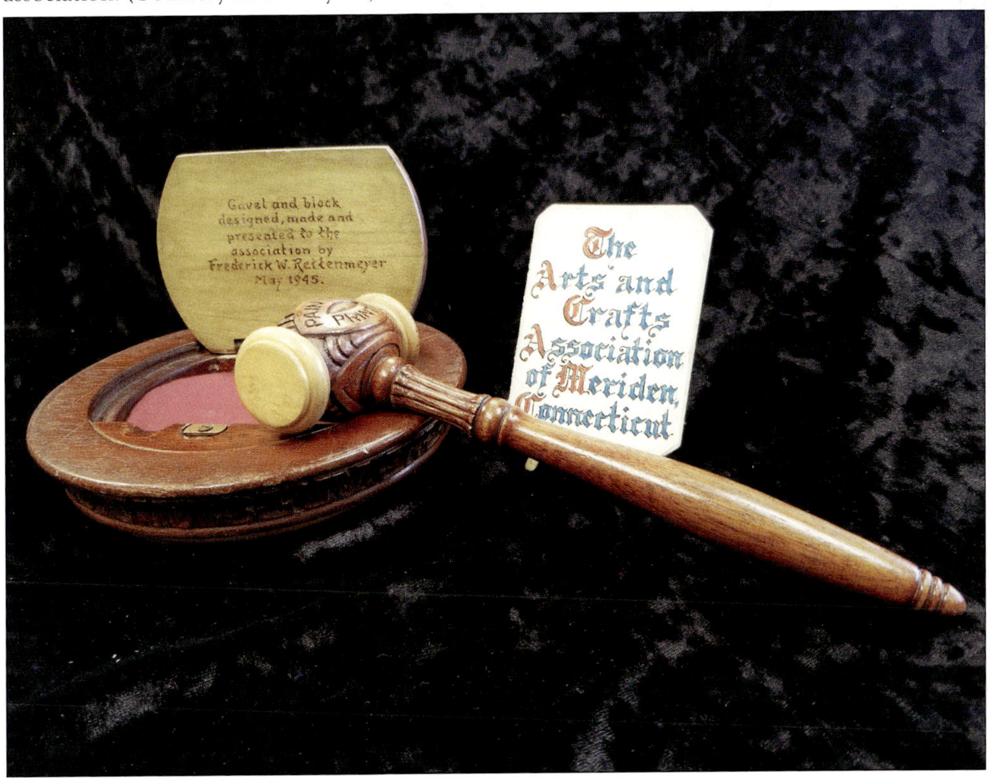

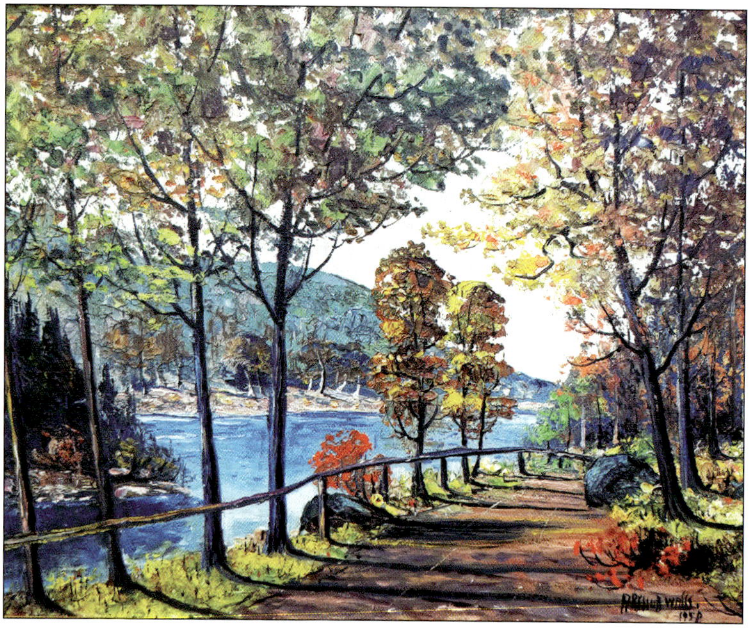

Arthur Watts. In 1944, after a lifetime as a minstrel, vaudeville, and Hollywood soundstage performer, Arthur Watts traded in his dancing shoes for a career as a painter. Studying under the tutelage of Meriden artist Frederick Matzow, Watts painted similarly beautiful, local scenic landscapes, but Watts offered a much bolder, wider-ranging color palette than Matzow.

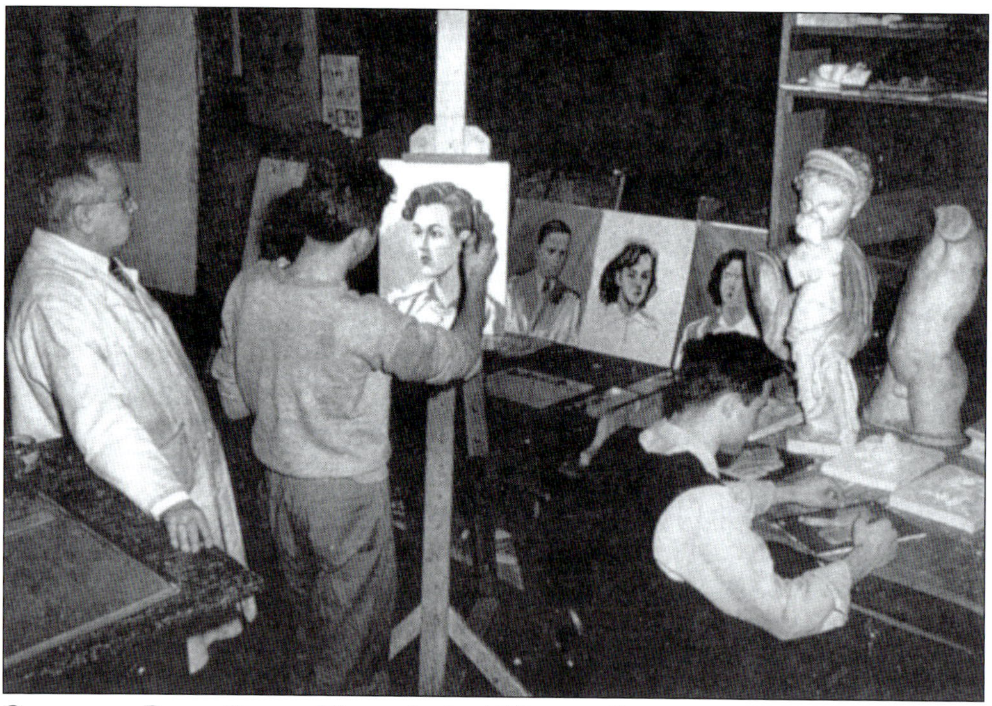

Ornamental Design Class at Wilcox. In this 1950 image, Horace C. Wilcox Technical School's ornamental design instructor Ernst Lohrmann peers over the shoulder of student Nicholas Scalise as he paints a portrait of a woman. To their right, classmate Siro Toffolon is working on a clay relief sculpture. At one time, 13 out of the 16 designers at International Silver Company had received their training from Lohrmann. (Courtesy of Henrietta Scalise.)

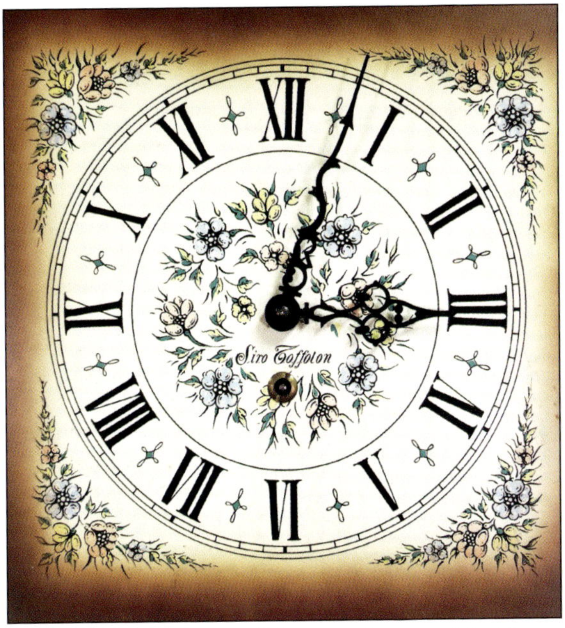

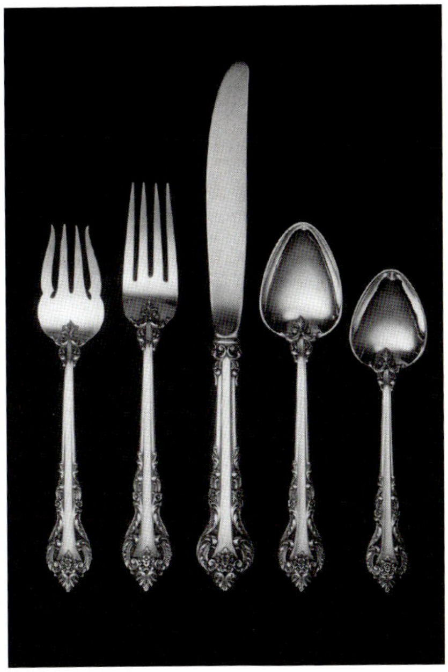

Siro Toffolon. Siro Toffolon was born in Meriden and attended the local schools, graduating from Horace C. Wilcox Technical School in 1951. Following Wilcox, Toffolon worked for the International Silver Company as a designer, and his classic styles catapulted him to worldwide acclaim as one of America's most revered designers of silverware, jewelry, antique guns, and clocks. His passion for colonial Americana was unparalleled. Toffolon died in 2015.

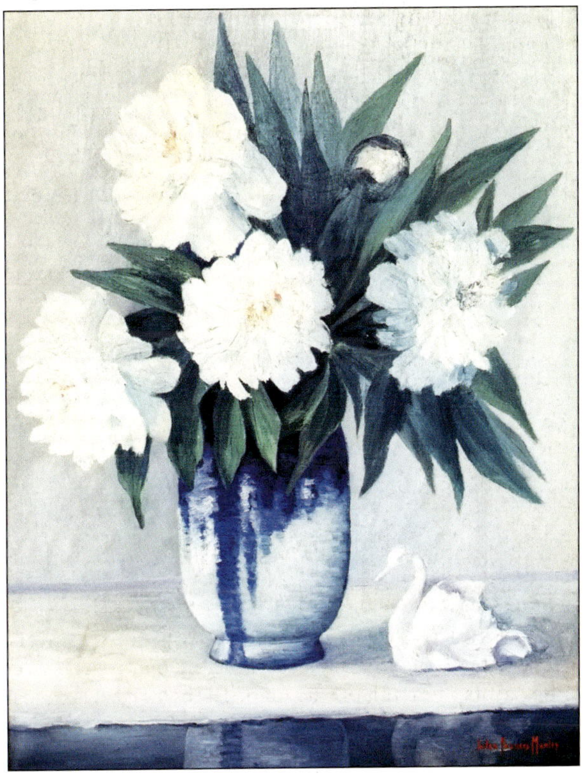

Julia Manley. Julia Manley was born in 1880. A native Meriden resident, she received her first drawing instructions from local artist Charlotte Lilla Yale. She continued her studies in illustration and portrait painting and became an accomplished children's book illustrator. Having published many stories and poems herself, Manley was also a member of the New York Writers Guild. She married famed sculptor Louis Gudebrod in 1961 after their lifelong friendship, but he died that same year. Manley died in 1967.

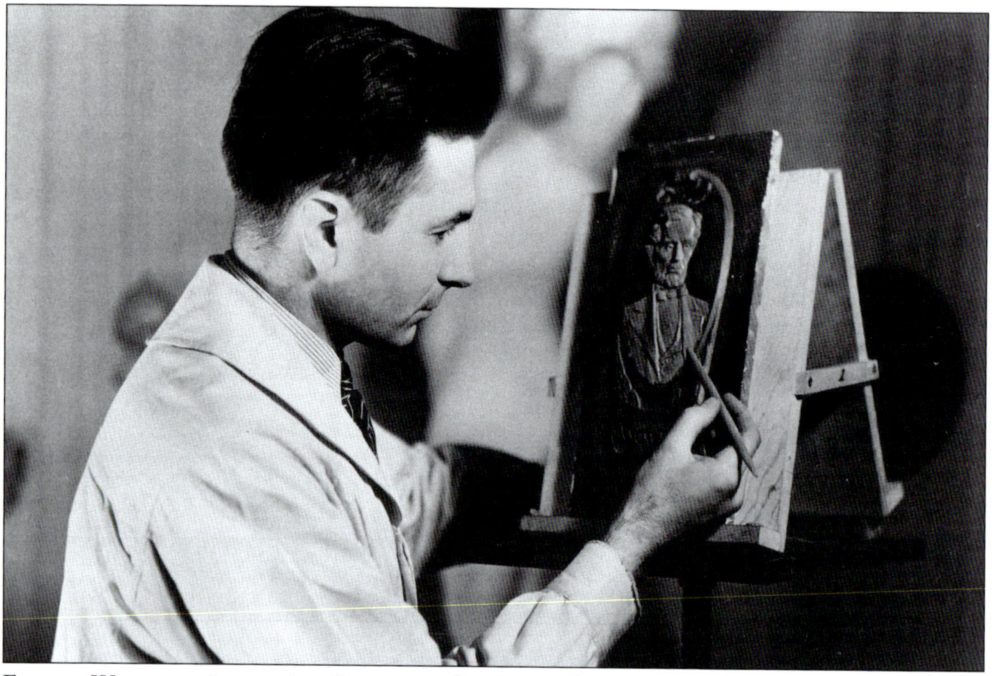

Edward Widstrom. Internationally renowned sculptor Edward Widstrom was born in Wallingford, Connecticut, in 1903. He studied at the Detroit School of Art and at the Art Students League in New York City. After his schooling, Widstrom moved to Meriden and for many years was a model maker for International Silver Company, specializing in bronze sculpture and other metals. Among his many achievements, he received the coveted Silver Medal of the National Sculpture Society and designed and modeled the portraits of 36 US presidential spoons and a series of medallions for International Silver Company. He also created *Jungle Runner,* a sculpture of a racing tropical rooster, which was sold to William Benton, publisher of Encyclopedia Britannica; a second casting is in the permanent collection of Brookgreen Gardens in South Carolina. Listed in the *Who's Who of American Art,* Widstrom died in 1989.

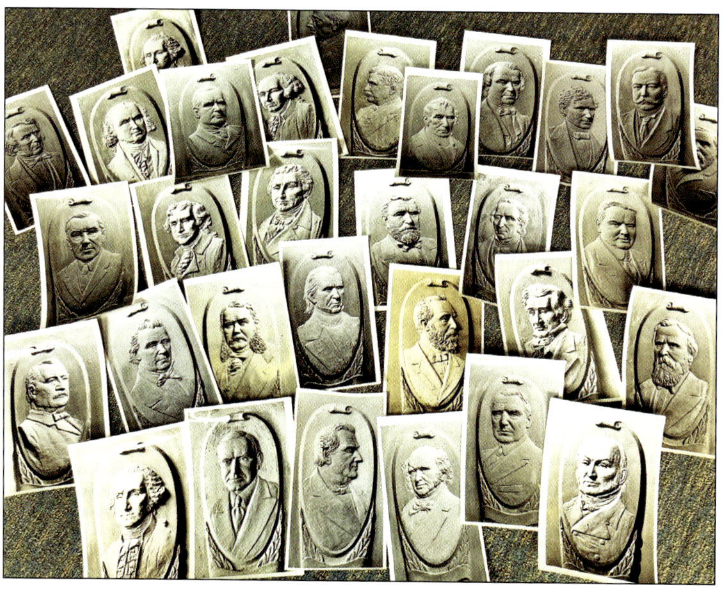

Meriden Sesquicentennial Art Retrospective Exhibit. Arranged in honor of the Meriden sesquicentennial celebration in 1956, this local art retrospective exhibit was presented by the Arts and Crafts Association of Meriden. It featured artists whose works had been exhibited throughout the organization's first 50 years, including notables like American landscape painter Winslow Homer and renowned local artist Edwin Augustus Moore. (Courtesy of Gallery 53.)

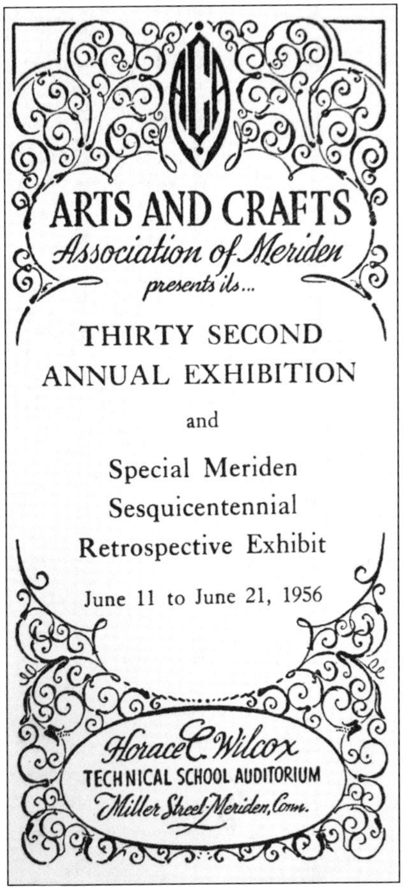

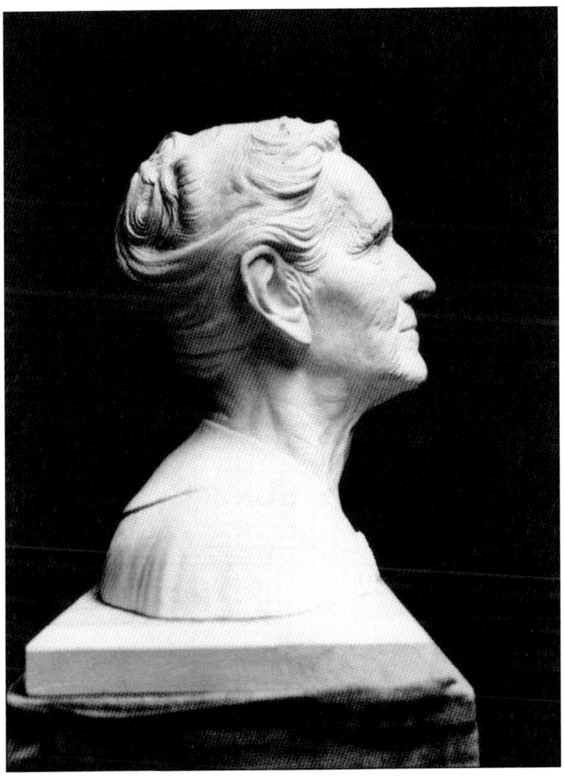

Indianna Thomas. This bust of the late Indianna Thomas, a passionate leader and advocate in artistic circles in and around Meriden for many years, was created by Meriden sculptor Edward Widstrom. It was used as a centerpiece for the Arts and Crafts Association of Meriden's 32nd annual exhibition, held in conjunction with the city's sesquicentennial celebrations. (Courtesy of the Meriden Historical Society.)

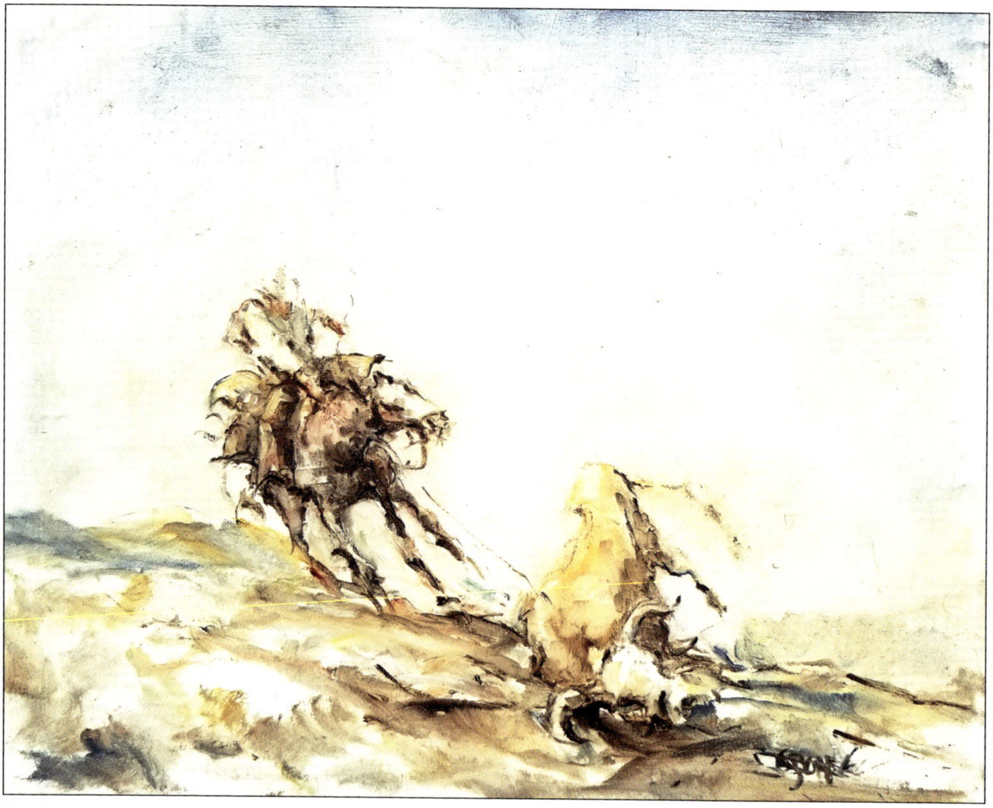

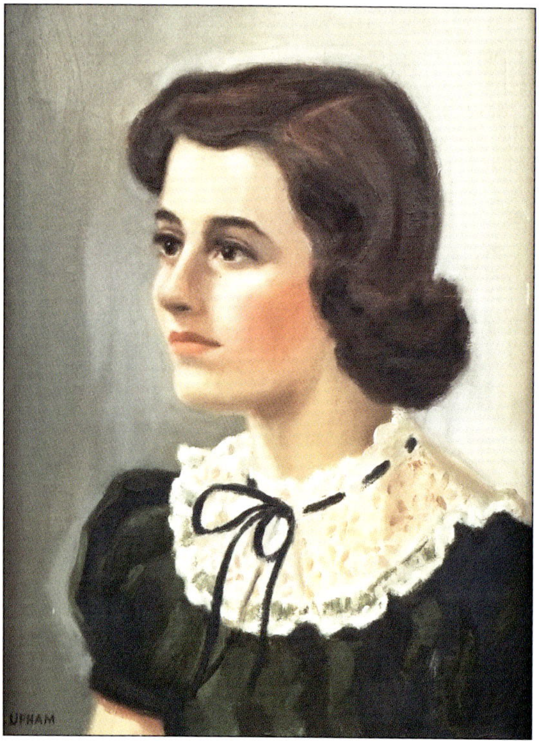

George Osbourne. George Osbourne was a talented artist whose favorite medium was oil painting. He was also a sculptor and whittler, and he made interesting caricatures of people—particularly fishermen—in rural Maine. In the 1960s, he taught art from his home and at the YMCA in Meriden. After leaving Meriden, he maintained a studio in Kennebunk, Maine, for several years. He was shot dead in Texas after a barroom brawl. (Courtesy of Gallery 53.)

Lucy Upham. Lucy Upham was born in Meriden in 1924 and from an early age had an interest in art. She studied at Horace C. Wilcox Technical School under the tutelage of Ernst Lohrmann and became a well-known portrait artist in the city, preferring pastels as her medium of choice because of their softness and vibrancy. In later years, she also ran a nursery school. Upham died in 2003.

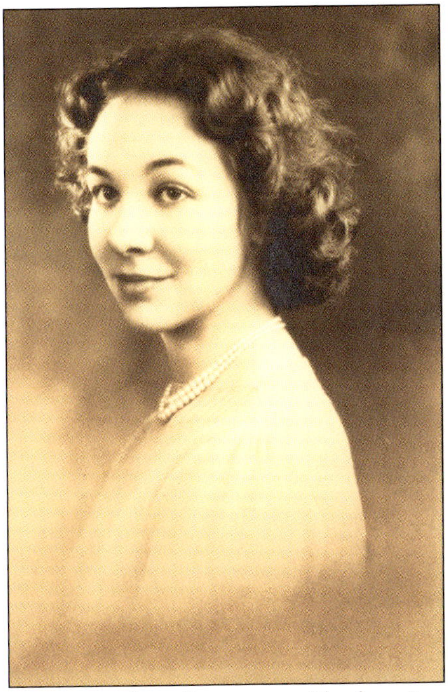

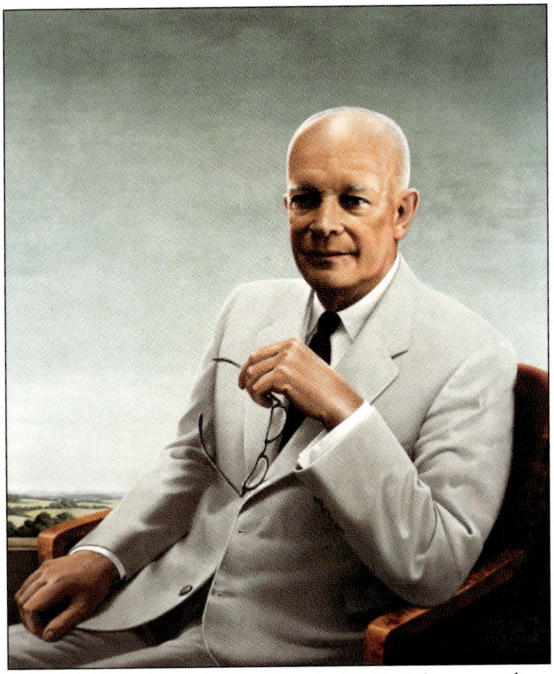

CHARLOTTE JOAN STERNBERG. Charlotte Joan Sternberg was born in Meriden in 1920. After attending public schools, she went to the Yale School of Art and graduated in 1942. It was at Yale that Sternberg learned how to paint in egg tempera, her choice of medium. She had a long career in commercial illustration painting a variety of subjects, although she was best known for her Americana-themed art. Sternberg was commissioned to paint several portraits, including those of Connecticut governor John Lodge and Pres. Dwight D. Eisenhower. Her artwork has been exhibited at the New Britain Museum of American Art in Connecticut and the Bennington Museum in Vermont. Later in her career, Sternberg focused on landscape painting, and Greenwich Workshop, a leading publisher of fine art, produced a line of limited-edition prints of her work. Sternberg died in 2003. (Top right, courtesy of the Eisenhower Presidential Library and Museum; bottom, courtesy of Carla Sternberg Koch.)

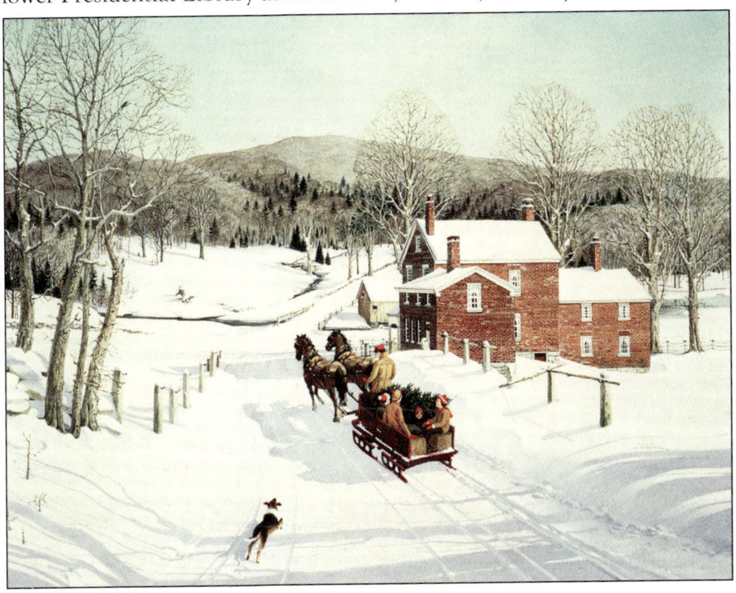

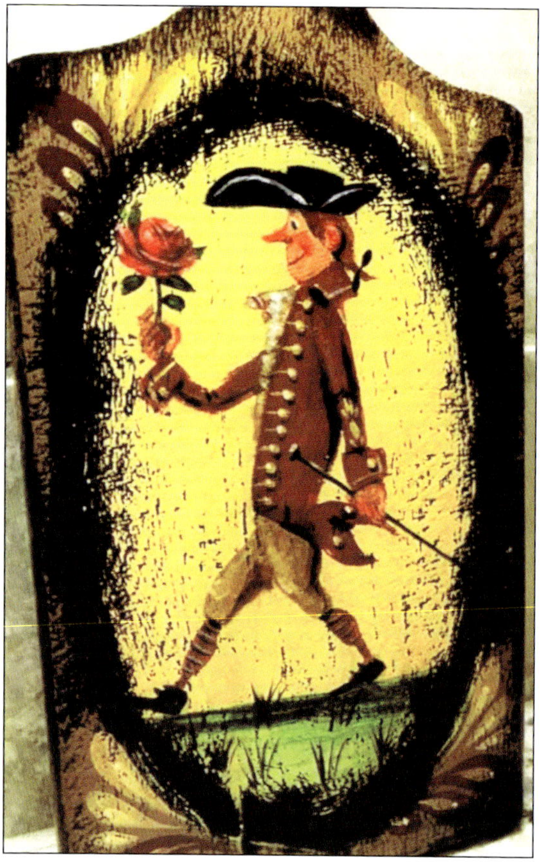

Robert Berger. Robert Berger was born in Buffalo, New York, in 1918. After World War II, Berger graduated from the Randall Art School in Hartford and settled in Meriden. He was a commercial artist who was employed by the Randall Advertising Agency in Hartford for 20 years. During this time, he was also involved with the State Line Potato Chip advertising campaign. Upon retirement, Berger remained active as a specialized decorative painter.

William Brinley. William Brinley was a pioneer among folk art circus model builders. For over a quarter century, he created a grandiose miniature circus, and in 1950, television legend Hopalong Cassidy had Brinley travel with his circus to drum up publicity for the Cole Brothers Circus, which was soon to follow. His miniature circus was displayed at the New York World's Fair and likely seen by millions. In 1967, it found a permanent home in the Barnum Museum in Bridgeport, Connecticut. Brinley died in 2016.

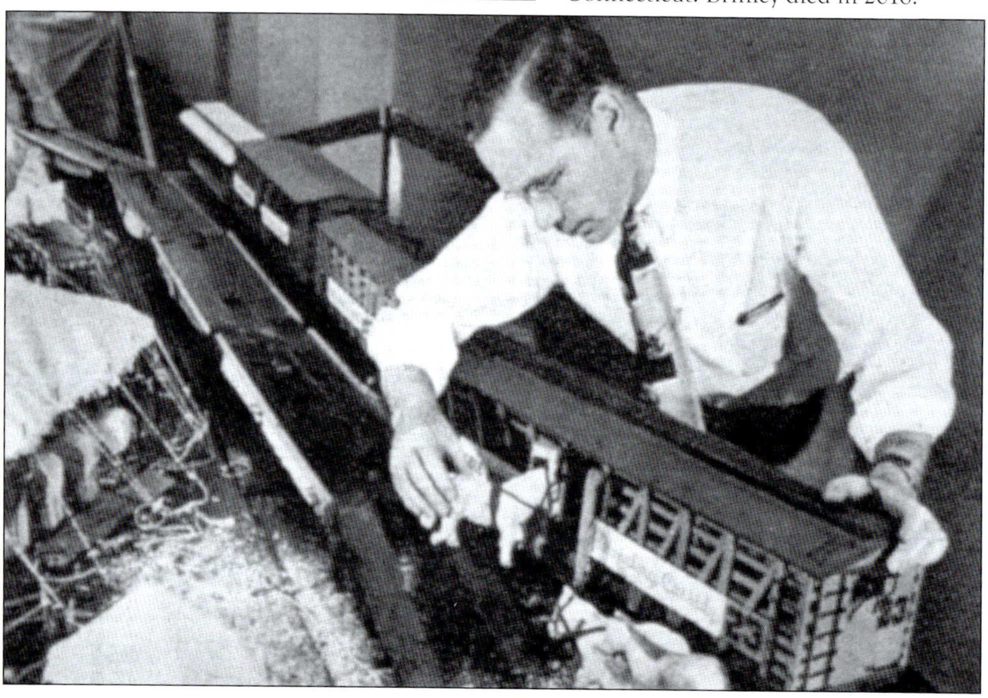

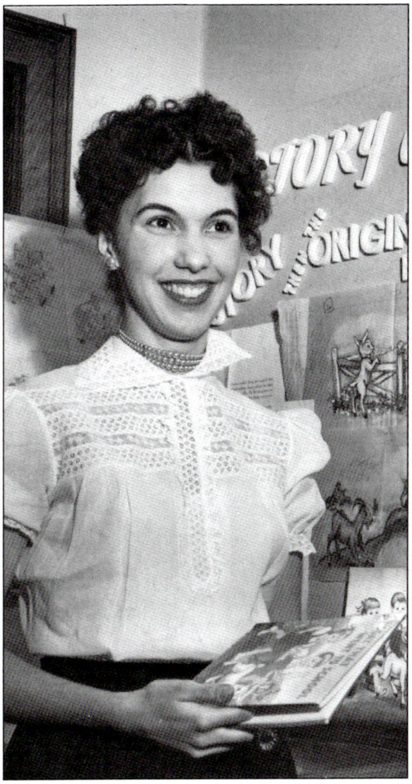

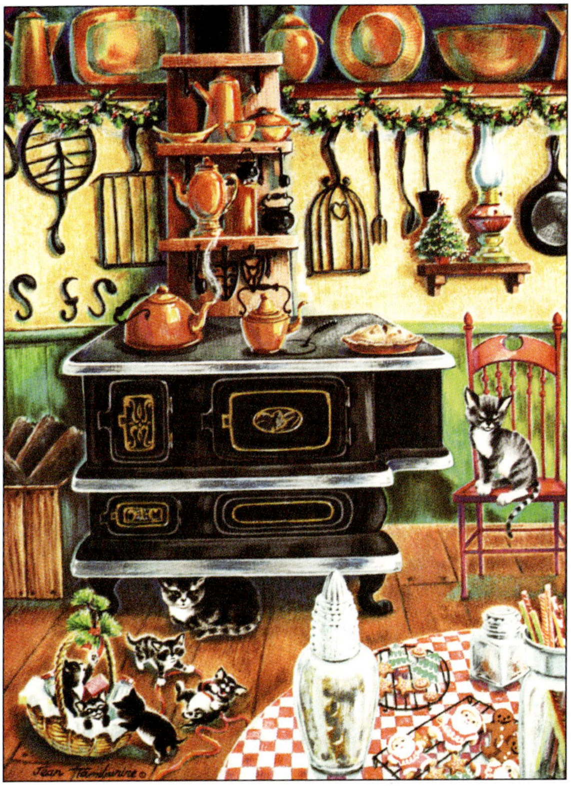

Jean Tamburine Bertolli. Jean Tamburine Bertolli was born in Meriden in 1930 and graduated from Meriden High School in 1941. Bertolli was an award-winning artist, author, and illustrator. Her paintings, drawings, and sculpture are in public and private collections all over the world. She was selected by famed writer and novelist Pearl S. Buck to produce renderings of Asian American children and created the bronze sculpture *Heritage* for the Wallingford Public Library in 1986. Additionally, she was one of the 15 original commissioners appointed by Gov. John Dempsey to form the Connecticut Commission on the Arts. She is listed in the *Who's Who in American Art*, *Who's Who in American Women*, *Who's Who in the East*, and in *Contemporary Authors*. Bertolli died in 2013 at the age of 83. (All, courtesy of the Meriden Public Library.)

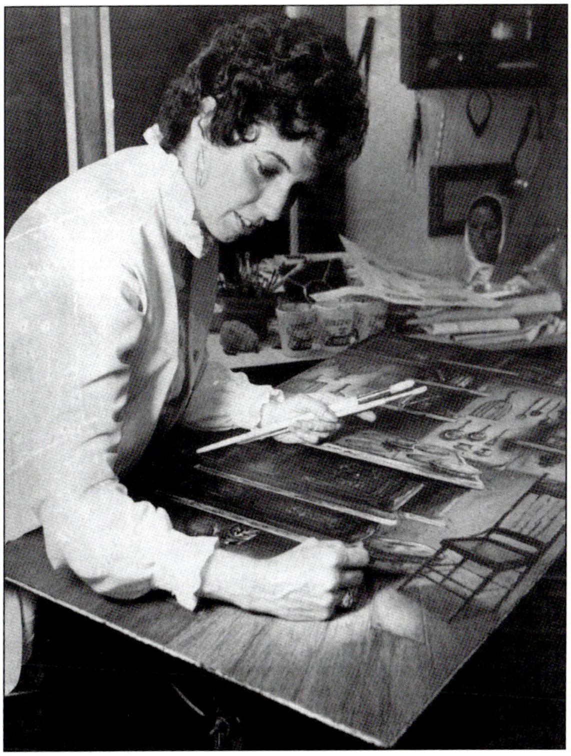

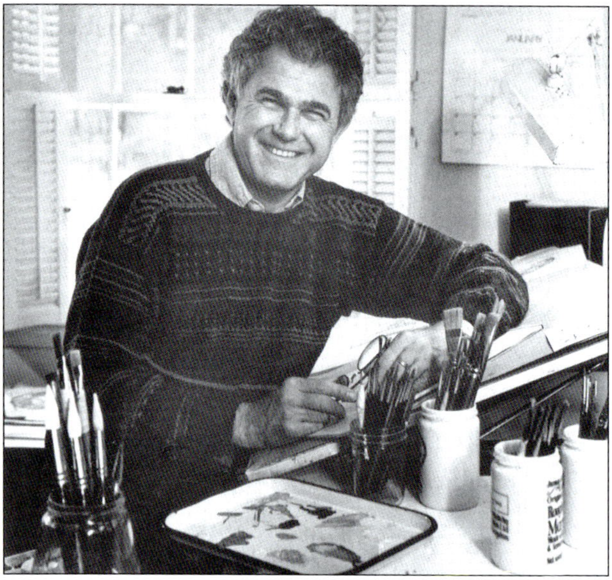

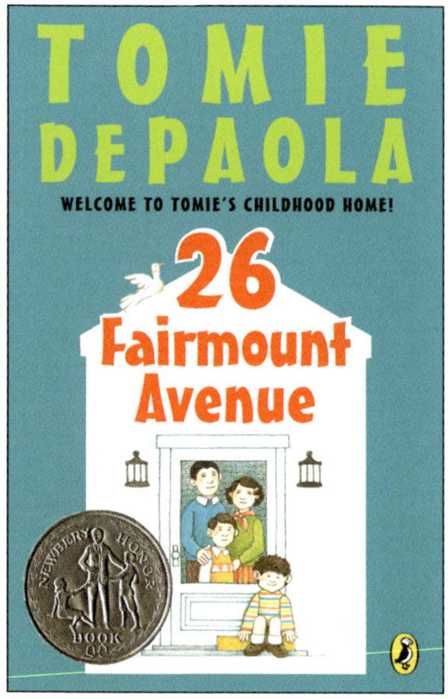

TOMIE DEPAOLA. Meriden native Tomie dePaola forecasted his future when he told his first-grade teacher that he was going to make books with pictures when he grew up. DePaola wrote and/or illustrated over 270 books, including *Strega Nona*, *Tomie dePaola's Mother Goose*, and *26 Fairmount Avenue*. He has been recognized with the Smithson Medal from the Smithsonian Institution and the Society of Illustrators Original Art Show Lifetime Achievement Award, and the American Library Association has honored him with the Caldecott Honor and Newbery Honor awards. As a painter and muralist, his works adorn many Catholic churches and monasteries in New England. In 1984, dePaola illustrated the Neiman Marcus Christmas catalog, and a year later, he was chosen to create both the American Book Awards poster and the Metropolitan Museum of Art advent calendar. He passed away in 2020 at age of 85. (Top left and bottom, courtesy of the *Record-Journal*; top right, courtesy of Penguin Random House LLC.)

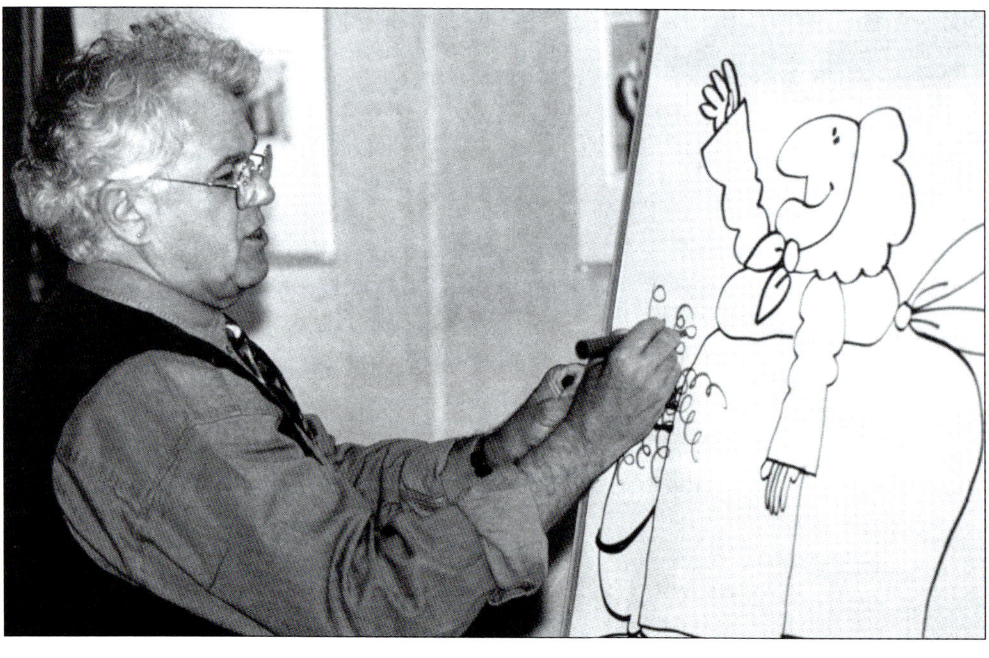

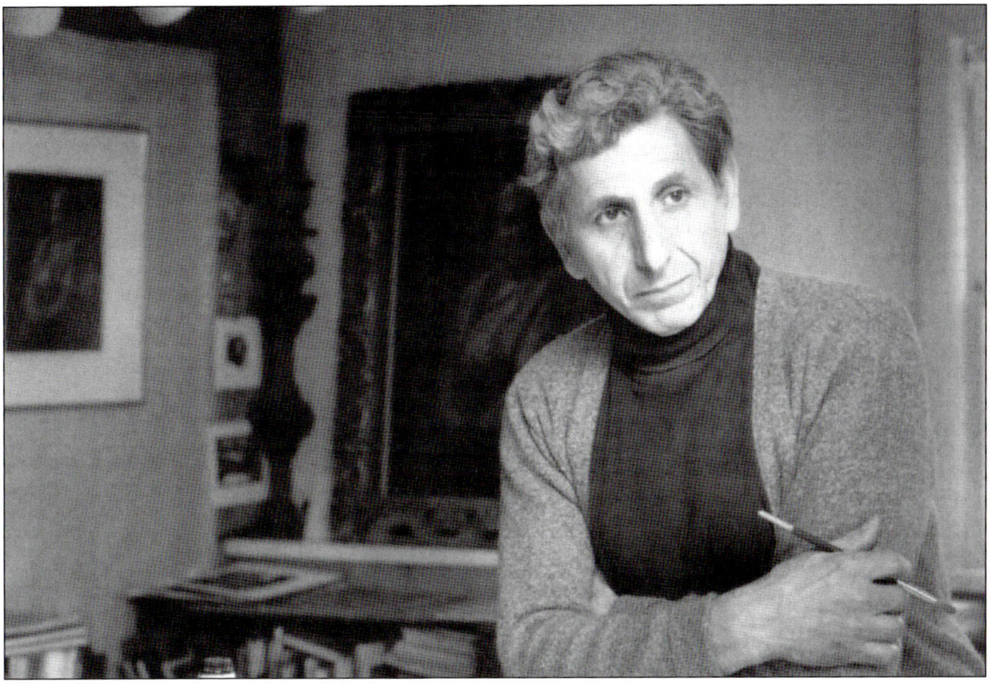

Nicholas Scalise. Nicholas Scalise was born in Meriden in 1932 during the height of the Depression. He received his art education at Horace C. Wilcox Technical School in Meriden and at Paier School of Art in Hamden, Connecticut, from which he graduated with honors. From 1959 to 1970, Scalise taught commercial art at the Famous Artists School in Westport, Connecticut. Scalise's artistic achievements earned him national recognition and his art can be found in public and private collections throughout the United States and abroad. He had exhibited in several one-man shows and was the recipient of many prestigious awards. Scalise died in 2009.

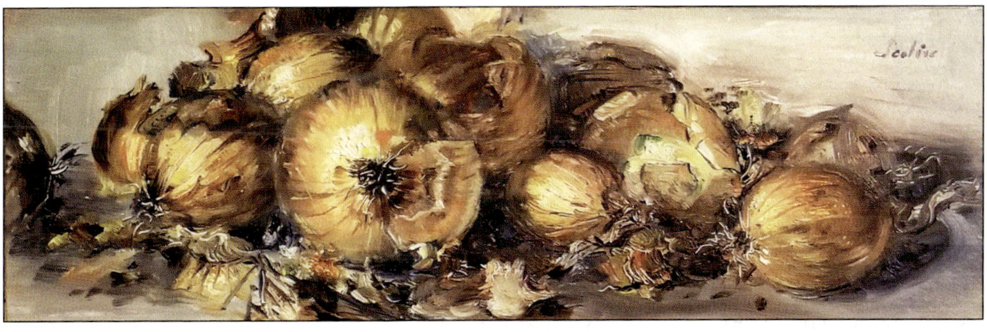

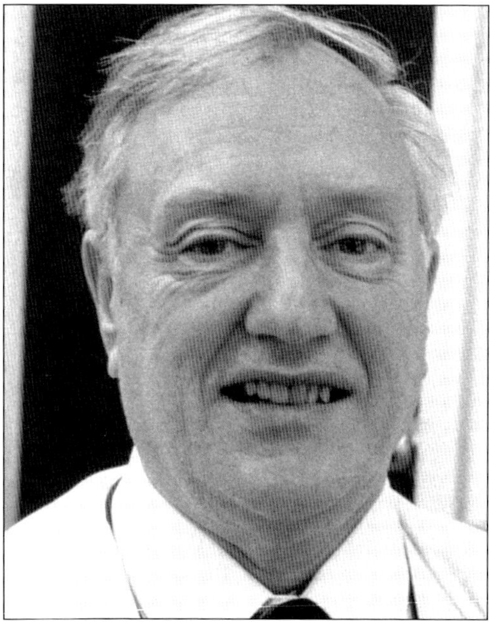

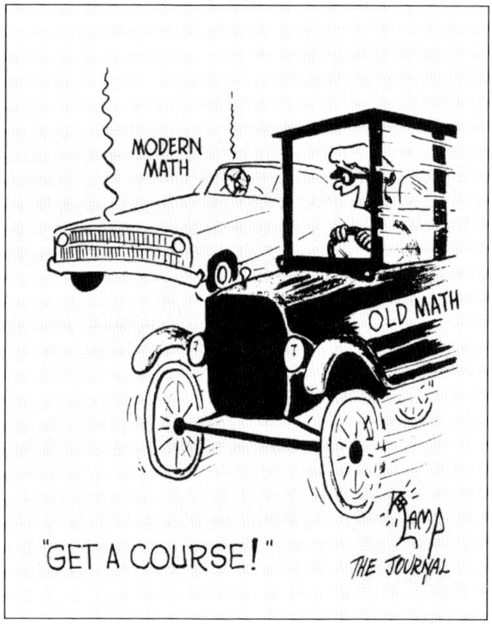

Frank Lamphier. Frank Lamphier sold his first cartoon to the *Providence Journal* at age 12. After his high school graduation and a successful stint in the military, he came to Meriden and made it his permanent home. Lamphier took the ornamental design class at Horace C. Wilcox Technical High School, studying under Ernst Lohrmann. In May 1947, the *Meriden Morning Record* published Lamphier's first editorial cartoon under the pen name of "Lamp." He continued as an editorial cartoonist for the rest of his life, creating about 10,000 cartoons. In 1974, his editorial cartoon on "modern math" was included in the book *The Best 100 Cartoons of the Year.* Through the years, Lamphier's work has appeared in magazines, books, and pamphlets, and he designed the logos of the world champion Connecticut Falcons women's professional softball team and of the Antique Veterans World Post No. 1 of Meriden. He drew two editorial cartoons each week for the *Record-Journal* until his passing in 2010.

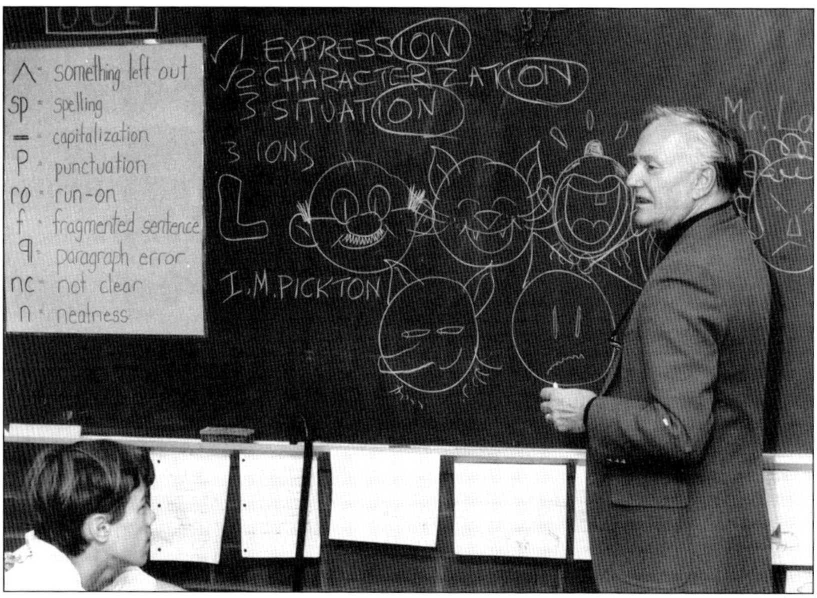

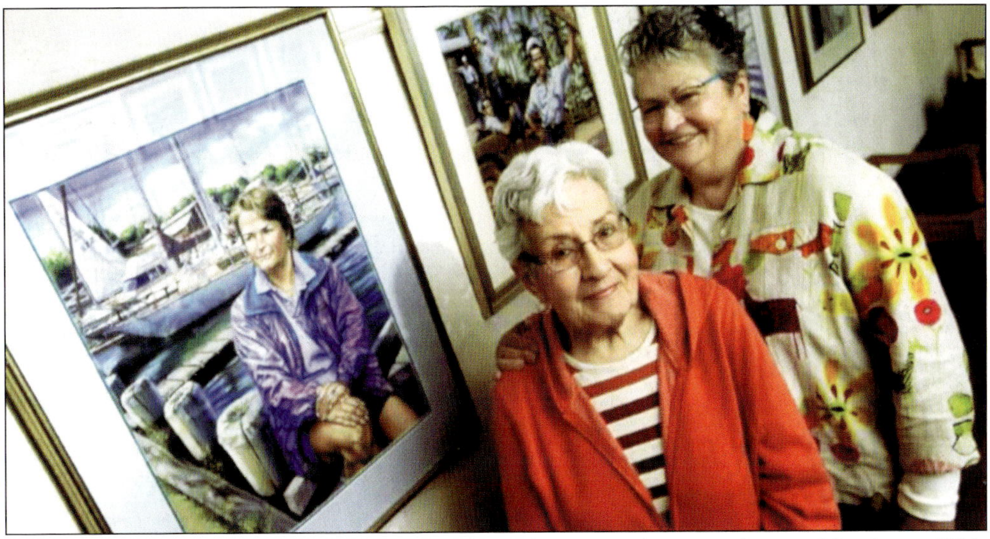

Ellie Bender. Ellie Bender, seen here with daughter Christine Webster, was born in Meriden in 1928. She attended Meriden schools and graduated from the Art School of Fashion in Hartford, Connecticut. She later studied oil and watercolor painting at the Hartford Art School. For over 35 years, she was employed in the fashion industry as a commercial artist, specializing in fashion illustration. Her love for art and a changing job market led her to take portraiture and pastel classes with the nationally renowned Claudia Post, after which she embarked on a new career as a portrait artist and educator. Bender is active in Meriden's arts community and is a signature member of the Connecticut Pastel Society and Gallery 53, formerly known as the Arts and Crafts Association of Meriden. She has earned over 125 national and regional awards, and her pastel portraits and landscapes have been exhibited in galleries in Connecticut, New York, and Massachusetts.

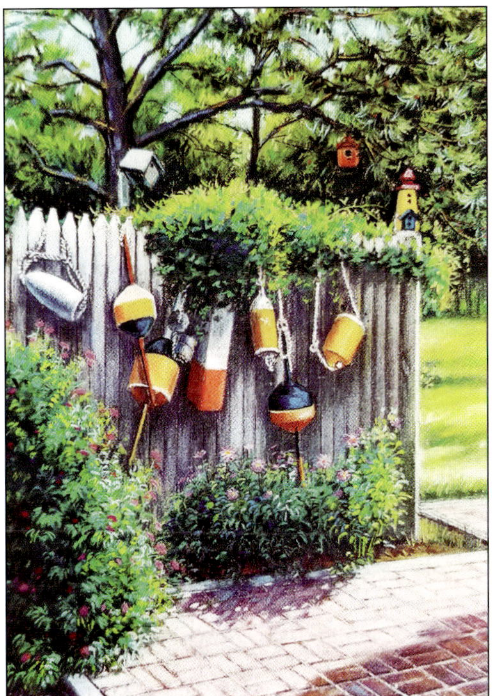

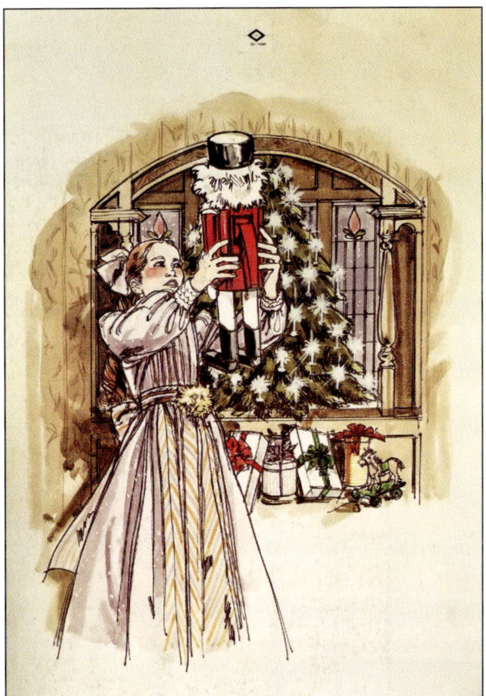

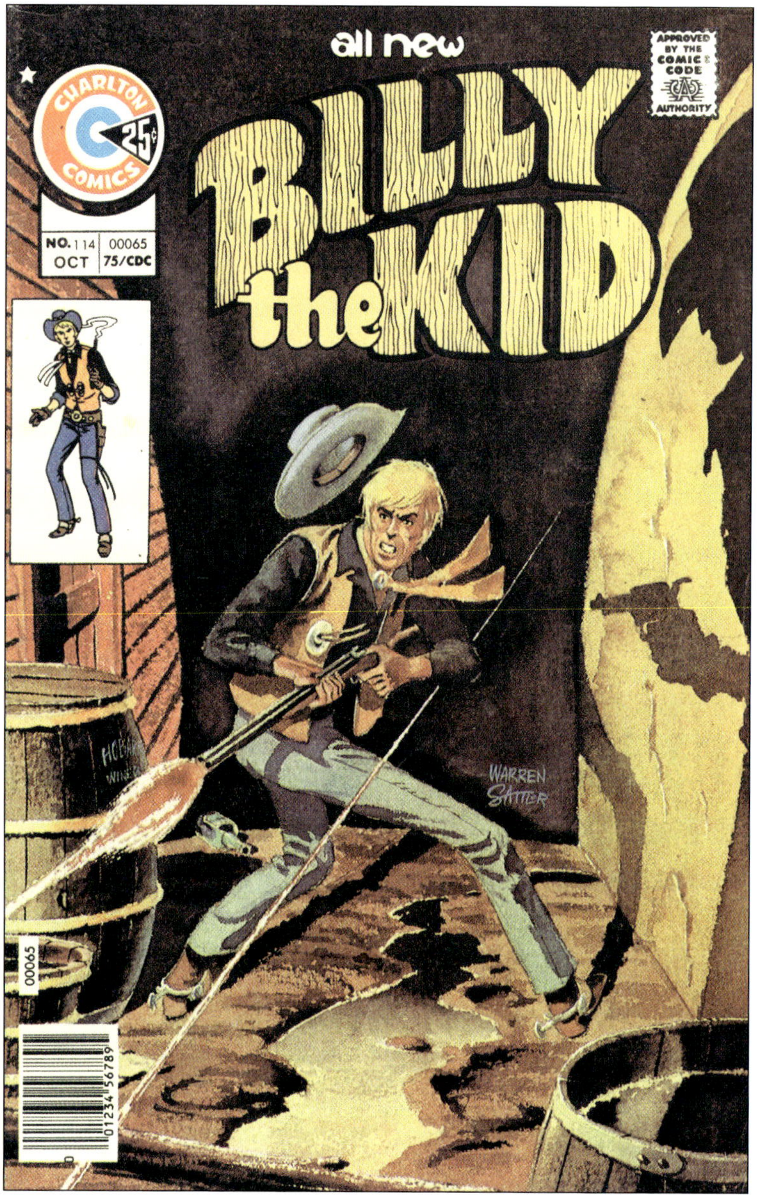

WARREN SATTLER. Warren Sattler was born on September 7, 1934. As a cartoonist, he contributed to many popular publications from the early 1960s through the 1990s. A lifelong Meriden resident, Sattler began drawing cartoons at an early age and was first published at age 15. He later taught at the Famous Artists School from 1957 to 1962, and in the 1960s, he assisted on the comic strips *Barnaby* and *The Jackson Twins*. Sattler also drew comics that appeared in *Help* magazine under the direction of Harvey Kurtzman. His own strip, *Grubby*, ran from 1964 to 1997. In the 1970s, Sattler produced art for comic books, particularly for Charlton Comics, including titles *Billy the Kid, Fightin' Army, Fightin' Marines, Ghostly Haunts,* and *Yang*. He illustrated for *Cracked* magazine, *National Lampoon*, and *Playboy*. Sattler created a second syndicated comic strip, *Swamp Brats*, in 1980 and ghosted on newspaper strips like *Bringing Up Father, Comics for Kids*, and *Gil Thorp* during the 1980s and 1990s. In 2003, he was inducted into the Meriden Hall of Fame in the category of art. (Courtesy of Warren Sattler.)

Seven

A Persevering Arts Community

The strength of the arts in Meriden has ebbed and flowed over the years, with periods of revival countered by economic hardship, global conflict, and waning community interest. But Meriden's arts community has remained steadfast, and its most committed individuals and organizations have maintained their dedication in keeping the arts alive.

As the 1960s drew to a close, Meriden's art scene was struggling with little community support. This reality was a hurdle to the revived Arts and Crafts Association of Meriden and its new goals of creating a gallery space, serving as a teaching residence, and supporting local artisans. The association determined that a physical presence in downtown Meriden could be a turning point for the arts. In 1981, under the leadership of then president Irma Peckham Morse, they purchased the building at 53 Colony Street, which also housed the century-old Butler Paint. This strategic and forward-thinking purchase fueled the association's campaign to reinvigorate the arts in the city. Rebranding itself as Gallery 53 after its new street address, the organization flourished, using its permanent space to increase its number of exhibitions, host frequent live art demonstrations, and offer community programs. It continued to attract and cultivate talented artists as member and exhibitors, building public awareness of artists with local, regional, and national notoriety.

Despite its successes, Gallery 53's enthusiastic work was challenged by the urbanization of Meriden in the 1980s and 1990s, which reduced traffic to downtown. In another strategic move, Gallery 53 spearheaded a collaborative effort to promote broad interest in the arts by partnering with the Meriden Symphony Orchestra to form the Meriden Arts Council in 1993. The council was active for more than 20 years, elevating a variety of art forms, including visual arts, theater, music, history, and recreation.

By the mid-2000s, Meriden's municipal leaders supported an arts revival in the city. They pinned their hopes on a revitalized downtown with a refurbished train station, a new city green and new residential spaces. The arts were a key element in this overall plan to breathe life into Meriden's city center, though momentum was stalled in 2020 by the global coronavirus pandemic.

Today's outlook for the arts in Meriden is bright. With a variety of art forms as diverse as its population, Meriden's innovative and talented artists continue to put the city on the map and keep the arts alive.

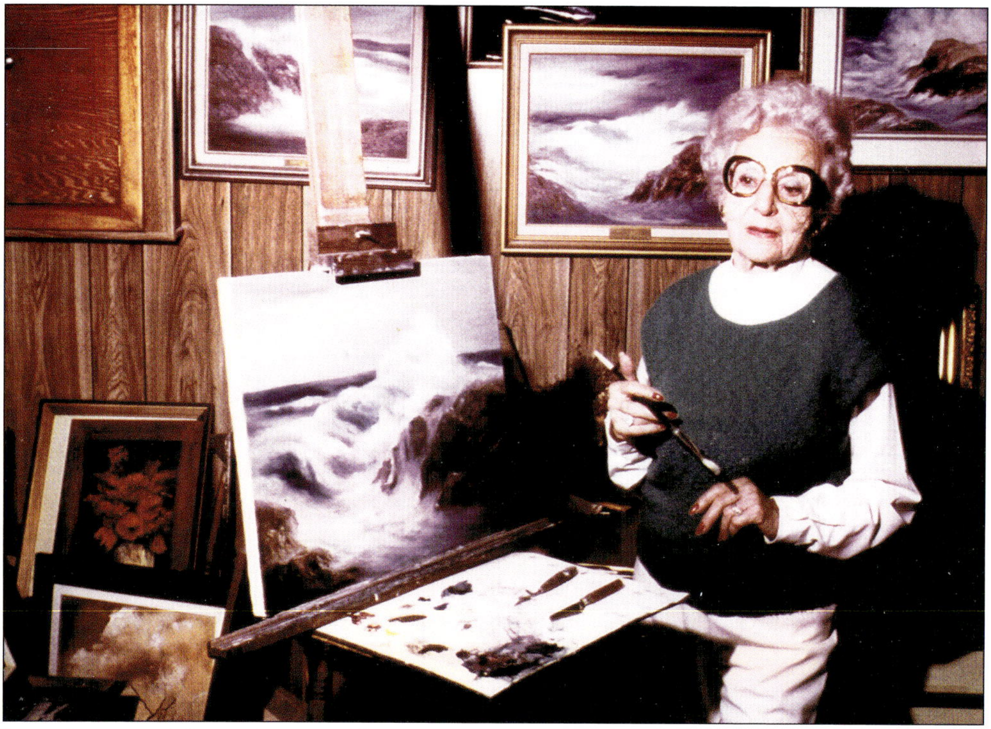

Irma Peckham Morse. Irma Peckham Morse was born in Middlefield, Connecticut, in 1907. Morse's first love was art, and after graduating from high school, she attended Pratt Institute in New York. She was the recipient of various local and regional awards for her paintings in oil, watercolor, acrylic, and pastel. She shared her talents with the community through teaching oil and watercolor classes at the Meriden Senior Center and art classes for local hospital patients for 17 years. She was active in the Arts and Crafts Association of Meriden for over 50 years and served in many capacities. Her leadership as president gave direction to the association after the purchase of its present home at 53 Colony Street. Morse died in 2000 in Meriden at the age of 92. (Both, courtesy of Diantha Morse.)

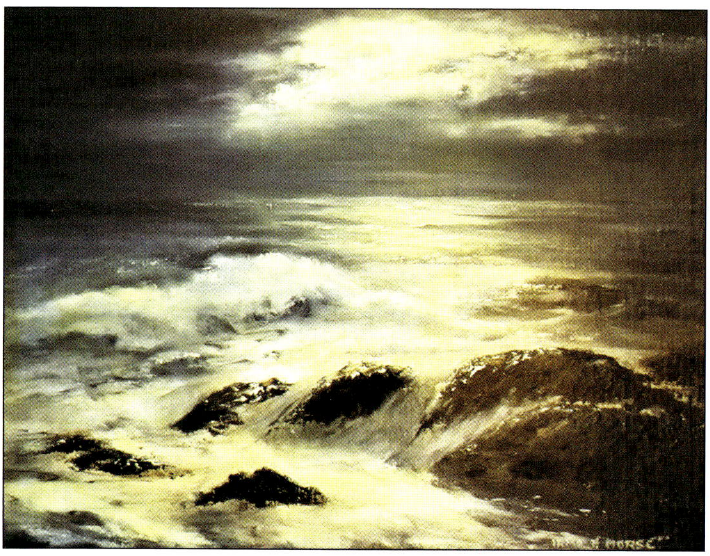

Meriden Artists in Retrospect Exhibition. In 1977, the Meriden Historical Society offered a unique exhibit featuring rare views of Meriden as created by the artists of the city's past. It spotlighted artwork from 40 men and women, pulled from private collections in and around the city. Meriden industry from around the turn of the 20th century was responsible for several of the talents represented in the show. This retrospective introduced a newer generation to the talented and renowned artists and artisans of Meriden.

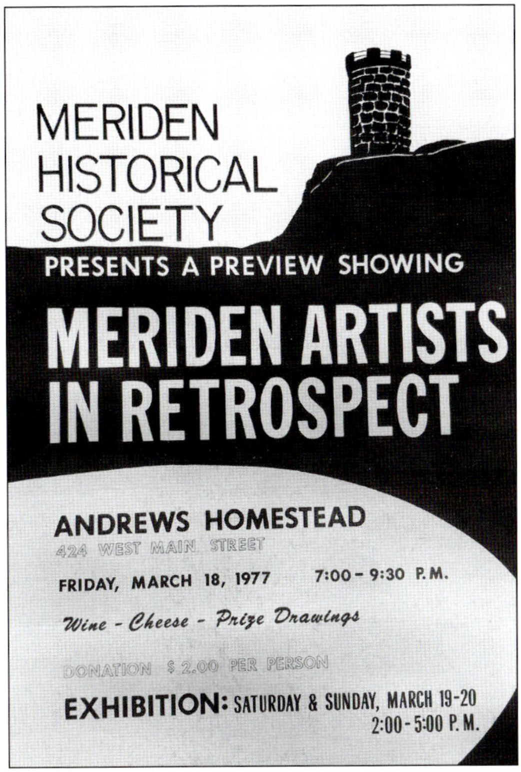

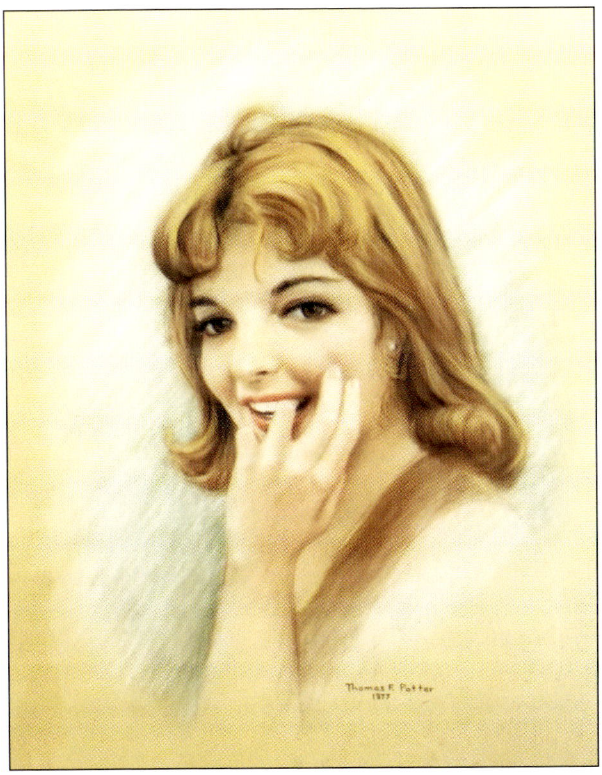

Thomas F. Potter. Thomas F. Potter earned degrees in art education and school administration, which led to his appointment as supervisor of art for the Meriden public schools in 1959. He served in that role until his retirement in 1987. For years, he was an avid painter in both oils and pastels. Potter was also a veteran of World War II, earning the rank of captain and receiving the Purple Heart after fighting in the Battle of the Bulge. Potter passed away in 2007. (Courtesy of the Meriden Historical Society.)

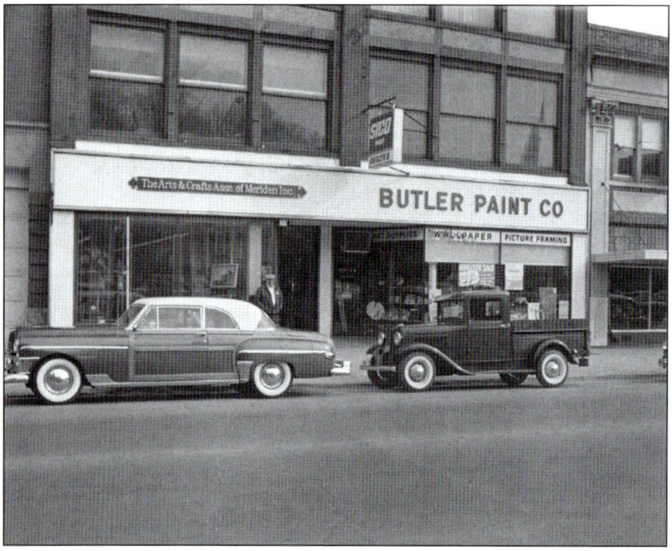

53 Colony Street. The Arts and Crafts Association of Meriden took a big yet strategic step in June 1981 when it purchased the building at 53 Colony Street as a permanent home. Association volunteers worked hard to make this goal a reality and did so with the vision of turning the building into an artist colony, complete with a school, gallery, repository for the association's permanent art collection, and a sales area for local artists.

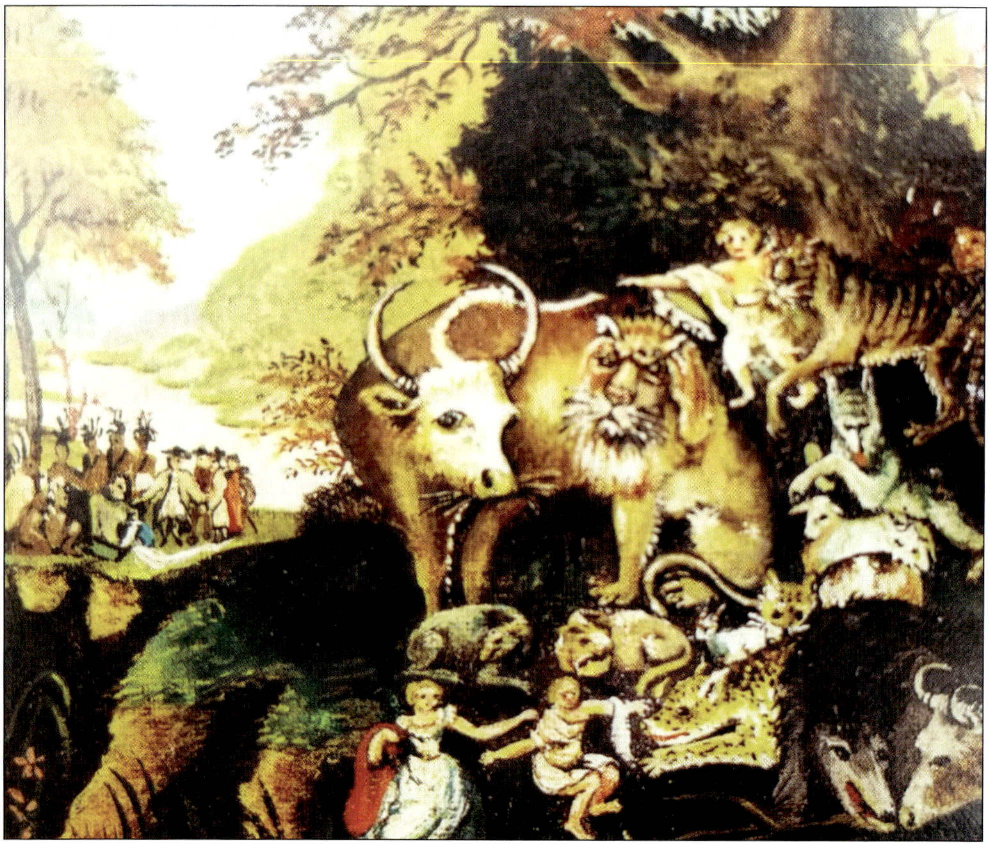

George Schlosser. After retiring as a corporate executive, George Schlosser launched a second career as a painter. He produced miniature paintings, which today are sought by collectors all over the world. During Christmas 1981, his scaled-down copies of five famous painting were displayed among the holiday decorations at the White House in Washington, DC. He was named a "fellow" by the International Guild of Miniature Artisans Ltd. in 1985 and died in 1994.

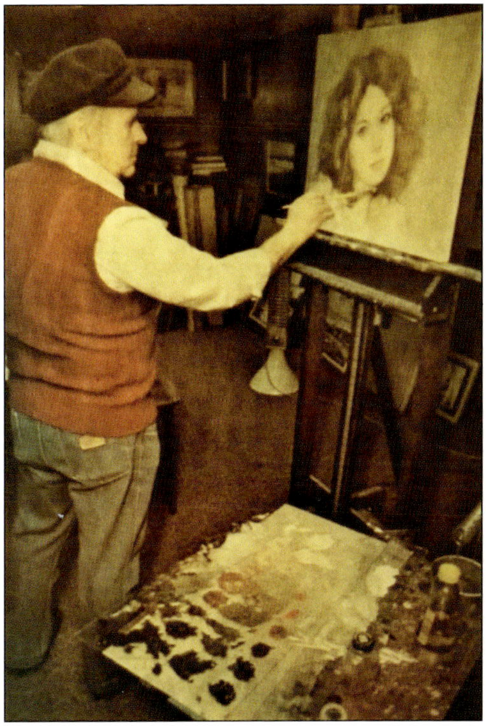

Earl Bushnell. Earl Bushnell was born in New London, Connecticut, in 1922. He moved to Meriden as a child, and his interest in art began at the age of 14. He was a self-taught artist and experimented with various mediums. He attended Horace C. Wilcox Technical School, learning the die-cutting trade, and later studied at the Art Students League in New York City. After serving in the US Coast Guard during World War II, he worked for the International Silver Company making ornamental dies. In 1952, he started the Jade Die Company and managed it until his retirement in 1979. Bushnell was a past president of the Arts and Crafts Association of Meriden and a member of several art associations. He exhibited extensively throughout the Northeast and won many awards. Bushnell died in 2006.

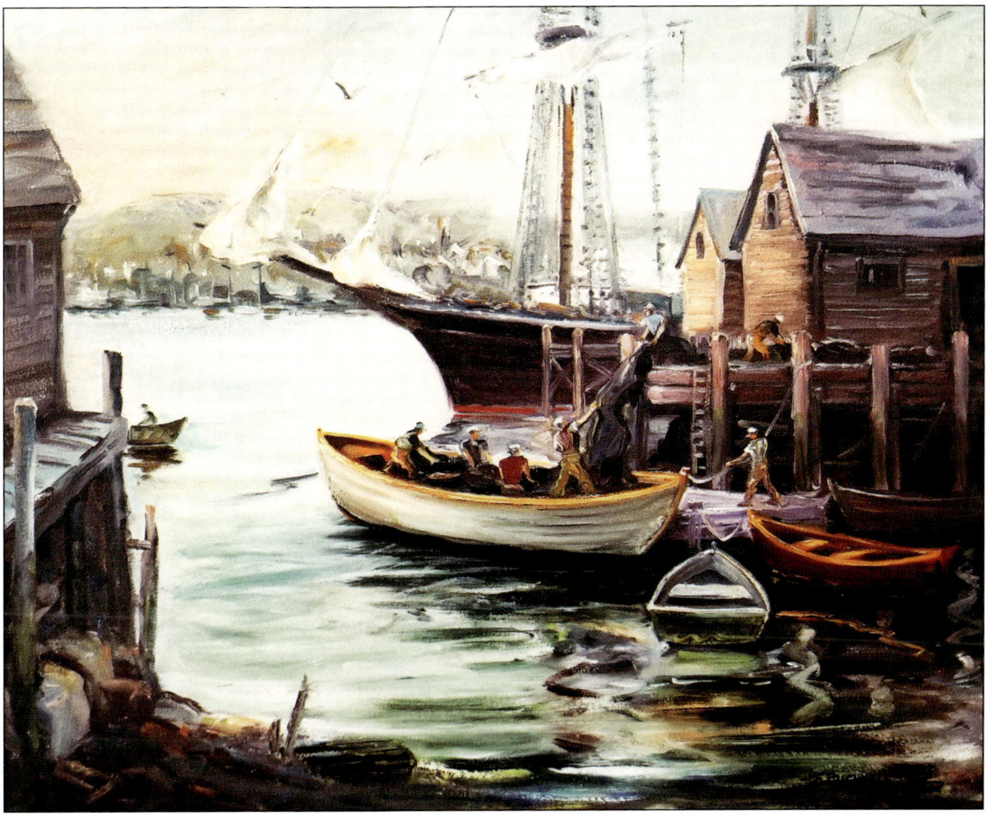

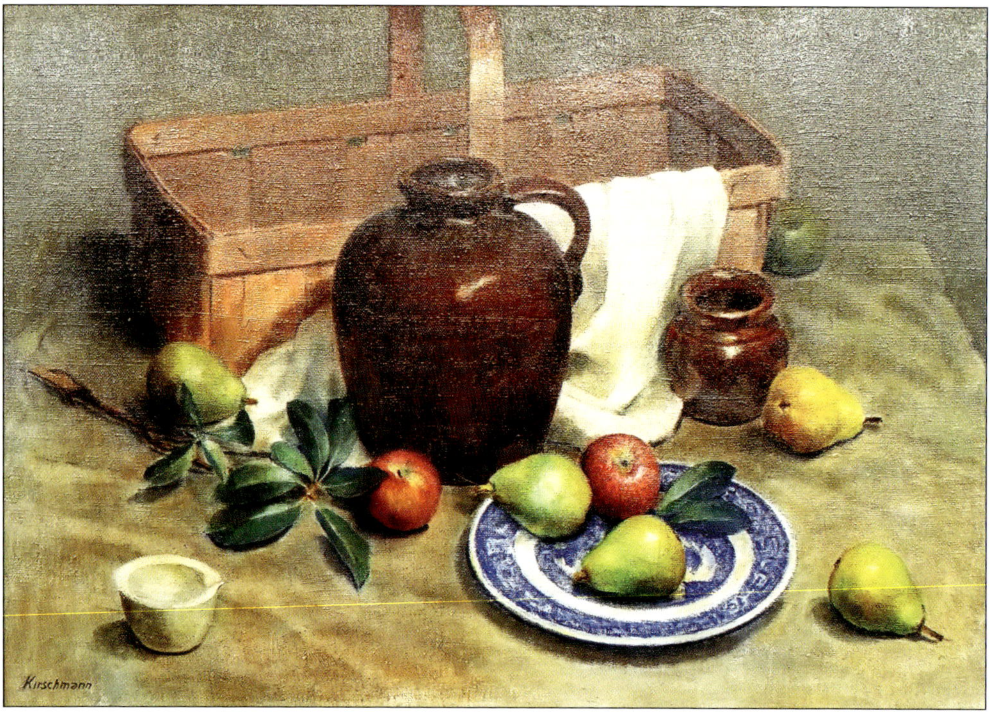

GEORGE KIRSCHMANN. George Kirschmann was born in Germany in 1914 and immigrated to America in 1925. He studied art with Robert Brackman, Emil Gruppe, and Ivan Olinski and painted many watercolor landscapes as well as oils and pastels of still-life subjects. Kirschmann was a full member of the Pastel Society of America and lived in Meriden and Naugatuck, Connecticut, eventually settling in Myrtle Beach, South Carolina, until his death in 2003.

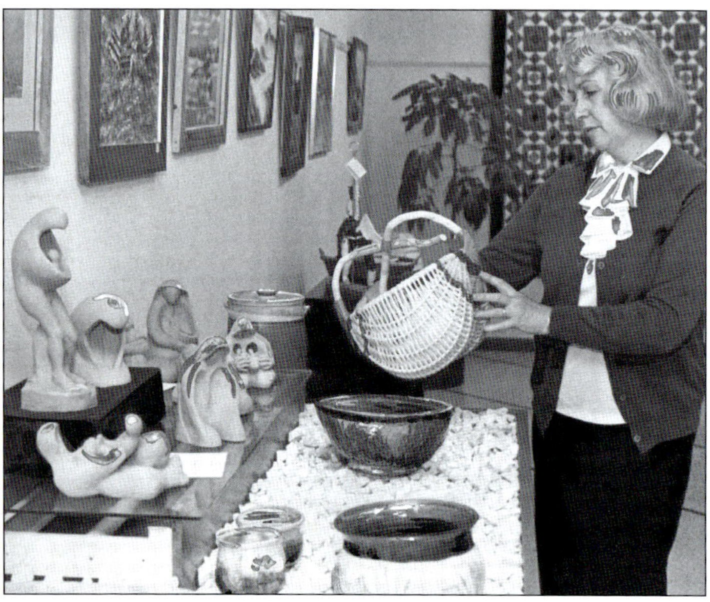

DOROTHY BUSHNELL. By the 20th century, the distinctions between fine art and "arts and crafts" were blurred; today, most art forms are considered "fine arts." Over the last century, the Arts and Crafts Association of Meriden has juried each medium separately in its annual exhibitions. Here, Dorothy Bushnell, wife of painter Earl Bushnell, looks over a table of fine artisan work of a variety of mediums. (Courtesy of Gallery 53.)

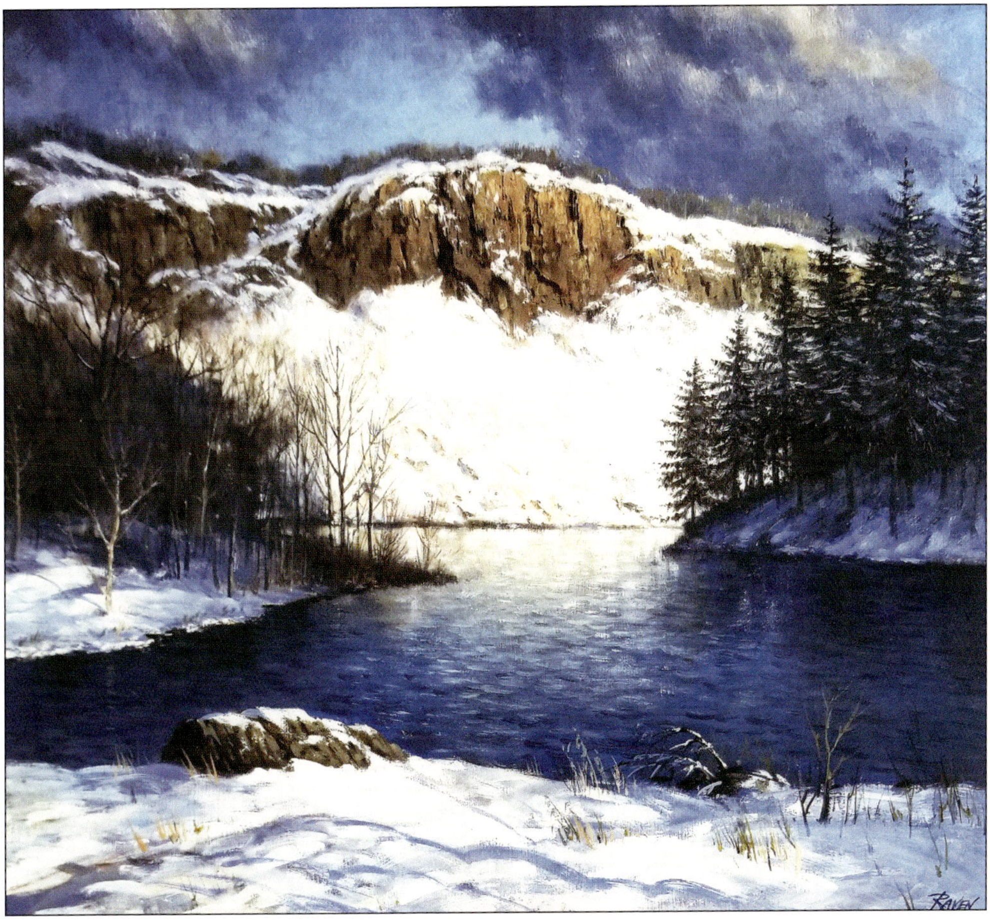

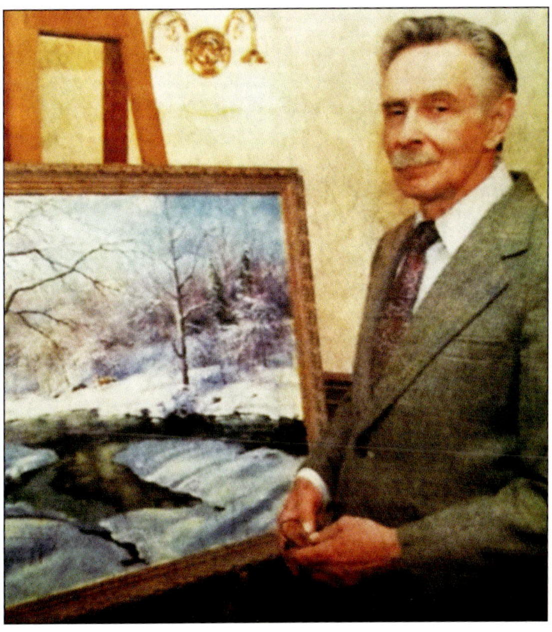

BRUCE RAVEN. John Bruce Raven, later known by his middle name, was born in Meriden in 1929. He attended Meriden schools and continued his education at the Hartford Art School in Connecticut and at the Instituto Allende in San Miguel, Mexico. Raven returned to Meriden and was employed in advertising and illustration for over 30 years, which included painting murals for residential and commercial venues. He also found employment as an interior decorator. Raven was very involved with the Arts and Crafts Association of Meriden, holding various volunteer positions and teaching regular painting classes. He also taught classes at the Meriden Senior Center for many years. Today, Raven's paintings are in public, private, and museum collections across the country. Raven died in 2009.

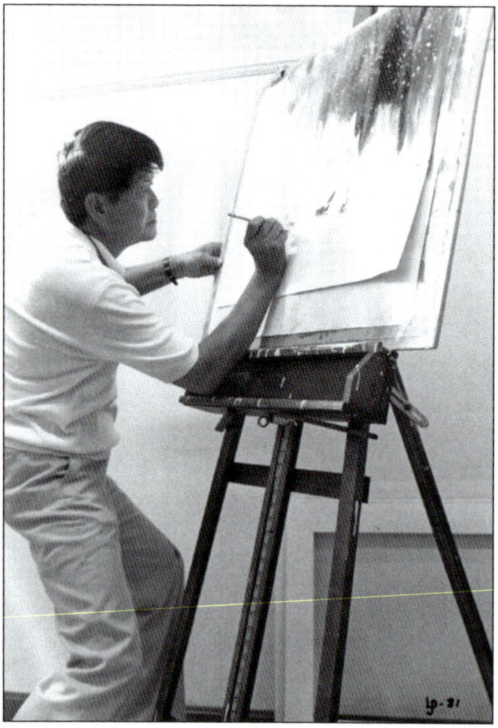

Chien Fei Chiang. A third-generation artist, Chien Fei Chiang was born in China in 1928 and received a degree from Taiwan Normal University Department of Fine Arts. He taught in Taiwan before coming to America in 1967. He worked at the Meriden Gravure Company for 20 years before retiring in 1986 to focus on his art. Chien Fei Chang is recognized in the *Who's Who in American Art*. He passed away in 2011. (Courtesy of Gallery 53.)

Doe Bartlett. Doe Bartlett graduated from Massachusetts Art School in 1949 and later studied throughout Connecticut. She taught art in Meriden schools and was the resident art teacher at the Meriden Senior Center for many years. Bartlett is a past president of the Arts and Crafts Association of Meriden, a former vice president of the New Haven Paint & Clay Club, and is widely represented in collections throughout the Northeast and Florida. (Courtesy of the Meriden Historical Society.)

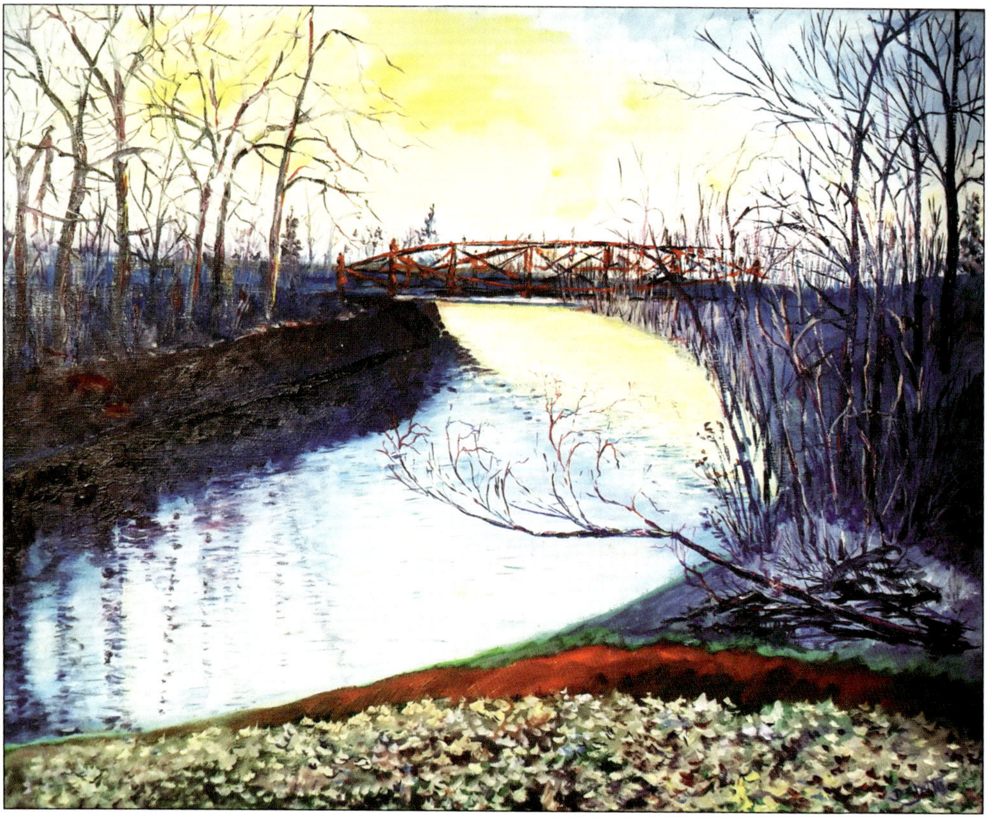

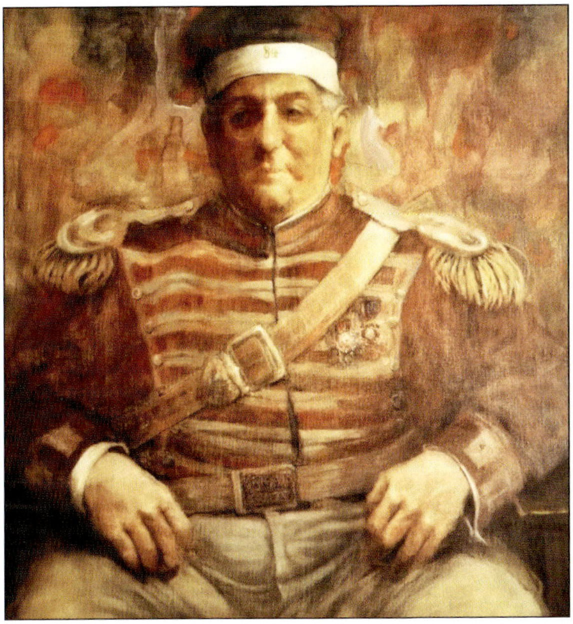

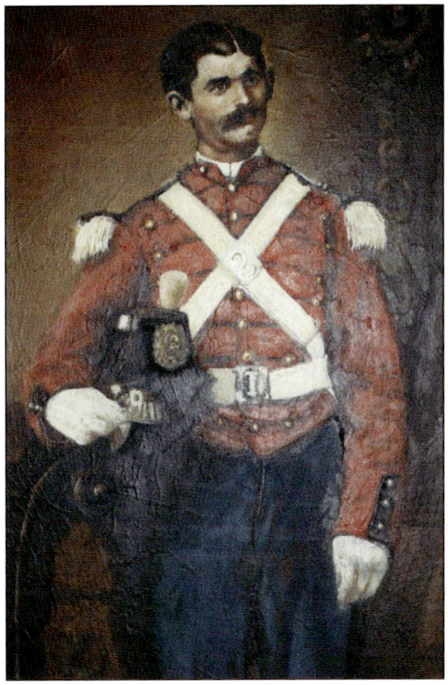

Sara Cambria. Sara Cambria was born in Brooklyn, New York, in 1916. After her schooling, she studied art at the Leonardo da Vinci Art School and also spent time at Valley College in California. Cambria was employed by New Departure in Meriden and later as a designer at Rockwell Silver Company. As an artist, she often sought out unorthodox subjects to paint and, similarly, peculiar surfaces to paint on such as flat rocks and dried fruits. She was a member of the Arts and Crafts Association of Meriden and the New Haven Paint & Clay Club and was a prominent artist who exhibited widely throughout New England. Her work is in many private collections and museums throughout the area, such as the New Britain Museum of American Art in New Britain and the Mattatuck Museum in Waterbury, Connecticut. Cambria died in 2007. (All, courtesy of Sherwin Borsuk.)

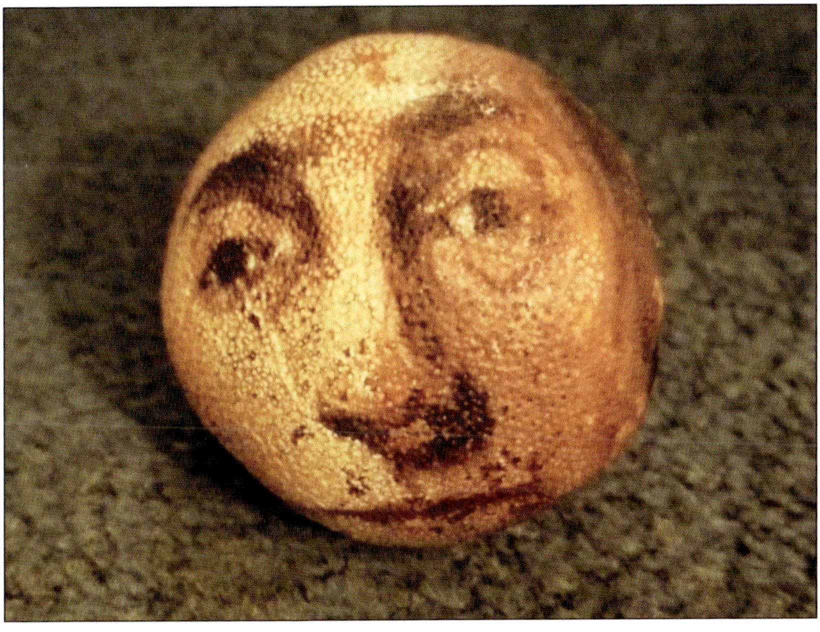

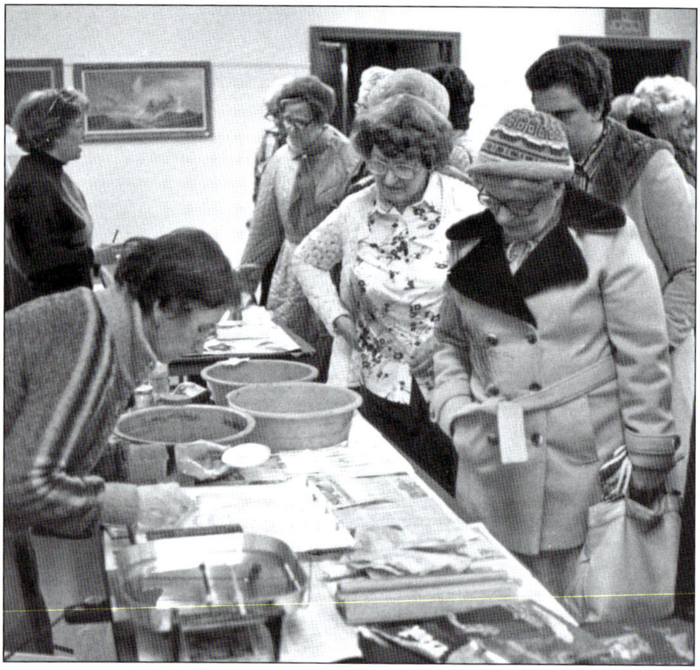

GALLEY 53 ART DEMONSTRATIONS. For years, Gallery 53 hosted a regular monthly series of workshops and art demonstrations led by key members of the organization. These free community presentations and live demonstrations highlighted the artists' influences, their techniques and processes, and their works. Unfortunately, due to the disrespect of incoming public onlookers, the community demonstrations were discontinued. (Courtesy of Gallery 53.)

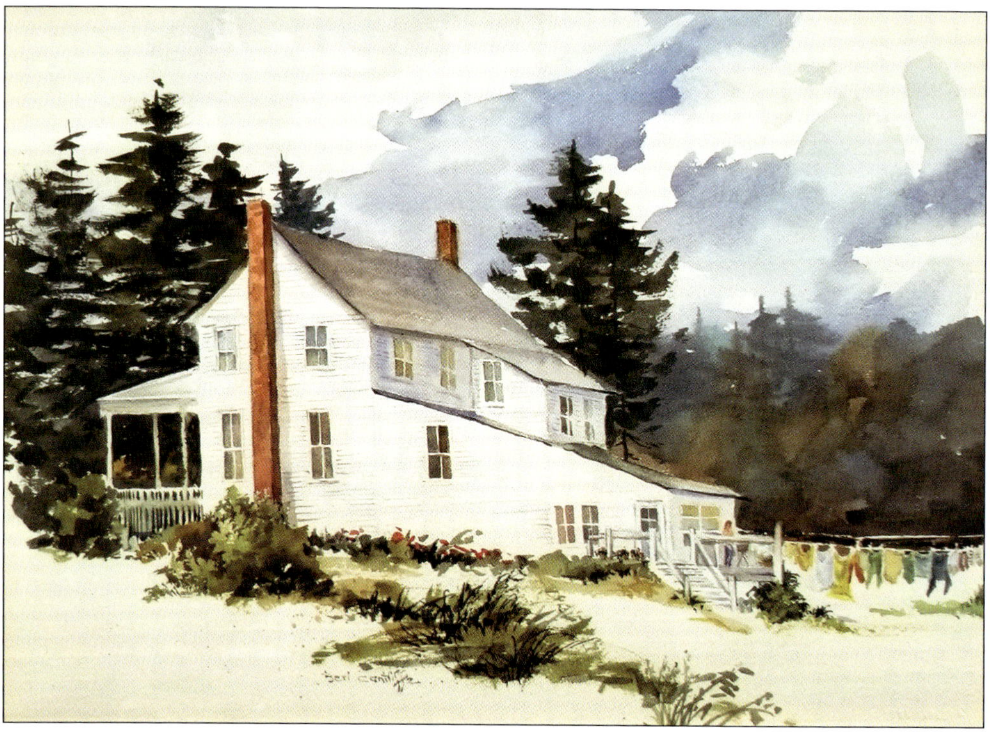

JERRI CANTLIFFE. Jeri Cantliffe was born in North Carolina in 1927. After moving to Meriden several years later, she earned her degree in art education from Wesleyan University in Middletown, Connecticut, and then studied at the Paier School of Art in Hamden, Connecticut. In addition to her private art students, Cantliffe taught in the state technical school system. Her personal work hangs in private collections around the world. Cantliffe died in 2019.

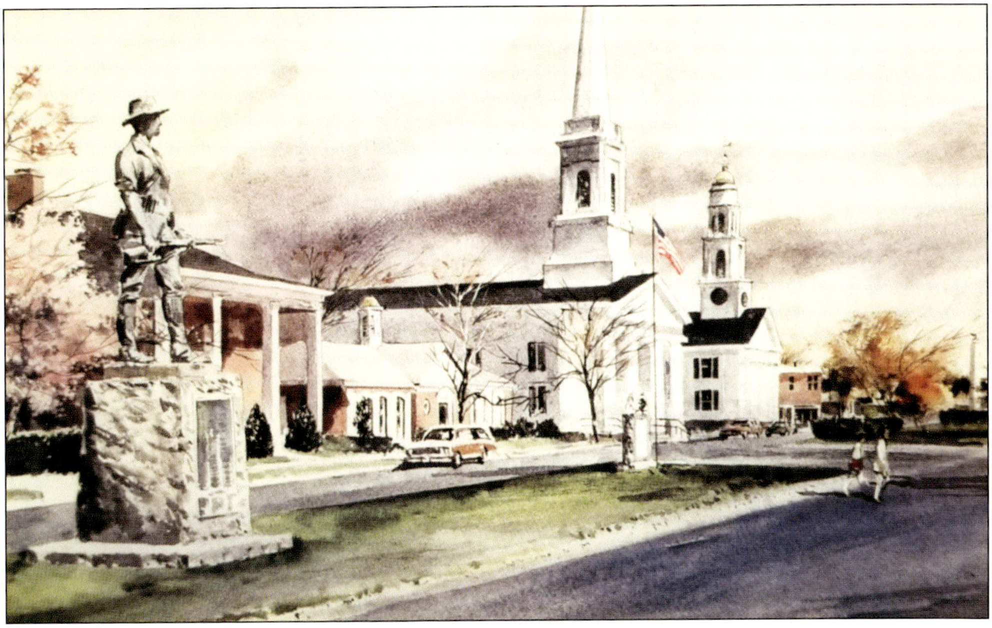

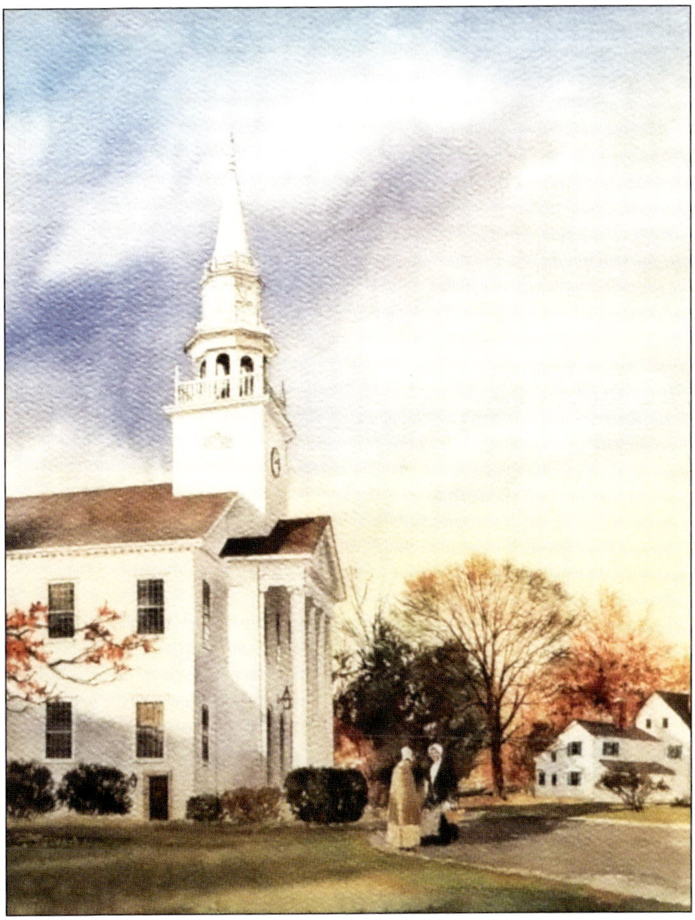

John Neff. A graduate of Whitney School of Art in New Haven, Connecticut, John Neff was a well-known watercolor artist. He was born in Pennsylvania in 1926, and shortly after, his family moved to Connecticut. Neff's artwork focused on landscapes, historic homes, and maritime scenes. He was particularly interested in whiskey painting, a technique in which the artist mixes paint with liquor. He is represented in many museum collections, including the Smithsonian Institution in Washington, DC. Neff is listed in the *Who's Who of American Art* and was a member of the American Watercolor Society and of the Whiskey Painters of America. Neff died in 2017. (Both, courtesy of the Meriden Historical Society.)

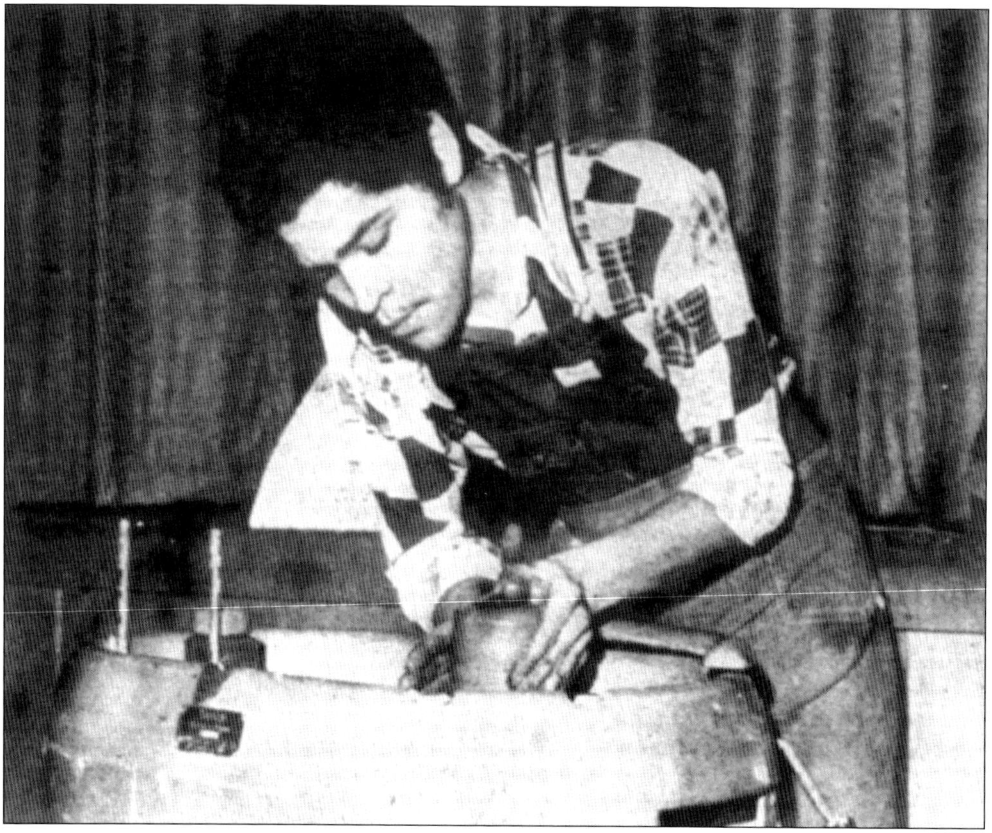

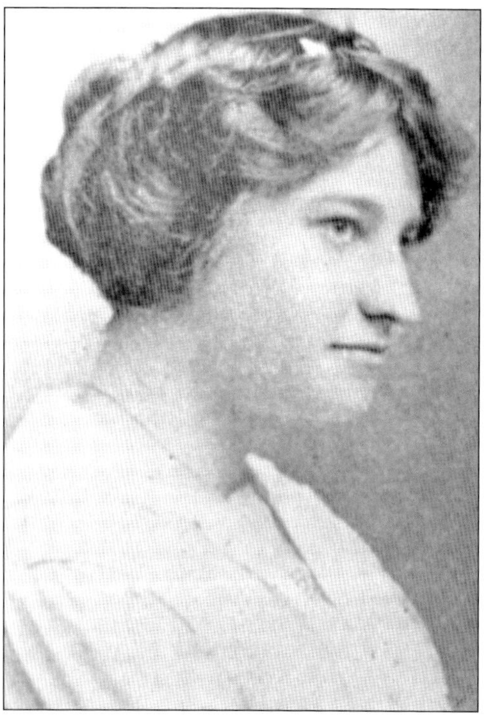

GARY O'NEIL. After his graduation from Maryland Institute's College of Art and further study in Mexico, Gary O'Neil began a nearly half-century career educating the art students of Meriden. In addition to his classroom teaching, O'Neil's professional art resume is equally impressive, exhibiting his clay and hand-building pieces widely from Cape Cod to Mexico and teaching with the Wesleyan Potters of Middletown. (Courtesy of the *Record-Journal*.)

ANNE RETTENMEYER. Anne Rettenmeyer was one of Meriden's most distinguished citizens and greatest art benefactors. Born in Meriden in 1897, Rettenmeyer was surrounded by an artistic family. Her father, Emil Koffinke, was a successful wood carver, and her husband, Frederick, was an accomplished painter and sculptor. Rettenmeyer was a poet and published two books of original verse and was a generous supporter and donor to the Arts and Crafts Association of Meriden. She passed away in 1984.

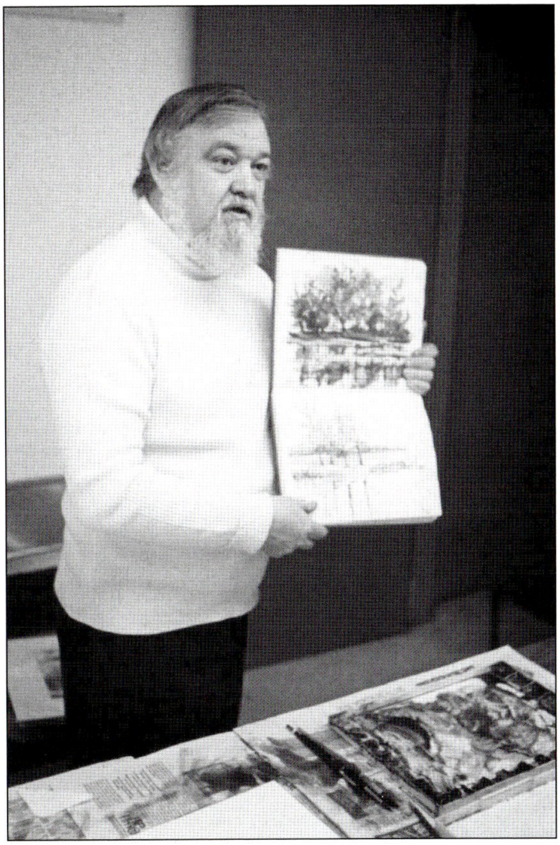

Stuart Grandy. Stuart Grandy was born in Meriden in 1932. He studied commercial advertising at the New England School of Art in Boston, Massachusetts, for three years before serving in the US Army during the Korean War for three years. Upon his return, Grandy continued studying and took private art lessons with such notables as Don Stone and Harry Ballinger. He was most known for his landscapes in watercolor. He was associated with a number of organizations, such as the Arts and Crafts Association of Meriden, the Essex Art Association, the North Shore Arts Association, the Connecticut Pastel Society, and the Connecticut Watercolor Society. In 1990, Grandy received the esteemed DeWitt Brevard Memorial Watercolor Award. Stuart Grandy died in 2014.

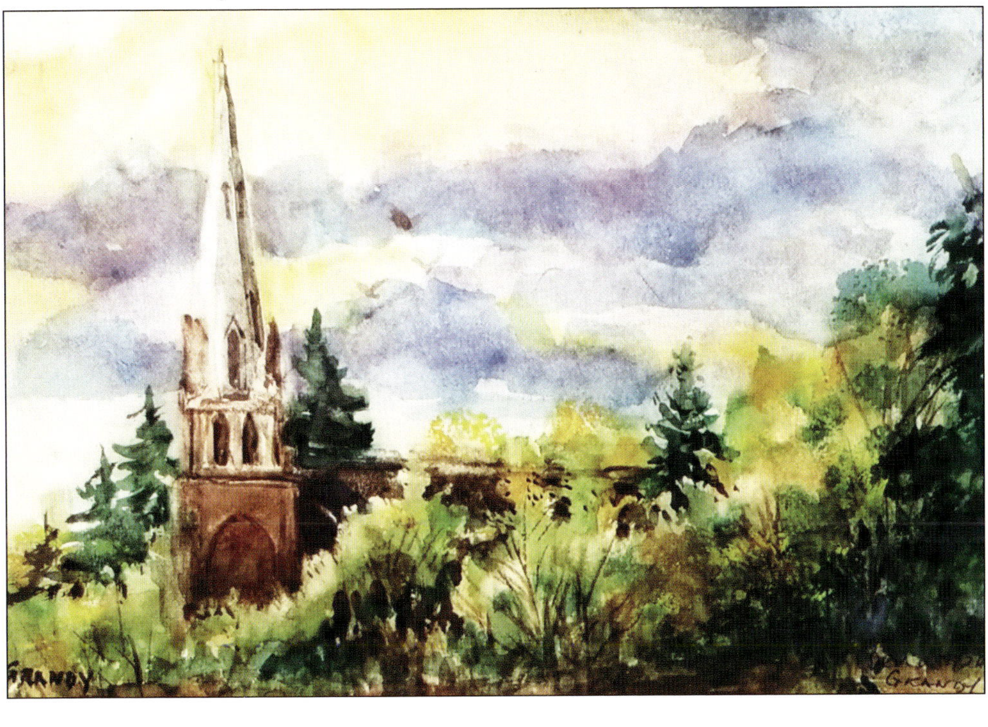

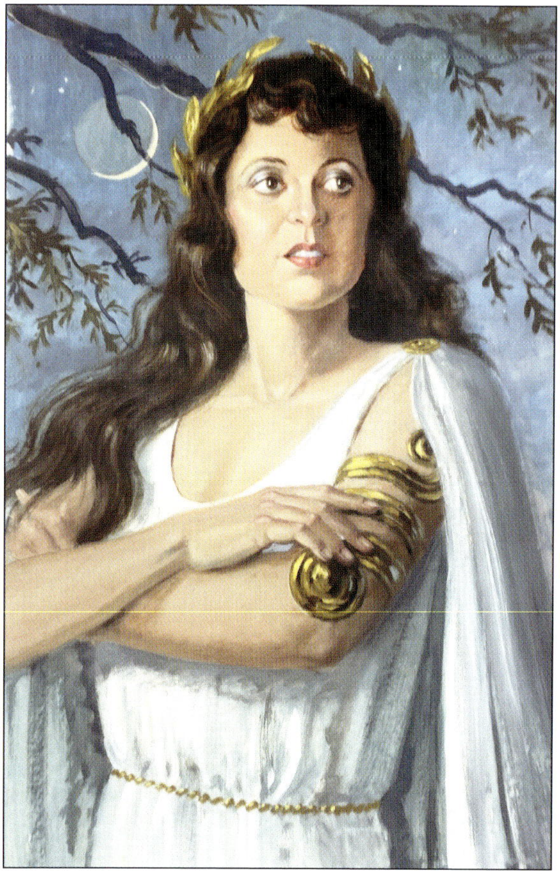

PAINTING OF ROSA PONSELLE. In early 1987, John Bruce Raven embarked upon one of his most endearing projects, a portrait of Meriden's own Rosa Ponselle, one of the greatest sopranos of the 20th century. Based upon a black-and-white still photograph from her classic role in the opera *Norma*, this oil-on-canvas was commissioned to hang in the Augusta Curtis Cultural Center in Meriden. (Courtesy of the Meriden Historical Society.)

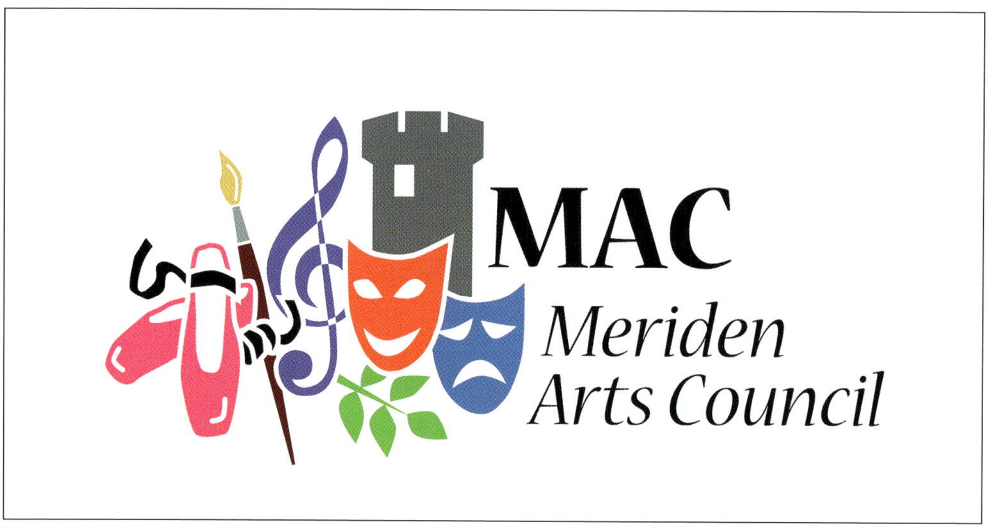

INTRODUCTION OF THE MERIDEN ART COUNCIL. In the late 1980s, local artisans of all disciplines were eager for an alternative, community-based art group. In February 1993, Gallery 53 and the Meriden Symphony Orchestra joined together to present two shows, the first steps in a collaboration that resulted in the formation of the Meriden Arts Council. The council remained a staple in Meriden's art landscape for over 20 years, unifying artists, musicians, actors and actresses, and dancers.

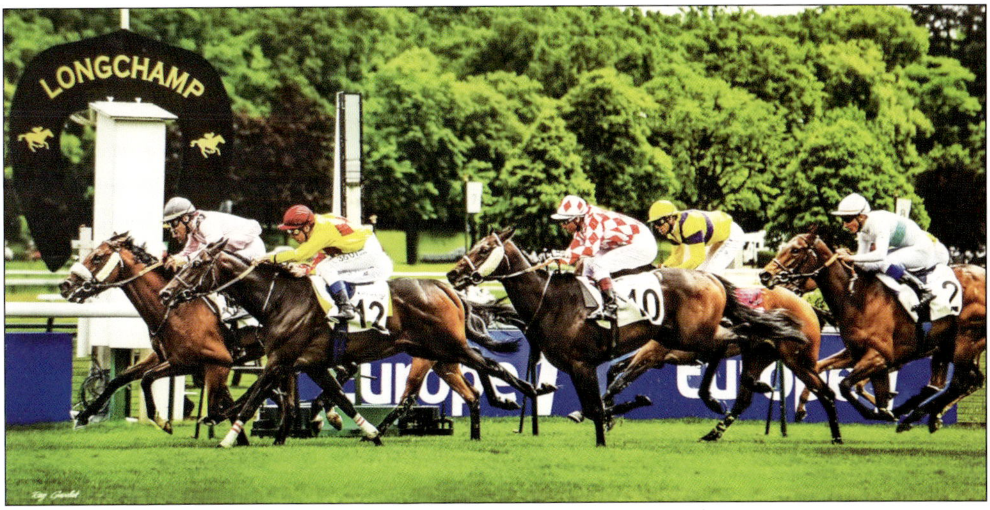

RAY GAWLAK. Photographer Ray Gawlak has traveled the world over to capture some of its most beautiful landscapes. After a brief six-year teaching stint in the early 1960s, Gawlak began working for the Meriden newspapers, where he contributed sports photography. In 1968, Gawlak, established locally as a cameraman, opened and successfully ran his own photography studio, which he maintained for decades. (Courtesy of Gallery 53.)

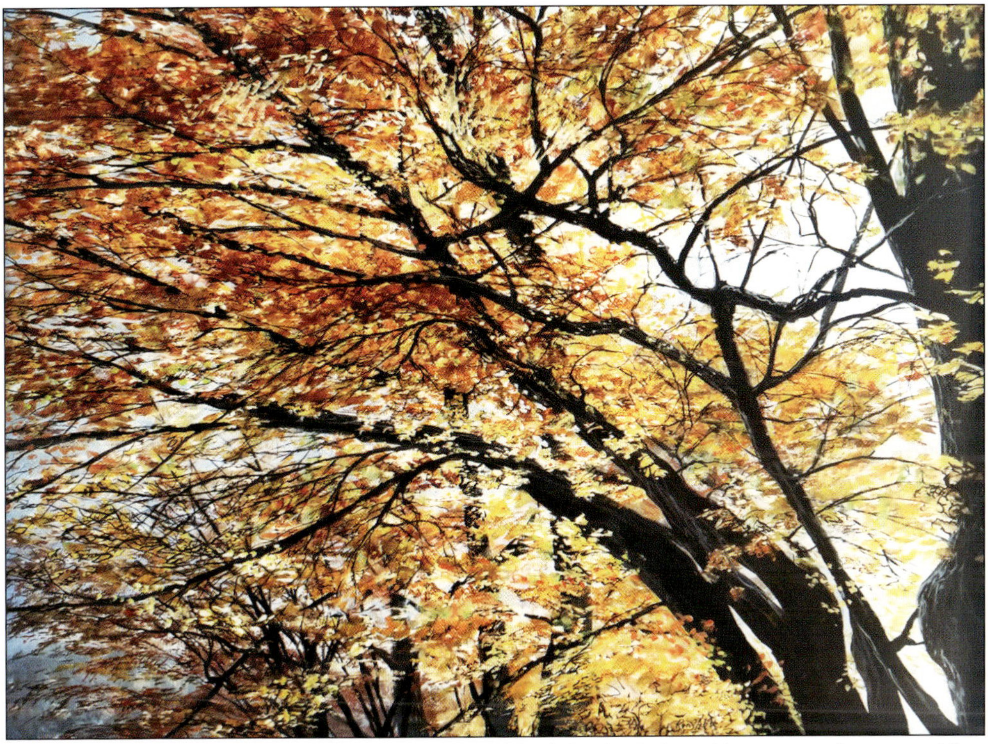

RONALD ABBE. Meriden artist Ronald Abbe earned both his bachelor of fine arts and master of fine arts degrees from the School of the Art Institute of Chicago. Working in oil, watercolor, or pastel, Abbe strikes a balance between realism and abstraction through his use of a signature paint-layering technique that draws the viewer into the details. Abbe has exhibited throughout the region and country but finds most of his inspiration in the quiet pockets of nature throughout Connecticut.

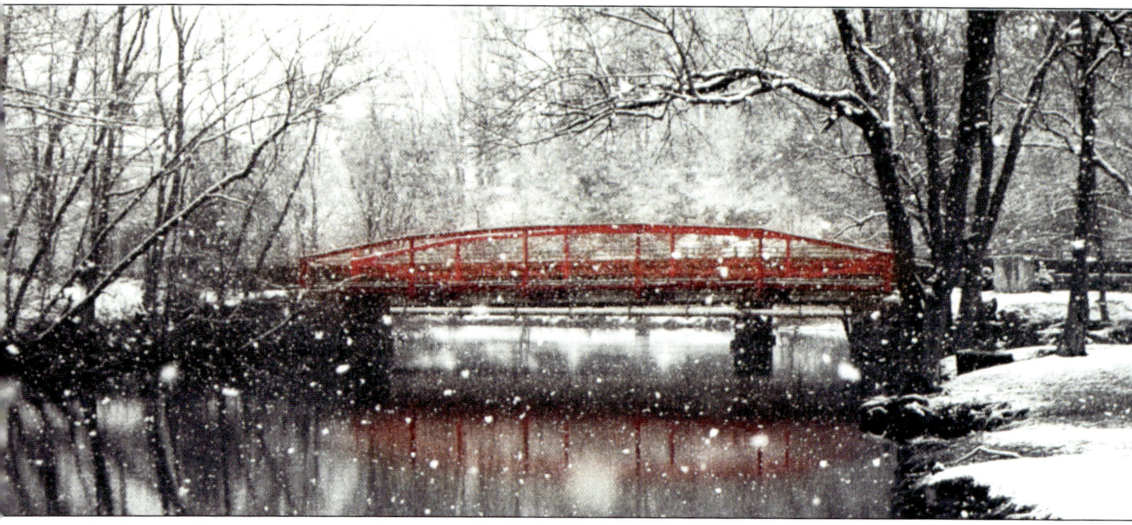

PETER WNEK. Meriden-born photographer Peter Wnek graduated from the Rhode Island School of Photography and quickly set out upon a freelance and commercial career in the field. His versatility as a photographer is demonstrated in his range of skill, spanning from the altered and image-composite photographs of the digital realm to the more ethereal, romantic feeling of nature and the natural landscape. Inspired by the Hudson Valley River School of painting, each of Wnek's photographic compositions strives for similar attributes: purity, innocence, light, and details. "I am looking for the charm of yesteryear," he once said. (Courtesy of Peter Wnek.)

Igor Karpov. Russian-born artist Igor Karpov graduated from the St. Petersburg Fine Arts School in 1987, where he specialized in drawing and the rendering of landscapes. Since 1990, he has lived and worked in Montreal, Canada, and Meriden. Karpov's choice of media includes both oil and gouache. Today, his works can be found in the Heritage Art Gallery in St. Petersburg and in private collections in Sweden, Israel, Germany, Belgium, Canada, and the United States.

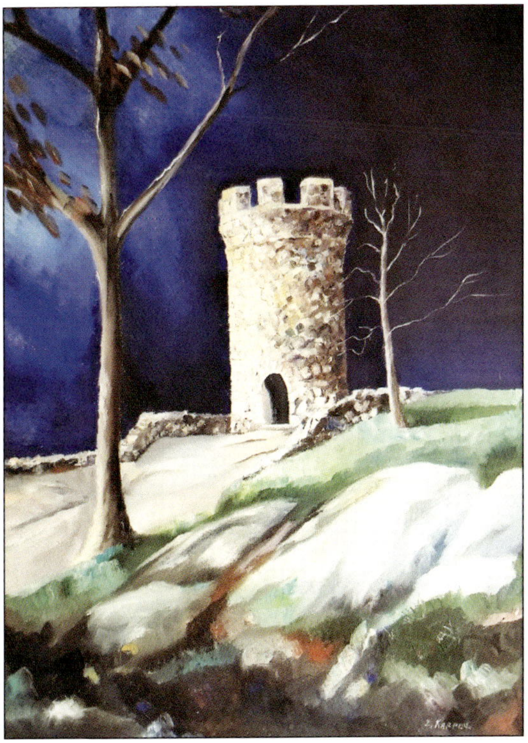

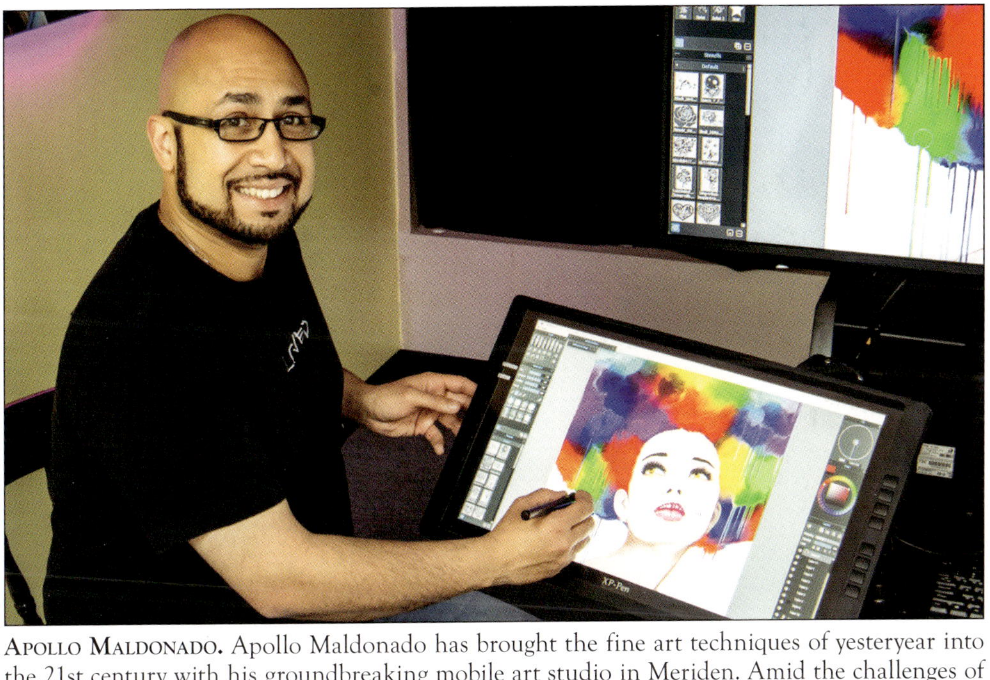

Apollo Maldonado. Apollo Maldonado has brought the fine art techniques of yesteryear into the 21st century with his groundbreaking mobile art studio in Meriden. Amid the challenges of the COVID-19 pandemic, Maldonado refurbished an old school bus and converted it into a fully functional digital art lab. This traveling lab provides the flexibility and capability to teach the masses of today. He remains active in Meriden's art community and is a highly sought-after artisan. (Courtesy of David Emmett Cooley.)

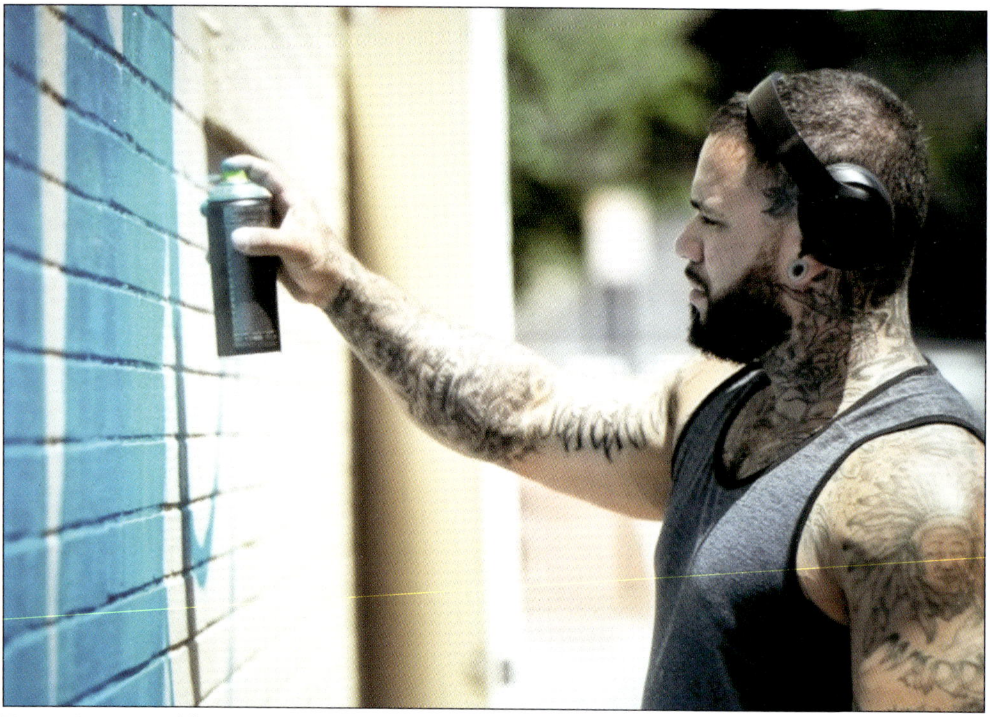

Eddie Rivera. Eddie Rivera moved to Meriden from Puerto Rico at an early age. With interests in hair design, music, and art, Rivera is an inspiration to many local artisans. Aside from his personal artistic merits, he has organized community-based endeavors, including multiple group efforts to help beautify Meriden's downtown. Rivera continues to mentor aspiring artists in Meriden. (Courtesy of the *Record-Journal.*)

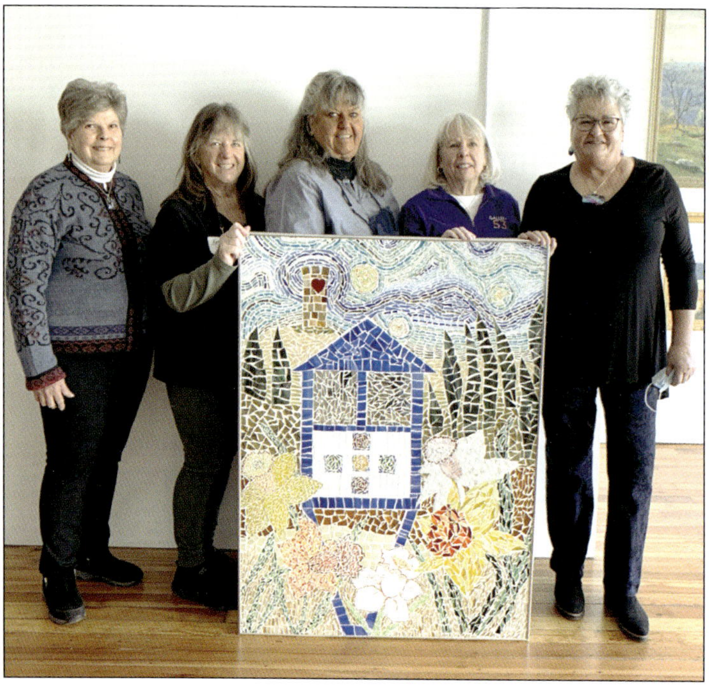

Raise the Roof. Soon after the COVID-19 pandemic shut down the world, Gallery 53—formerly the Arts and Crafts Association of Meriden—learned that its building was in desperate need of a new roof. This costly venture inspired "Raise the Roof," a campaign to raise the funds needed to replace the roof of 53 Colony Street. In this 2020 photograph, the gallery's Mosaic Magic Team poses with one of its large-scale stained-glass mosaics that would be sold to benefit the campaign. (Courtesy of Gallery 53.)

Eight

Beyond the Borders

Meriden has attracted the interest of a number of renown artists in the last two centuries. Some visited for projects based in the city, others designed art or manufactured pieces for local businesses and institutions, and others came seeking inspiration from the breathtaking, naturally built landscapes.

The Hanging Hills, a range of traprock hills to the west, and other mountains in the area have attracted the attention of artists for their graceful abruptness and boldness as they tower over the city. Printmaker and publisher John Warner Barber was perhaps one of the first nonlocal artists to depict Meriden's surrounding mountains in his engravings of the Broad Street churches and Cathole Pass, published in his 1836 book *Connecticut Historical Collections*. Nelson Augustus Moore, George Edward Candee, and Richard Benson are among other artists who later drew inspiration from Meriden's traprock ridges.

The city's booming manufacturing industry during the 19th and 20th centuries—particularly the silver companies—attracted big-name artists to design signature pieces. The Meriden Britannia Company commissioned nonlocals for a multitude of endeavors, including German-born sculptor Theodore Baur, who created *Buffalo Hunt*, the company's signature display piece at the 1876 Centennial International Exposition in Philadelphia. The International Silver Company also engaged outside talent like *Saturday Evening Post* artist Ben Stahl for its highly rendered advertising promotions.

Although he did not live in Meriden nor depict it, painter Emile Gruppe was extremely influential to the tradition of Meriden art. Gruppe lived in Gloucester, Massachusetts, and developed a unique bond with the Arts and Crafts Association of Meriden, visiting multiple times over decades to give live demonstrations. In return, association members made annual trips to Rockport, Massachusetts, and other scenic seaside towns where they studied with Gruppe and other regional and national artisans. These inspirational meetings brought about an artistic shift for Meriden's local artists like Irma Peckham Morse and Earl Bushnell who began focusing on seascapes and water elements.

While Meriden has been home to a cadre of distinguished artists who achieved notoriety locally and elsewhere, out-of-town artists have also shaped the city's artistic tradition. Regardless of the duration of their Meriden connection, these artists have left a lasting impact on the local art history.

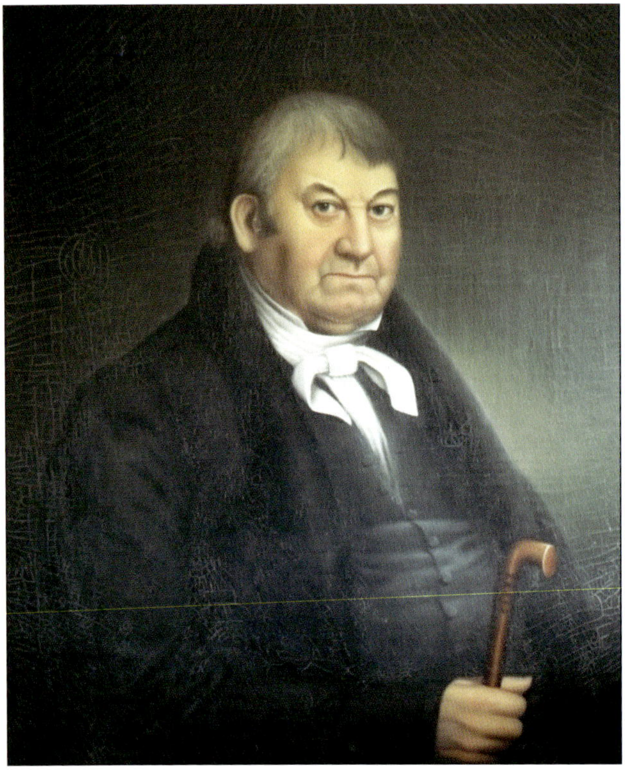

A. Patrick. As interest in American painting increased in the early 19th century, a number of outstanding painters emerged. One such artist, the relatively obscured artist A. Patrick, never received his proper recognition. These early-19th-century oil-on-canvas paintings of Meriden's John and Betsey Yale by Patrick demonstrate his artistic merits, particularly in his brush technique and his use of light and shadow. As a travelling artist, Patrick would have learned these skills on his own or from neighboring artists and then traveled from town to town seeking customers who wanted portraits. Other examples of Patrick's work, although limited, are in the Smithsonian American Art Museum in Washington, DC. (Both, courtesy of the Meriden Historical Society.)

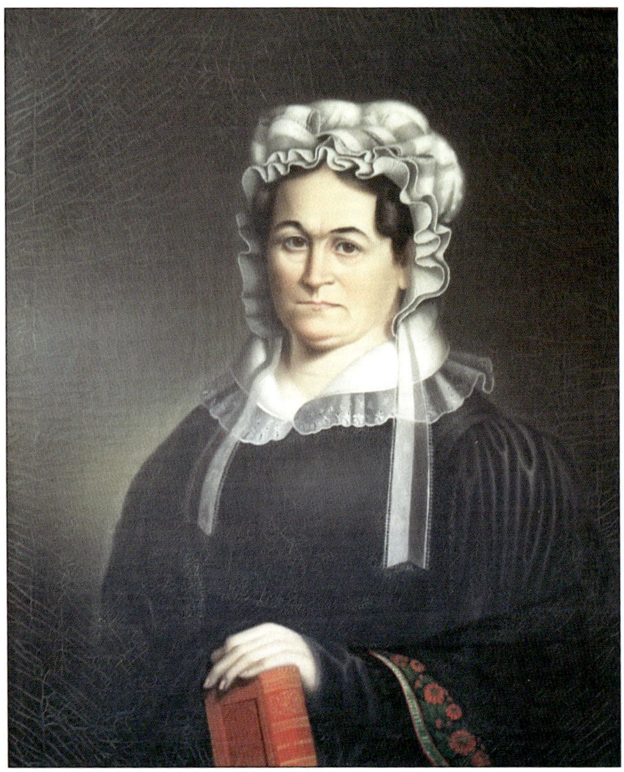

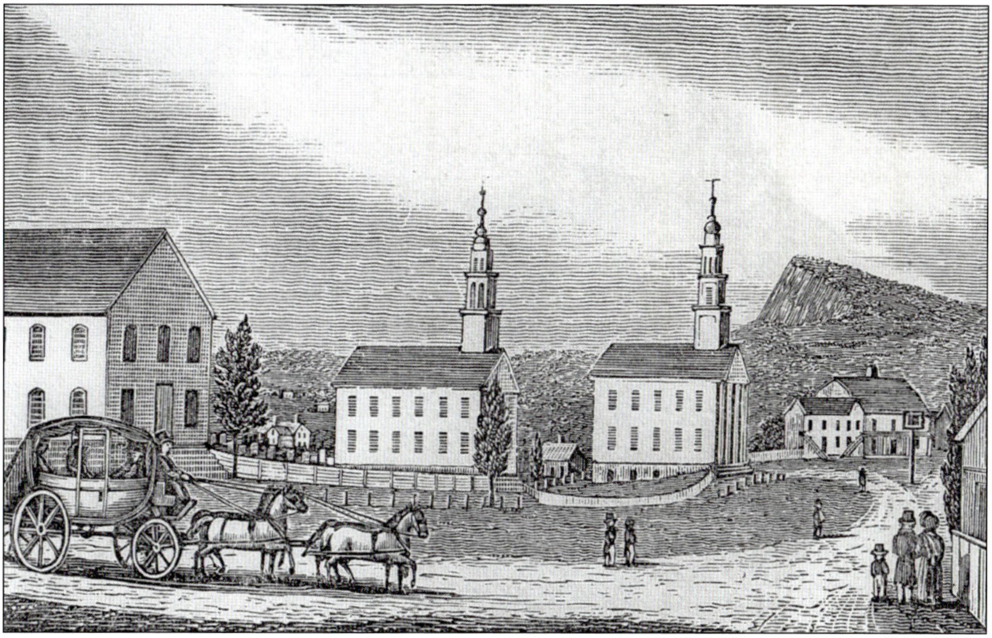

John Warner Barber. Born in 1798 in East Windsor, Connecticut, John Warner Barber was an artist, printmaker, author, and publisher. He studied with East Windsor printmaker Abner Reed before settling in New Haven in 1823. Although not a Meriden resident, Barber frequently visited Meriden. To prepare for his 1836 book *Historical Collections of Connecticut*, he traveled throughout the state to sketch characteristic buildings and views and collect information from local sources. He developed his rough pencil sketches into more detailed wash drawings, which were subsequently transferred directly to small blocks of boxwood, on which he engraved the designs. These wood engravings, including this c. 1836 southern view of the Meriden churches (above), were used to illustrate his 500-page book. The image below shows a young yet bustling Meriden just a few decades before the industrial boom transformed its downtown area. Barber died in 1885.

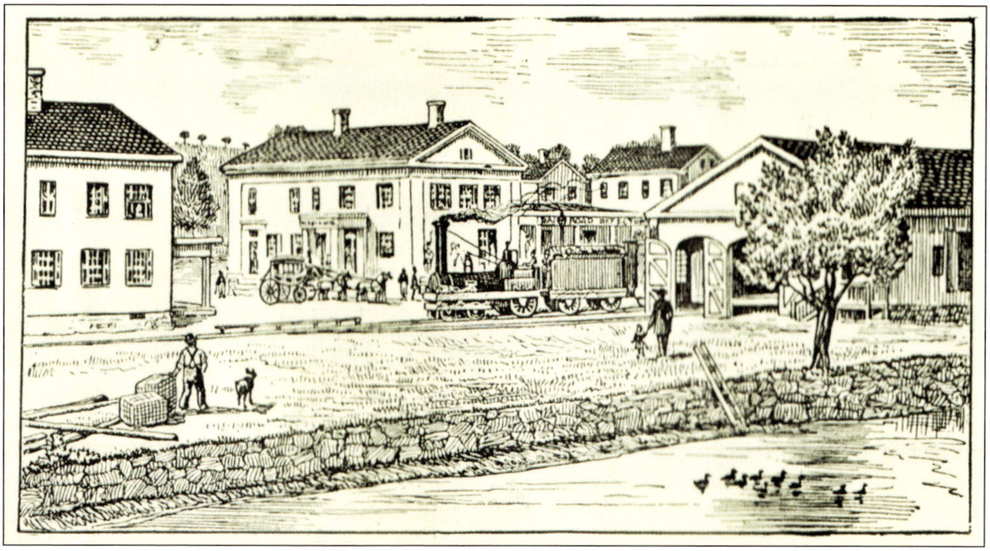

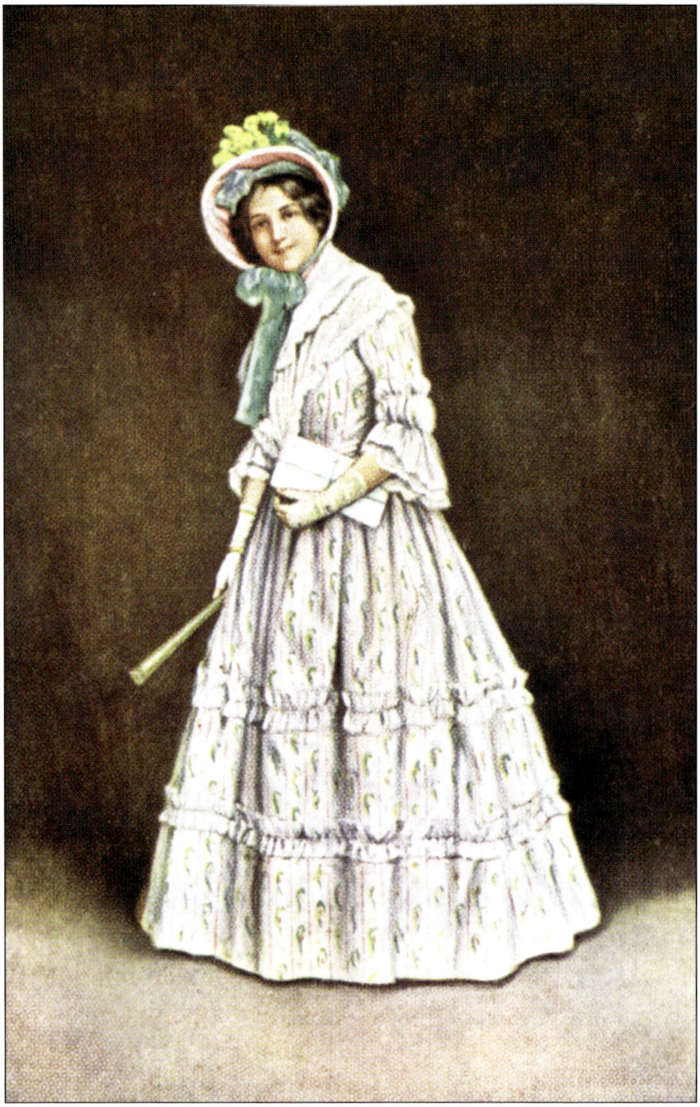

The 1847 Rogers Girl. Effective advertising requires creativity and imagination, two qualities that William G. Snow brought to the Meriden's silver industry. In 1899, Snow, advertising manager at the International Silver Company, visualized an advertisement featuring "an entrancing Miss who might lead purchasing multitudes to a promised land alight with silverplating." With the original photography of F.W. Kurtz of New York City, Snow's *1847 Rogers Girl* came to life to promote International's *1847 Rogers Brothers* line of plated silverware. In Meriden, Stella F. Brooks impersonated Snow's creation, sitting in the window of Fred Weber's jewelry store on Valentine's Day 1912. Soon, all across the nation, young ladies posed as the 1847 Rogers Girl in store windows, drawing flowery comments in local newspapers while also boosting product sales. As a result of Snow's creative advertising campaign, International broadened its artistic scope and entered in the costume business, distributing 1847 Rogers Girl costumes to department stores and organizations eager to put on an 1847 show. The Butterick Company of New York City was retained to make a complete set of costume patterns. During his last years at International, Snow resigned as advertising director but remained as the company historian and authority on the history of American silverware. (Courtesy of the *Record-Journal*.)

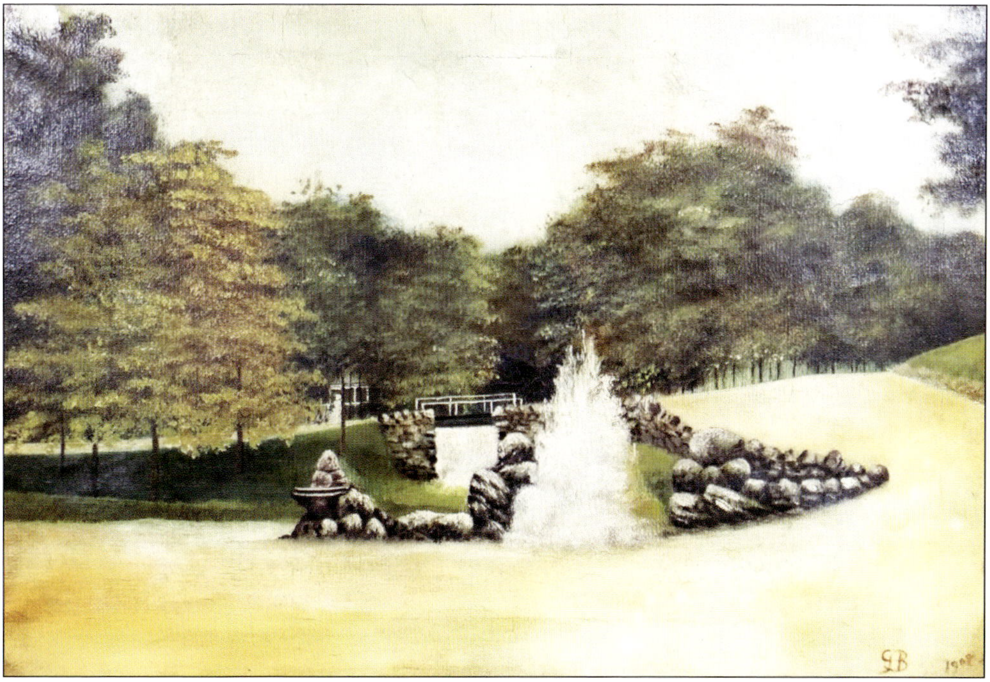

G.H. Brown. These two Hubbard Park scenes were painted by G.H. Brown (or Braun) of Glasgow, Scotland. Rendered from early-20th-century Meriden postcards, these oil-on-canvas paintings captured Meriden's crown jewel park. The above painting depicts the Hubbard Park entrance with the waterfalls powered by Mirror Lake cascading downward toward an erupting fountain. The painting below shows the lower park area complete with central wading pool, fountain, and round goldfish pool. These paintings were a wedding present to a couple living on Bunker Avenue in Meriden, and they remained in their possession for many years. Today, they are in the collection of the Meriden Historical Society. (Both, courtesy of the Meriden Historical Society.)

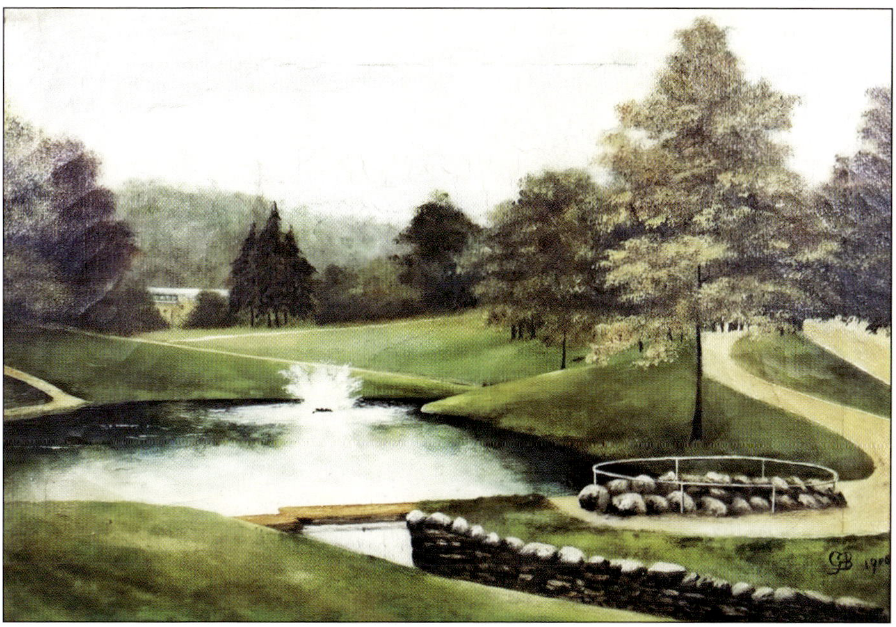

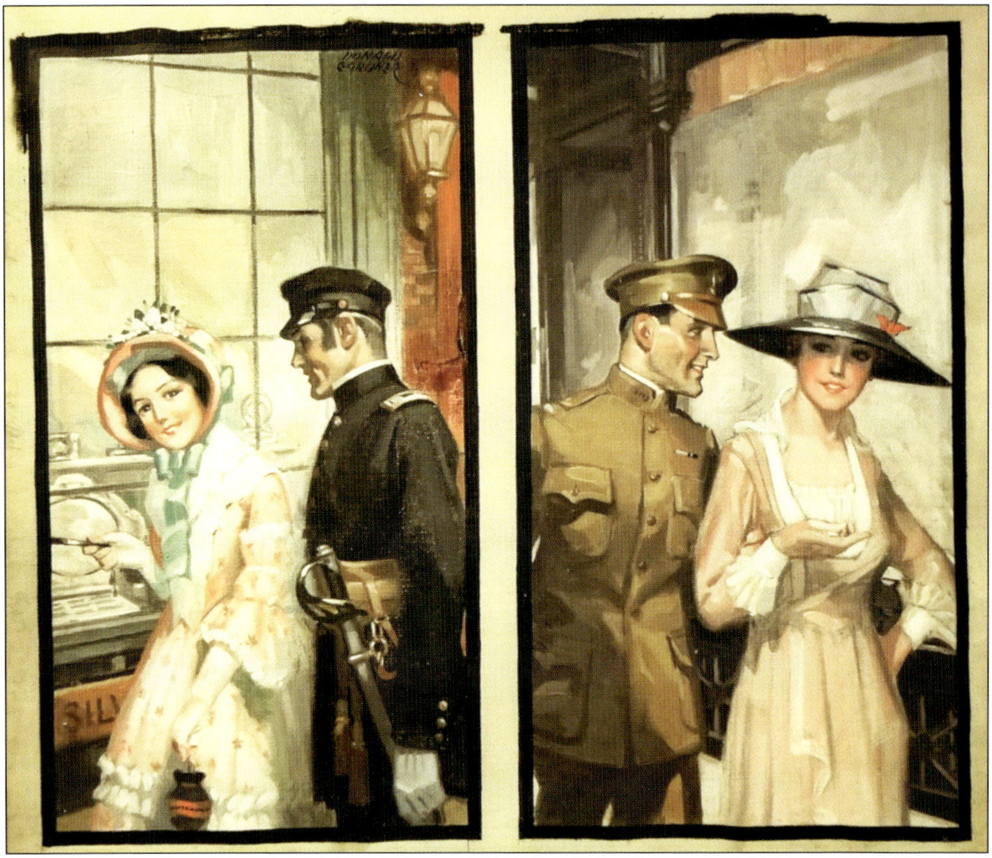

MERIDEN IN ADVERTISING. The great success of Meriden's many manufacturers was no doubt the result of their advertising and promotion. Advertising had become an art form in its own right as artists were now encouraged to elevate the artistic value of promotional advertisements. These images were part of International Silver Company's early-1900s campaign to highlight and sell its silverware lines. International commissioned the top illustrators to promote its brand with eye-catching, full-color layouts, and advertising became paramount to the success and longevity of such leading companies. (Both, courtesy of the Meriden Historical Society.)

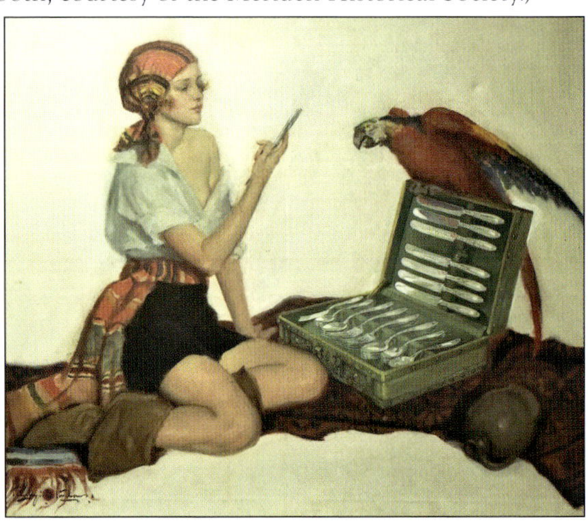

Ben Albert Stahl. Born in Chicago in 1910, Ben Albert Stahl was introduced to the world of art by his grandmother. After high school, Stahl worked as an apprentice at a commercial art studio where one of the partners recognized his ambition and talent and encouraged him to draw and paint to start amassing a portfolio. The contents of this portfolio landed him a job at Chicago's most prestigious art studio. Stahl developed a unique style, influenced by Impressionism, which he felt would carry the mood and the emotional impact of commercial illustrations. He illustrated over 750 stories for the *Saturday Evening Post* and a number of other magazines. Pictured here are original oil paintings that were used to commemorate the 100th anniversary of the 1847 Roger Bros. in Meriden. Stahl died in 1987. (Both, courtesy of the Meriden Historical Society.)

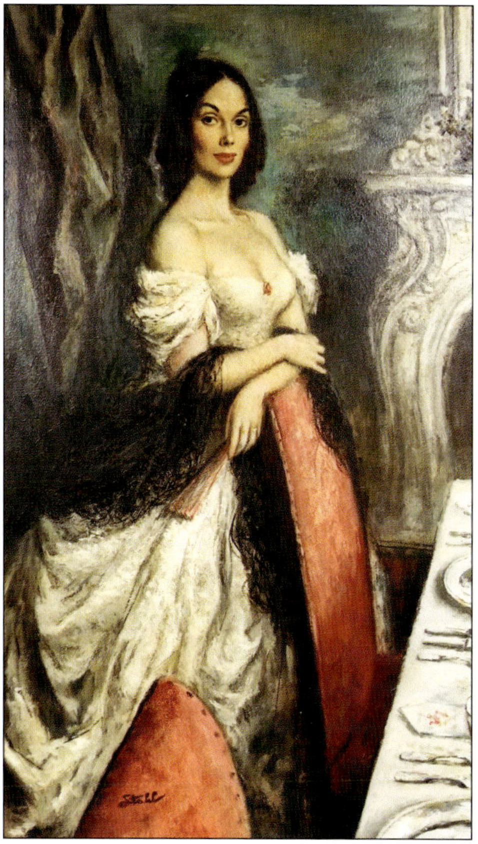

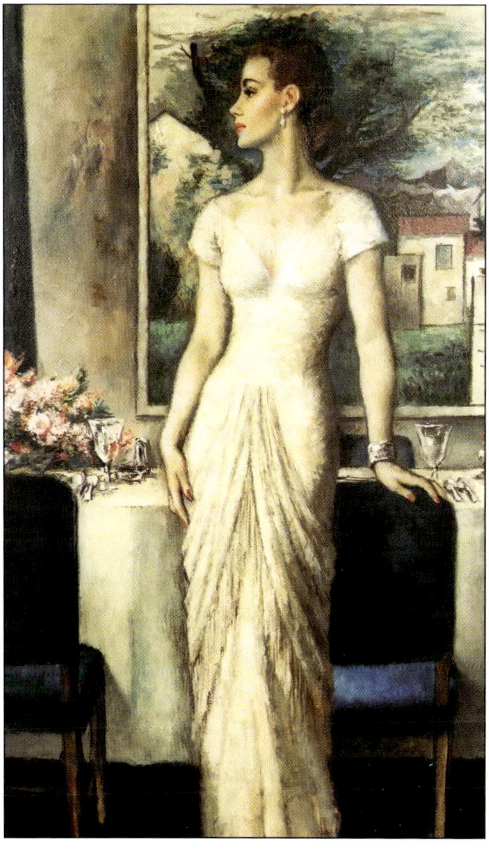

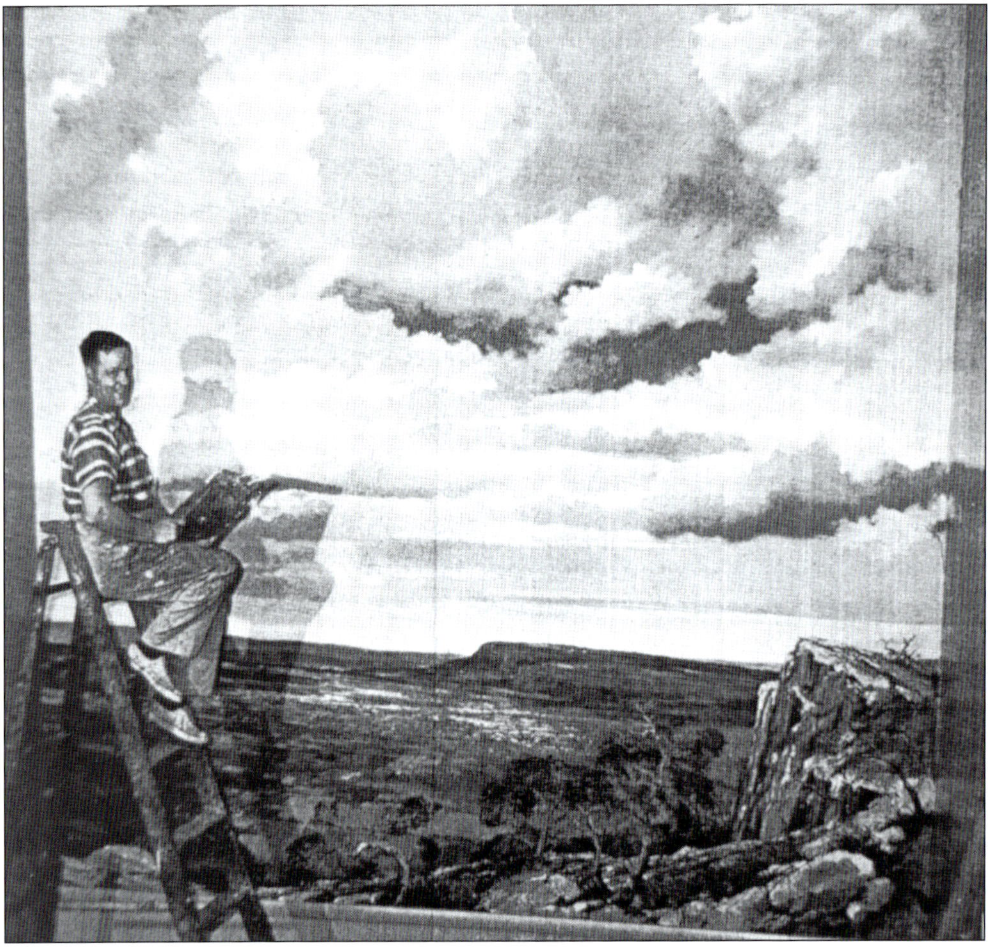

Eric Sloane. Eric Sloane was an American landscape painter, illustrator, author, and folklorist. Born in 1905, he is best known for his paintings of New England farmscapes and books on early Americana. While working on an early assignment that included aviation pioneers flying out of Roosevelt Field, Sloane fell in love with the clouds and sky. Among his early clients was Amelia Earhardt, who bought his first cloud painting. Although Sloane died in 1985, he is considered to be the finest cloud painter of his generation. His clouds are featured in his mural, *The Silver City*, depicting the Hanging Hills from a distance across the 1950s-era Meriden valley. Painted from the vantage point of Chauncey Peak, this mural was commissioned by the International Silver Company in 1957 to commemorate the opening of its new headquarters on South Broad Street in Meriden. The mural remains intact today in the staircase of the former International building, which is currently owned by the *Record-Journal*. (Both, courtesy of the *Record-Journal*.)

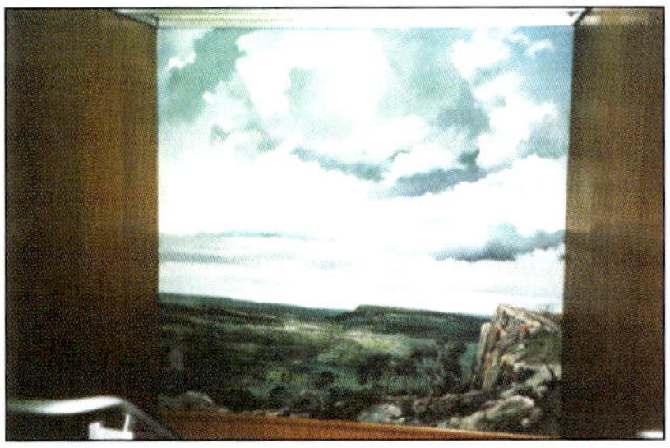

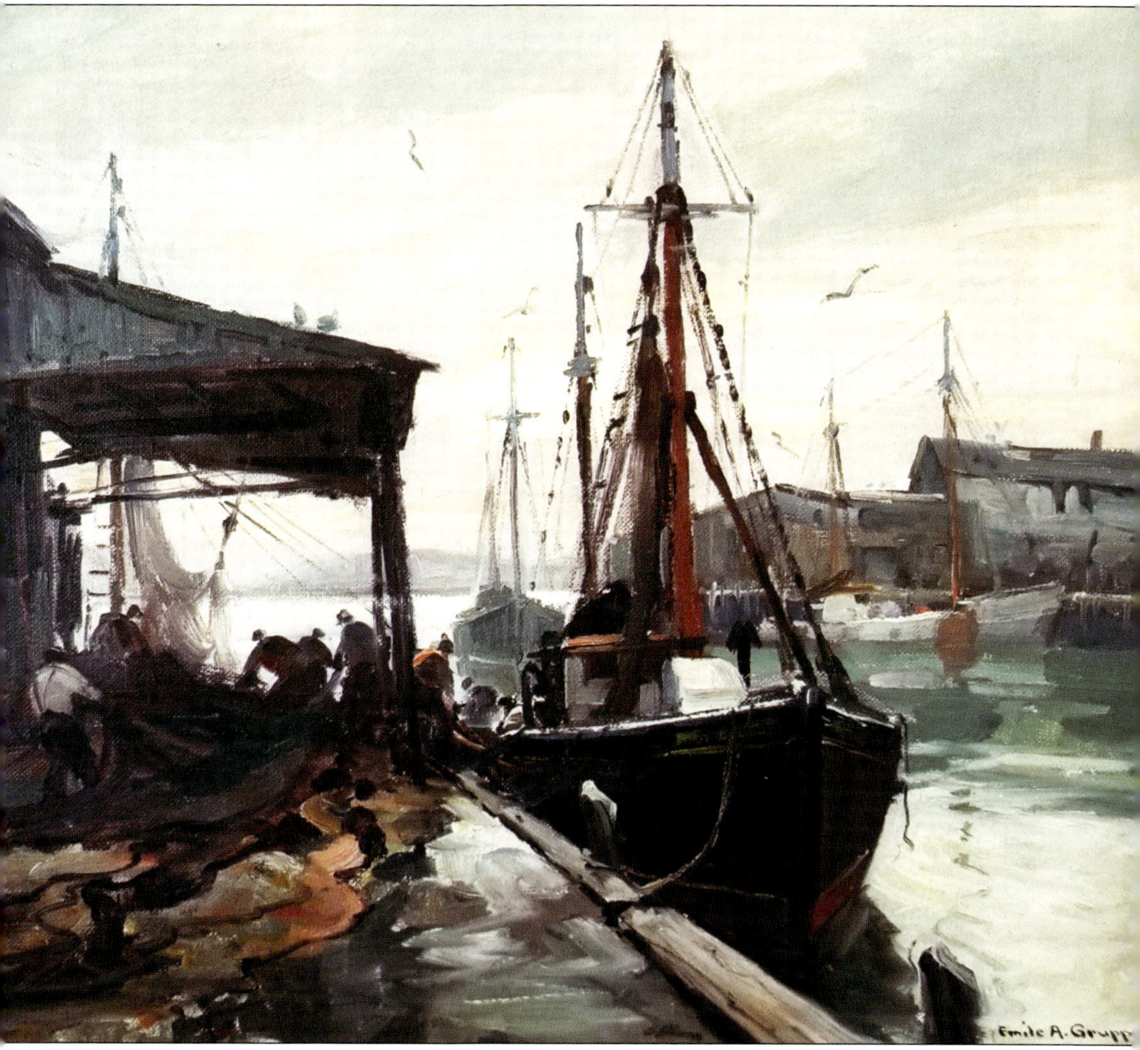

Emile Gruppe. Although he was not a Meriden resident nor were his subjects Meriden-related, Emile Gruppe had a profound influence upon a number of Meriden artists. Son of renowned painter Charles Gruppe, Gruppe was born in 1896 and attended the Carnegie Art School, the Art Students League in New York City, and the Cape Cod School of Art in Provincetown, Massachusetts, although his studies were briefly interrupted for one year when he entered the US Navy in 1917. Gruppe felt compelled to teach, and painting in his adopted hometown of Gloucester, Massachusetts, he founded the Gloucester School of Painting in 1942. Located on Rocky Neck in East Gloucester, the school boasted an impressive faculty, which included Gruppe and many of his own teachers. For decades, the Arts and Crafts Association of Meriden traveled to Gloucester to take advantage of the school's painting workshops. Gruppe's tutelage was so inspiring that Meriden artists like Irma Morse and Earl Bushnell began changing their own subject matter to include water and seascapes. Gruppe died in Gloucester in 1978 at the age of 81.

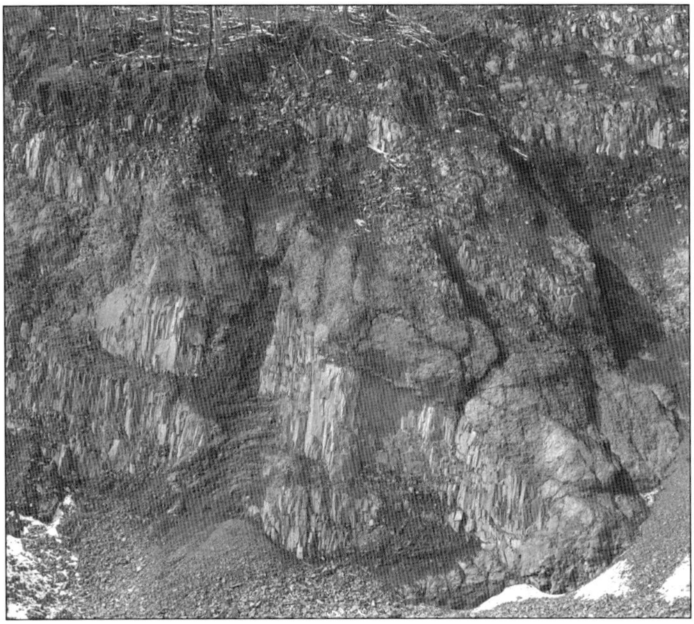

Richard Benson. Richard Benson was a famed American photographer, printer, and educator who was best known for his innovations in photographic offset printing techniques and later inkjet printing. This gelatin silver print, *Trap Rock Cliffs*, was taken by Benson in Meriden in 1969. Benson's work is held in major museums such as the Metropolitan Museum of Art in New York and the San Francisco Museum of Modern Art in California. (Courtesy of the Yale University Art Gallery.)

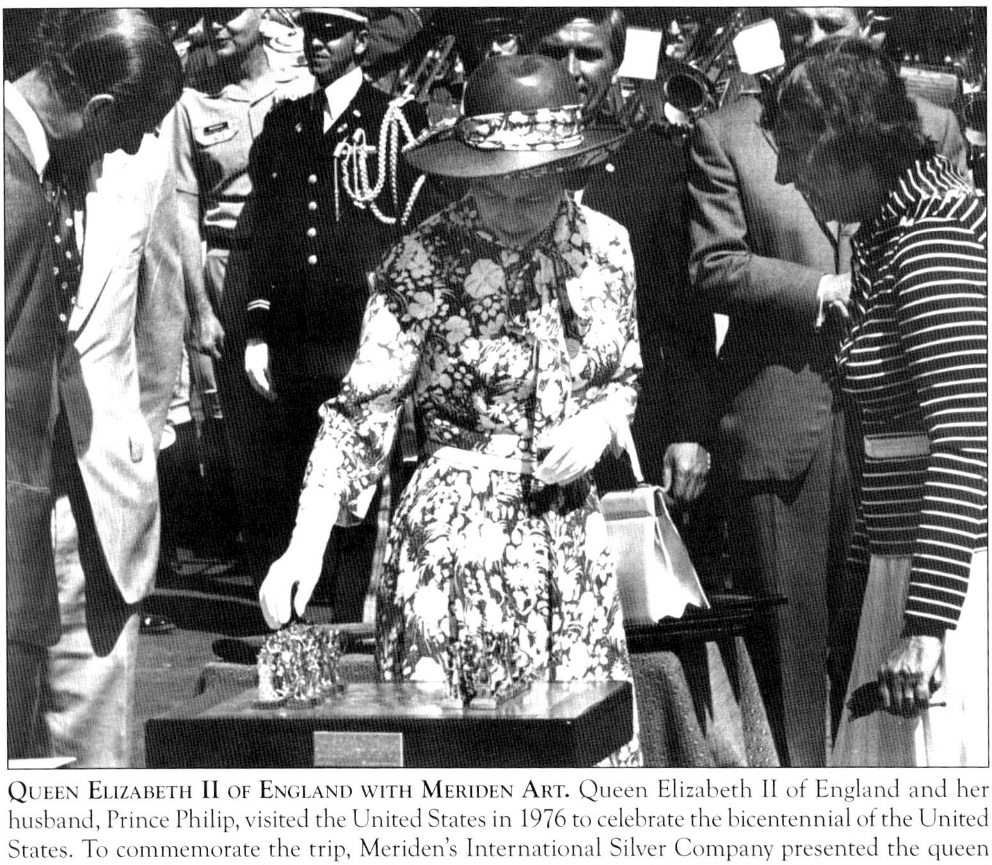

Queen Elizabeth II of England with Meriden Art. Queen Elizabeth II of England and her husband, Prince Philip, visited the United States in 1976 to celebrate the bicentennial of the United States. To commemorate the trip, Meriden's International Silver Company presented the queen with a custom chess set. A duplicate of this chess set is in the collection of the Meriden Historical Society. (Courtesy of the Meriden Historical Society.)

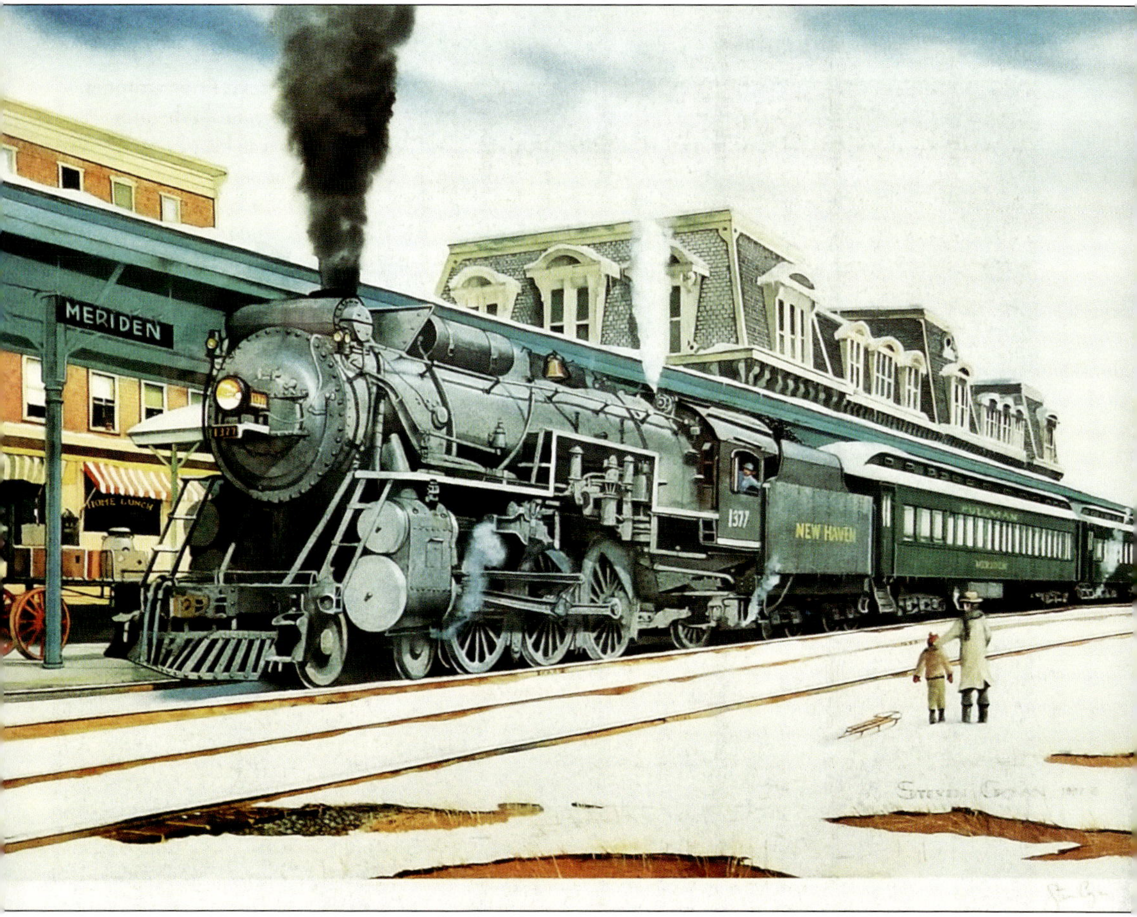

Steven Cryan. Connecticut artist Steven Cryan graduated from Paier College of Art in Hamden, Connecticut, in the early 1970s. He has become known for painting maritime and railroad subjects, and his luminous, realistic watercolors have won numerous awards. His artwork hangs in private and corporate collections throughout the world, including the Quinnipiac Club in New Haven, Connecticut, and the Connecticut River Museum in Essex, Connecticut. Additionally, one of his paintings was added to the art collection on board the RMS *Queen Mary II* ocean liner. As an illustrator, Cryan has created many magazine cover designs and center spreads for *Keystone*, *Steamboat Bill*, *Shoreliner*, *Trains Magazine*, *Nautical World*, and Moran Corporation's *Towline Magazine*. His illustrations can be seen in the books *Where Rails Meet the Sea* and *Tugboats* and has been featured on the cover of Lionel Trains' catalog. Cryan is a leading authority on trains and maritime history, and his photography collection on the subject is one of the largest in the United States. (Courtesy of Steven Cryan.)

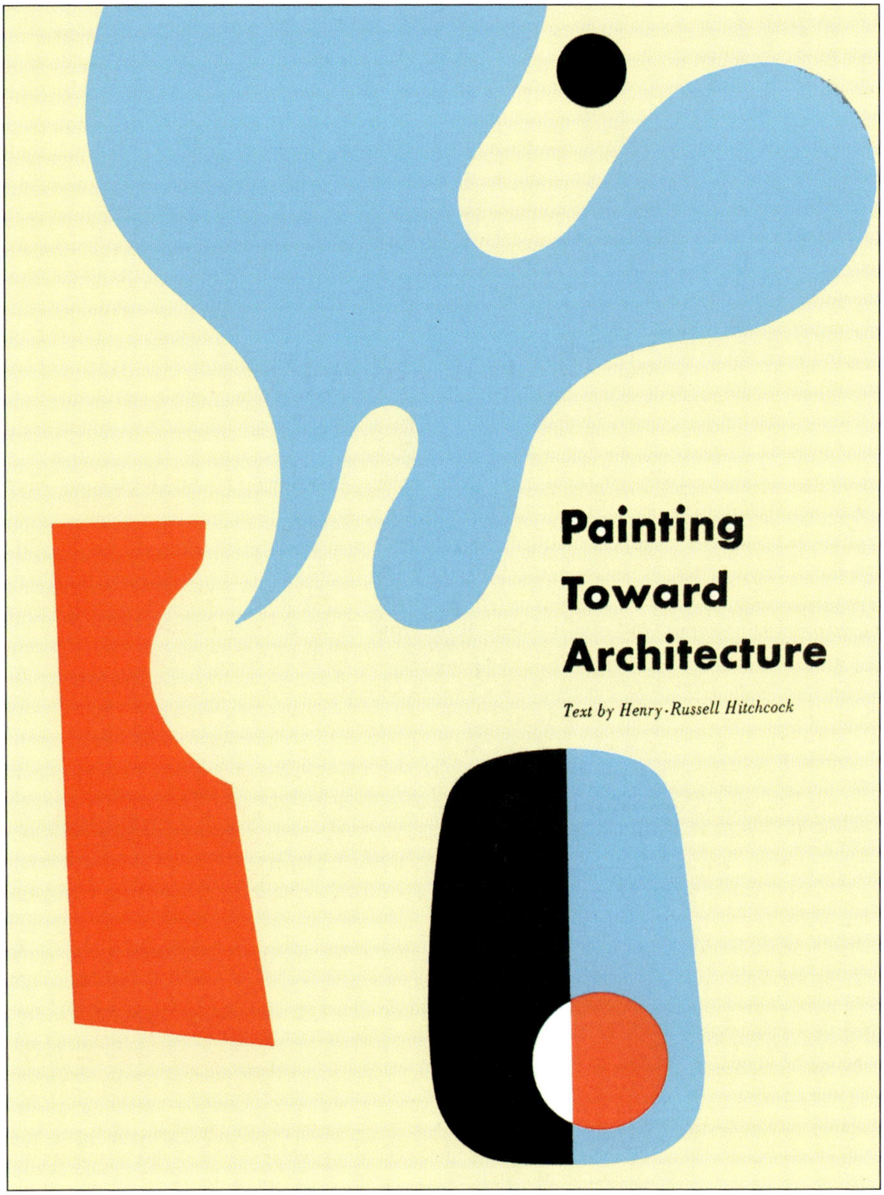

THE EMILY HALL TREMAINE ART COLLECTION. Emily Hall Tremaine and her husband, Burton G. Tremaine, were avid collectors of 20th-century art with a particular interest in work done after 1945. As owner of the Meriden-based Miller Lighting Company, Burton Tremaine commissioned the 1948 book *Painting Toward Architecture: The Miller Company Collection of Abstract Art* by Henry Hitchcock. Encouraged by the book's success, the couple continued to acquire more than 400 works over the years for their collection. Artists in their collection included Andy Warhol, Jasper Johns, and Robert Rauschenberg. When the Tremaines began to build their collection, these innovative artists were not yet recognized in the art world. The Tremaine Collection was widely considered one of the finest reflections of contemporary art in the nation and stood as a visual testament to the refined and courageous taste of Burton and Emily Hall Tremaine. This one-of-a-kind collection was sold and dispersed to create the asset base for the Emily Hall Tremaine Foundation, which remains active today carrying on Emily Hall Tremaine's legacy. (Courtesy of the Meriden Public Library.)

Bibliography

Baur, David and Agnes. *Frederick Matzow (1861–1938), Meriden's Artist-in Residence.* Meriden, CT: Konica Minolta Business Solutions, 2006.

Creps, Bob. *Biographical Encyclopedia of American Painters, Sculptors & Engravers of the U.S., Colonial to 2002, Volumes 1 and 2.* Land O' Lakes, FL: Dealer's Choice Books, Inc., 2002.

Curtis, George Munson. *A century of Meriden: A Historic Record and Pictorial Description of the Town of Meriden, Connecticut and the Men Who Have Made It, from Earliest Settlement to Close of its First century of Incorporation.* Meriden, CT: Journal Publishing Company, 1906.

Falk, Peter Hastings. *Who Was Who in American Art, Compiled from the Original Thirty-four Volumes of American Art Annual; Who's Who in Art.* Madison, CT: Sound View Press, 1985.

French, Harry Willard. *Art and Artists in Connecticut.* New York: Da Capo Press, 1970.

Gibson, Arthur Hopkin. *Artists of Early Michigan, A Biographical Dictionary of Artists Native to or Active in Michigan, 1701–1900.* Detroit, MI: Wane State University Press, 1975.

Gillespie, C.B. *Art Souvenir Edition of The Meriden Daily Journal Illustrating the City of Meriden, Connecticut in the Year 1895.* Meriden, CT: The Journal Publishing Company, 1895.

Golman-Hibel, Carole, John Hibel, and John Fontaine. *The Handel Lamps Book.* Pittsfield, MA: Fontaine Publishers. 1999.

Hogan, Edmund P. *An American Heritage, A Book About the International Silver Company.* Dallas, TX: Taylor Publishing Company, 1977.

Koch, Carla Sternberg. *Favorite Places, the Life of Charlotte Joan Sternberg.* Cheshire, CT: Sternberg Koch Publishers, 2017.

Little, Nina Fletcher. *Country Art in New England, 1790–1840.* Meriden, CT: The Meriden Gravure Company, 1965.

Scalise, Roseann. *The Brushstrokes That Shaped My Life.* Meriden, CT: self-published, 2014.

Sherman, Frederic Fairchild. *Early Connecticut Artists & Craftsmen.* New York: privately printed, 1925.

Van Dusen, Albert E. *Connecticut: A Fully Illustrated History of the State from the Seventeenth century to the Present.* New York: Random House, 1961.

Wendover, Sanford H. *150 Years of Meriden: Published in Connection with the Observance of the City's Sesquicentennial, June 17–23, 1956.* Meriden, CT: Meriden Sesquicentennial Committee, 1956.